50 pies, 50 states

An Immigrant's Love Letter to the United States Through Pie

STACEY MEI YAN FONG

PHOTOGRAPHS BY ALANNA HALE
ILLUSTRATIONS BY SHELBY WARWOOD

VORACIOUS

LITTLE, BROWN AND COMPANY
NEW YORK BOSTON LONDON

Voracious / Little, Brown and Company
Hachette Book Group
1290 Avenue of the Americas, New York, NY 10104
voraciousbooks.com

First Edition: June 2023

Voracious is an imprint of Little, Brown and Company, a division of Hachette Book Group, Inc.
The Voracious name and logo are trademarks of Hachette Book Group, Inc.

The publisher is not responsible for websites (or their content) that are not owned by the publisher.

The Hachette Speakers Bureau provides a wide range of authors for speaking events.
To find out more, go to hachettespeakersbureau.com or email hachettespeakers@hbgusa.com.

Little, Brown and Company books may be purchased in bulk for business, educational, or promotional
use. For information, please contact your local bookseller or the Hachette Book Group Special Markets
Department at special.markets@hbgusa.com.

Photographer: Alanna Hale
Designer: Tree Abraham
Illustrator: Shelby Warwood
Hand lettering: Brian Kaspr
Food stylist: Caitlin Haught Brown
Assistant food stylists: Namrata Hegde and Kathryn Irizarry
Prop stylist: Maeve Sheridan

ISBN 9780316394512
LCCN 2022946108

10 9 8 7 6 5 4 3 2 1

TC

Printed in Canada

This book is dedicated to my 爷爷 *and* 嫲嫲.
I can't wait to bake them pie in the great beyond.
My grandma will say, "It's okay, it's not too sweet,"
and ask if I've gotten married yet and why I have so many
tattoos that are so unbecoming. My grandpa will just hug
me tightly for a long while and ask me if I've eaten yet.
我爱你.

Candy might be sweet, but it's a traveling carnival blowing through town. Pie is home. People always come home.

—Ned, *Pushing Daisies*

For is there any practice less selfish, any labor less alienating, any time less wasted, than preparing something delicious and nourishing for the people you love?

—Michael Pollan

Pie is the American synonym of prosperity and its varying contents the calendar of the changing seasons. Pie is the food of the heroic. No pie-eating people can ever be permanently vanquished.

—*New York Times*, 1902

CONTENTS

PIE GUIDE

CRUSTS

PERSONAL PIES

PIES BY STATE

PIES BY TYPE

MINNESOTA
160

WISCONSIN
306

MICHIGAN
155

IOWA
115

ILLINOIS
105

INDIANA
110

OHIO
233

MISSOURI
171

KENTUCKY
127

W. VIRGINIA
301

TENNESSE
270

ARKANSAS
55

MISSISSIPPI
166

ALABAMA
40

GEORGIA
87

LOUISIANA
132

FLORIDA
82

NEW YORK
214

PENNSYLVANIA
248

VIRGINIA
290

N. CAROLINA
221

S. CAROLINA
258

MAINE
138

VERMONT 285

NEW HAMPSHIRE 198

MASSACHUSETTS 149

RHODE ISLAND 253

CONNECTICUT 72

NEW JERSEY 203

DELAWARE 77

MARYLAND 144

WASHINGTON DC 318

ALASKA
45

HAWAII
91

INTRODUCTION

HI! I'M STACEY AND I BAKE PIES.

People deal with feelings, stress, and trauma in different ways. You might process it through writing, long walks, or talking to your therapist or partner. I lie on the ground and listen to music, and then I bake a pie. Every time I am feeling a little too much, or sometimes not enough, I bake a pie. I bake a pie when I celebrate something, make a new friend, figure out something hard, go on an inspiring trip, and, most of all, when I am trying to create a feeling of home.

That's how this project started: as a valiant way to process the feelings I had of belonging nowhere and to no one, pining for that sense of home.

Pies have become my connection to my past and to my present, to where I've come from and to where I'll go. I use pies as mile markers to pinpoint the periods of my life. With every new core memory I make, I bake a pie.

This is my journey home. I hope you're home, or on your way there, too. You never know where a pie can take you.

"Where are you from?"
"Where do you call home?"

These are simple questions for some people, but for me they are two of the most loaded questions. The idea of "home" has always been foreign to me. I was born in Singapore, grew up in Indonesia and Hong Kong, and now live in Brooklyn, New York. I am the definition of a third culture kid, figuring out who I am in between different worlds.

My dad worked in the hotel business, and my family moved constantly. The minute I felt settled, we packed up and moved again. It taught me resilience and how to adapt, but I also spent life bracing for the moment I'd have to put on a brave face and start over. This constant movement gave me a deep appreciation for personal connections, no matter how fleeting. Any chance I could talk to someone and hear their story felt special, a shared experience to hold onto and find comfort in when I moved somewhere new. Another thing I appreciated about my dad's job was the traveling it allowed us to do. We went anywhere my dad's job took us, and I was particularly excited every time we got to go on a long flight to America.

American music and movies were a constant in my childhood. I spent hours with my dad in the car listening to Simon and Garfunkel or at home watching countless movies. I loved movies that featured road trips, stopping at diners for pie, and drinking out of red Solo cups. As a teenager growing up on the other side of the world, I loved to listen to classic country music, especially Dolly Parton. The lyrics in those songs just made sense to me as I gazed out of my bedroom window onto the South China Sea.

When the time came for college, I threw caution to the wind and uprooted my life again—this time on my own terms. I moved from Hong Kong to Savannah, Georgia. I felt I had grown a little comfortable in Hong Kong with my bubble of friends and family and I needed to test myself. Plus, I had always dreamed of going on a really long road trip, something you can't really do when you grow up on an island. Savannah was the perfect starting point to the adventure that led to where I am now.

At the Savannah College of Art and Design, most of my friends went home on holiday breaks to the houses they grew up in. Hearing their stories about sleeping in the same room they did as a child made me yearn for that "homecoming" feeling. With my family so far away, I spent countless holidays with my friends' families, who always made sure I felt special. I got to see all my friends' childhood bedrooms, a gift that also underscored that I didn't have my own to show. My sense of belonging would have to be created not by childhood bedrooms and attics filled with old toys, but by the relationships I forged.

By 2016, I had spent ten years in the United States, living, working, and having a hell of a time with my friends. I had exhausted my ability to reapply for the work visa I was on, and it was time to apply for permanent residency. This was a turning point. I finally realized that home doesn't have to be something you inherit. It can be a place you make for yourself. Ever the headstrong independent woman my dad raised, I had been laying that foundation for ten years with the friends who had become my family. America already felt like home; I was just making it official.

Adopting a new country is kind of a big move. As I went through the immigration process, I wanted to take on a project that would teach me about the country I chose to call home. I also wanted to make a grand gesture to show the friends who make this country so special that I love them.

In Singapore, a way you greet someone you love is by asking, "Have you eaten yet?" No one in my family is a professional cook or baker, but we are all eaters. All my most joyous moments growing up were spent around a table. No matter where we were, family dinner was always at 6 p.m. The best way I know to experience a new place or show someone how much I care is through food. I learned to cook by thumbing through cookbooks and watching countless hours of food TV. Whenever life became tumultuous, I went to the kitchen, where things just made sense.

When I began the application for my permanent residency, I was at the peak of feeling lost about my place in the world. I was in my mid-twenties, had gotten my heart broken, my grandmother had passed away, and I was under so much stress I got a case of shingles—all while wondering if I made the right decision to come to New York. In my job as a handbag designer, I found something I was good at that paid the bills, but I felt a lack of purpose. I hardly had the motivation to get up every day.

That Christmas, my best friend, Patrick, bought me *The Four & Twenty Blackbirds Pie Book*, from the Brooklyn pie shop we both loved. I decided to work through it, to try to bake myself out of my emotional hole. When I was baking, I felt a sense of emotional calm and peace that I hadn't experienced in a long while. Studying the seasonality of the ingredients for the fillings and their origin stories was so fulfilling (ha) and interesting to me. It gave me a sense of purpose I hadn't felt in so long. And I realized: What is more American than pie?

That's when my project, 50 Pies, 50 States, was born. I decided to learn about America by creating a pie for each state that said something about its people and included meaningful regional ingredients. I would gift the pie to someone I knew from that state as a token of my affection. Along the way, I would learn state facts that would make me the perfect team member on pub trivia nights. What an adventure: I would learn, bake, eat, and get to share my love for this country with those who made me fall in love with it in the first place.

I love America, from coast to coast and from sea to shining sea. It has constantly brought me a sense of wonder and excitement, from the lush forests of Oregon to the driest deserts of Arizona and the snow-capped mountains of Colorado. Its wide open spaces and sprawling skies are like none where I grew up. Yet for all its splendor, this country constantly tests my love for it. It is a country of contradictions and disparities, immense privilege and painful hardship. Like a bad boyfriend, it lets me down when I need it the most, then builds me back up to loving it again. But it's the people I have met during my time here that drive my desire and need to stay.

Come along and join me on this pie road trip through the United States of America. I have included some bonus pies on top of the ones for each state, each of which tells part of my journey. I am in so many ways a different person than I was when I crimped my first state pie crust. I hope that, whether you are celebrating your own home state or feeling a little lost yourself, these pies bring you happiness and a little emotional release.

Thank you for being my pie trip buddy. Buckle up, it's a long drive, but the tunes are good and the pies are abundant. See you at home!

xoxo Stacey

HOW THIS BOOK WORKS

This book is your road trip companion through the United States and some pivotal pitstops in my life so far. I'll take you to the places I've seen, introduce you to the friends I've made along the way, and tell you all about the other places I cannot wait to visit.

The road trip starts with your usual cookbook or travel check list below, and then we jump into the pies. At the end, in the Making Crust section, you'll learn about the ingredients and tools that have helped me crimp and roll through my life of pie, along with all the crust recipes and basic pie-making techniques.

In the pages that follow, each state pie gets the same five-star treatment: You get some fun facts about the state, a description of a pie personalized with ingredients that define the state to me, and at the end my dedication to a friend. Occasionally I'll direct you to my website for a downloadable template you can use to help cut out a decorative crust or make a Dolly Parton portrait in pie.

I have yet to visit all fifty glorious states and don't (yet!!) have a friend who hails from all of them...so I want to hear from you if you are from a state I haven't visited. Let me know, I can't wait to share a slice with you!

BEFORE YOU START SLINGIN' PIES

1. **HAVE GOOD TUNES PLAYING** to set the vibe. I believe that how you feel gets baked into what you are making, and the people can taste it. So put your favorite music on, tie on that apron, LFG!

2. **READ THE RECIPE.** Read it multiple times. You know the carpentry saying, "Measure twice, cut once?" The same goes for recipe reading. Sometimes I read my own recipes seven times, just for luck.

3. **MAKE SURE YOUR EGGS, BUTTER, AND CREAM CHEESE ARE AT ROOM TEMP.** The only exception to this rule is when you are making crust. Keep that butter *cold!*

4. *MISE EN PLACE!* Have all your ingredients measured out and arranged in the order you need them, so you are ready to roll (hehe). Having ingredients measured and sorted can be time consuming, but makes assembly so much easier. When you are in the thick of it, you are going to be so happy you already measured out that 1 teaspoon of vanilla extract.

5. **KNOW YOUR INGREDIENTS.** Here, unless I say otherwise, the sugar is granulated, the salt is Diamond Crystal kosher salt, black pepper is freshly ground, the flour is all-purpose, and the eggs are large.

6. **PREHEAT YOUR OVEN AND ADJUST THOSE RACKS!** Almost every pie bakes on the center rack of the oven; I'll tell you if you should bake it otherwise.

7. **ALWAYS BAKE YOUR PIES ON A BAKING SHEET.** This will help prevent butter and fruit juices from dripping all over your oven and smoking up your kitchen, with you on a ladder waving a tea towel at the smoke detector. You can even line your baking sheet with parchment paper to make cleanup a breeze.

8. **REMEMBER: MISTAKES HAPPEN.** Not all your pies will come out incredible. At the end of the day, it is just pie. Cover it in ice cream and carry on.

9. **IF ALL ELSE FAILS,** pour yourself a stiff drink, listen to "Atlantic City" by the Band twice while singing along loudly, and start again.

10. **SAVOR EVERY BITE,** you made a pie, that's incredible! Enjoy the fruits of your labor and, better yet, share it with someone you love.

THE PIES

Before we start our road trip through the fifty states,
let's get to know each other a little first.
I'm going to start with pies for the places that
tell you the story of where I was born,
where I grew up, and how I eventually made
my way over to this country I have chosen to call
home. Everyone loves a spontaneous pit stop,
and really, what's better than a few bonus pies?

was born in the tiny Republic of Singapore in 1988 and lived there for the first years of my life. When people learn this about me, they always ask, "That's where you can't chew gum, right?" And, "Oh my god, is it just like *Crazy Rich Asians*?!" To answer those questions: Yes and no, but maybe?

I returned to Singapore throughout my childhood and teenage years to visit my grandparents and extended family and, most importantly (sorry fam!), to eat! The food in Singapore is next level and so unique: It is from everywhere and from nowhere exactly. There are flavors from Chinese, Malay, and Indian cuisines, to name a few, and all these flavors combine to create Singaporean cuisine. It is a melting pot of all things delicious. Singaporean cuisine hits on all flavor notes: spicy, savory, sweet, and sour. But most importantly, the food is so vibrant and bright that you'll be thinking about it for days to come after a meal. From nasi lemak to chili crab, there is truly something for everyone in Singapore.

My most vivid memories of the country are tied to my ye ye (my father's father), who always had a large tin of Khong Guan biscuits (from the 76-year-old Singaporean biscuit manufacturer) waiting for me to snack on whenever I returned. My ye ye would often hand me a biscuit so I would focus on the buttery, flaky treat and he could have a moment of silence. Otherwise, I would never stop talking! (Some things don't change.) My ye ye will always be my favorite person: No one has brought me the sense of calm and safety he did. This pie is in honor of him.

On every visit, just before we left, we picked up a pandan chiffon cake from the bakery Bengawan Solo to take back to Hong Kong. It came in a massive red box. I was always so mad at having to carry it on the plane, but so happy to have it when we got home. So the pie I dedicate to Singapore is a pandan cream pie with toasted coconut, mango, and coconut whipped cream. The crust is made of the Khong Guan biscuits my ye ye used to give me, which pair perfectly with the floral flavors of pandan, a tropical plant with long, blade-like aromatic leaves. Its amazing fragrance combines scents of vanilla and tea rose, and it turns whatever you're making a vibrant lime green. I was inspired by, and adapted this recipe from, Linda Ooi of the wonderful food blog Roti n Rice.

I am proud to have been born in such a tiny place so full of life, personality, and flavor. The Singaporean national anthem says it best: Rukon damai dan bantu mĕmbantu, Supayă kită samă-samă maju. With peace and effort, we move forward together.

PANDAN CREAM PIE

WITH TOASTED COCONUT, MANGO, AND COCONUT WHIPPED CREAM

ACTIVE TIME: 30 MINUTES — BAKE TIME: 15 TO 30 MINUTES — TOTAL TIME: 5 HOURS — MAKES ONE 10-INCH PIE

CRUST

Cream Cracker Crust (page 337, using Khong Guan biscuits, or McVitie's digestive biscuits if you can't find them), blind baked as directed

FILLING

4 large egg yolks

2 tablespoons unsalted butter

2 tablespoons cornstarch

1¼ cups condensed milk

1¼ cups full-fat coconut milk

1 teaspoon pandan extract

4 drops green food coloring (optional)

TOPPINGS

¼ cup unsweetened coconut flakes

1 (13.5-ounce) can full-fat coconut milk or coconut cream, chilled (do not shake)

¼ cup confectioners' sugar

½ teaspoon vanilla extract

1 medium mango, peeled, pitted, and cut into small cubes

SPECIAL EQUIPMENT

Stand mixer with whisk attachment or hand mixer

PRO TIP: *If your coconut milk didn't harden and separate in the fridge, you might have gotten a dud can or one that doesn't have the right fat content. You can salvage this by adding 1 to 4 tablespoons cornstarch during the whipping process.*

MAKE THE FILLING: In a small bowl, whisk the egg yolks just until they come together. Set aside. Over medium heat, melt the butter in a saucepan and add the cornstarch. Cook, whisking, until it is a light golden color. Pour in the condensed milk, coconut milk, pandan extract, and food coloring (if using). Stir constantly over medium heat until thick and bubbly, 4 to 5 minutes. Remove from the heat and stir in the egg yolks until well combined.

ASSEMBLE AND BAKE THE PIE: Preheat the oven to 350°F. Pour the warm filling into the fully baked pie crust and place the pie on a baking sheet. Bake the pie on the center rack for 15 to 30 minutes. Give the pie a jiggle to test for doneness: The filling should have a slight jiggle to it; look for the texture of a soft thigh. Cover with plastic wrap and chill for at least 4 hours in the fridge.

MAKE THE TOPPINGS

Toasted Coconut

In a medium saucepan over medium-low heat, cook the coconut flakes, stirring frequently, until mostly golden brown. This should take 5 to 10 minutes. Set aside to cool.

Recipe continues ★★★

Coconut Whipped Cream

Place a stand mixer bowl or a large mixing bowl in the refrigerator to chill for 10 minutes before whipping. This will help the cream whip faster.

Remove the coconut cream from the fridge without tipping or shaking the can. Open the can and scrape out the thickened cream from the top, leaving the liquid behind.

Place the hardened coconut cream in the chilled mixing bowl; beat with the whisk attachment for 30 seconds, until it becomes thick and soft peaks start to form. Add the confectioners' sugar and vanilla and continue to mix until the mixture thickens and has the same texture as whipped cream, about 1 additional minute. Avoid overwhipping the cream, which can cause separation.

FINISH THE PIE: Take the chilled pie from the fridge and top with the coconut whipped cream. Sprinkle toasted coconut and cubed mango all over the top. Slice and enjoy!

We moved to Jakarta, Indonesia, for my dad's job and lived there from when I was 3 to 5 years old. We lived in a gated compound that I loved to explore on my little white four-wheeler with lilac wheels and pink trim. The house was surrounded by massive bougainvillea plants that towered over baby Stacey. I spent my days riding around the compound and taking naps under the trees without a care in the world. I loved it. Although I never lived there, Bali also has a special place in my heart: While living in Indonesia and throughout my childhood, we would often vacation there, and it's still one of my favorite places on the planet. The beaches are like none other, with sand that looks like nonpareil sprinkles, or "hundred and thousands," which was what they were called there.

Like Singapore, Indonesia has incredible food. But the thing that takes me straight back to my childhood in Jakarta is the smell of kopi, or coffee. Kopi in Indonesia is dark and bold with a prominent earthiness that is almost savory. I would wake up in the morning to the smell of my dad's coffee in a big cup on the table next to his stack of newspapers. My sister and I would fight to add the milk to his coffee and stir it for him. We still do this morning ritual for my dad, just a small thing to show him that we care.

Coffee in Indonesia is often prepared in a process called "pulling." This means mixing and brewing the coffee by repeatedly pouring it from one container to another, using a cotton strainer that gives the coffee a special thickness and depth of flavor. One style of kopi that is popular specifically in the Java region where I lived is kopi jahe. Mixed with ginger and palm sugar, the flavor just lends itself to becoming a lovely custard pie.

So here we have it: a kopi jahe custard pie for my Indonesian home. One smell and a slice later and I'm back in that four-wheeler, causing mischief amongst the bougainvillea.

KOPI JAHE CUSTARD PIE

ACTIVE TIME: 30 MINUTES — BAKE TIME: 1 HOUR — TOTAL TIME: 6 HOURS 30 MINS — MAKES ONE 10-INCH PIE

CRUST

All-Butter Crust (single, page 332),
  fully blind baked (page 348)
  and cooled

FILLING

1 cup palm sugar

1 cup cold brew coffee

1 (3-inch piece) fresh ginger,
  peeled and smashed

½ cup (1 stick) unsalted butter,
  melted

2 tablespoons granulated sugar

¼ cup espresso powder

½ teaspoon kosher salt

2 large eggs plus 3 large egg yolks,
  at room temperature

1 cup heavy cream, at room
  temperature

1½ cups whole milk, at room
  temperature

1 tablespoon vanilla extract

MAKE THE FILLING: Preheat the oven to 325°F. In a saucepan over medium heat, whisk the palm sugar, coffee, and ginger. Cook the mixture, stirring occasionally, until it has reduced by one-third of its original volume, 15 to 20 minutes. Pour into a medium bowl and let cool.

Whisk the butter, sugar, espresso powder, and salt into the coffee mixture.

In a separate bowl, whisk together the eggs, egg yolks, cream, milk, and vanilla. Add the egg mixture to the coffee mixture and whisk to combine.

ASSEMBLE AND BAKE THE PIE: Place the fully baked pie crust on a baking sheet and pour the filling into the crust.

Bake the pie on the center rack for 40 to 60 minutes, rotating the pie every 15 minutes after the first 30 minutes. When the pie is done, the edges will puff a little and the center will jiggle slightly when shaken, but it will continue to set as it cools. Allow to cool at room temperature for at least 5 hours before slicing. Best enjoyed while listening to the wind rustle through the bougainvillea.

"Home" Kong is where I truly grew up. I was there from age 5 until I left for college at 18. It is one of the most wonderful cities in the world, the magic of it hard to envision if you didn't grow up there. The setting is one-of-a-kind, with a landscape of tall skyscrapers backed by towering mountains that are all flanked by the South China Sea. Growing up in Hong Kong when it was "one country, two systems" allowed me the privilege of thriving in an environment where the cultural mix of Western and Eastern influences found a happy medium. The friendships I made during my time there have stayed with me. How many people are lucky enough to still have the same best friend since they were 11 years old?

I grew up on the south side of the island in the Stanley/Tai Tam area, right on the beach and surrounded by lush rainforest, but only a 20- to 30-minute bus ride from the city center. I attended an English School Foundations school in Hong Kong, meaning I went through the British school system—halfway around the world from London. Just as in *Harry Potter*, we had "houses" and competed in sports for a house cup.

I lived in Hong Kong during the handover from British to Chinese rule and have seen the changes the country has gone through since then. It's bittersweet to see a place where I grew up with so many freedoms—when Hong Kong was allowed to retain its own economic and administrative systems while mainland China used socialism—be torn apart. Essentially, Hong Kong was completely independent from the Mainland, China's rebellious daughter. Nothing is more upsetting than watching my compatriots lose freedom of speech and seeing a place I called home fall apart.

This pie is inspired by cha chaan teng, which translates as "tea restaurant" or "Hong Kong–style café." This type of casual restaurant is known for eclectic and affordable dishes that include Hong Kong takes on Western classics like pasta, pork chops, and French toast.

This pie also encapsulates the battle I had while growing up, of trying to immerse myself in Western culture while suppressing my own Chinese culture. All I wanted to be when I was younger was a beautiful blonde girl. I tried to rid myself of everything that made me Chinese because I was weirdly embarrassed by it. But I have spent most of my adult life learning to love my culture and embracing how wonderful and unique it is. I have come to find a balance: I am a little bit of this and a little bit of that.

The cha chaan teng dish I love the most is macaroni soup. One key to this soup (which would make any Italian shudder) is overcooking the macaroni until it's soft. Another key is canned cream of chicken soup. The dish was created when Hong Kongers tried to emulate Western dishes they had never eaten, which is why the macaroni is absolutely hammered, but that soft texture is so comforting to me. Whenever I make the soup I am immediately transported home, so I took it a step further and made it into a pie. Like me, it's a product of two cultures and represents the best of both my homes, Hong Kong and America.

HONG KONG-STYLE MACARONI SOUP PIE

ACTIVE TIME: 30 MINUTES — BAKE TIME: 30 MINUTES — TOTAL TIME: 1 HOUR — MAKES ONE 10-INCH PIE

CRUST

All-Butter Crust (single, page 332), fully blind baked (see page 348)

FILLING

1 (10.5-ounce) can condensed cream of chicken soup (preferably Campbell's)

1 cup chicken stock

¼ cup green peas, frozen or fresh

½ cup corn kernels, frozen or canned

1 (12-ounce) can Spam, cubed and fried until crispy, reserve ¼ cup for topping

1 teaspoon soy sauce

1 teaspoon sesame oil

Kosher salt and freshly ground black pepper

2 large eggs, beaten

2 cups dried macaroni, cooked according to package directions, drained

TOPPING

3 large eggs, fried sunny side up

¼ cup thinly sliced scallions

MAKE THE FILLING: Preheat the oven to 350°F. In a medium saucepan over high heat, bring the chicken soup and chicken stock to a boil. Reduce the heat to maintain a simmer. Add the peas, corn, Spam, soy sauce, sesame oil, and pinch each of salt and pepper and cook for 5 minutes, until warmed through. Stir in the beaten eggs. Stir in the cooked macaroni and set aside.

ASSEMBLE AND BAKE THE PIE: Fill the fully baked pie crust with the macaroni filling.

Transfer the filled pie to a baking sheet and bake on the center rack for 30 to 40 minutes, until the center is firm. Let cool for 10 to 15 minutes. Top with the reserved Spam cubes and fried eggs and garnish with the scallions. Slice and serve. It's best eaten with a large cup of coffee the way you take it and a copy of the *South China Morning Post*.

I USED TO SLEEP AT THE FOOT OF OLD GLORY,
AND AWAKE IN THE DAWN'S EARLY LIGHT.
—JOHN PRINE

I listened to a lot of John Prine's music when first coming up with this little project of mine. His lyrics are pure poetry and inspiration; he's a storyteller and I needed guidance for telling my story. His music helped me feel less overwhelmed by the project I had chosen to undertake.

When starting off, it felt wrong to go straight to the first state. I had to set the scene in some way, so I decided to start with Old Glory. I always thought the American flag was so beautiful, with its stars and stripes, its red, white, and blue. Even now, I get a little emotional listening to "The Star-Spangled Banner" at the beginning of a hockey game. And if you haven't heard Whitney Houston sing it at Super Bowl XXV in 1991, get ready for full-body goosebumps and to shed a tear. It wasn't the anthem to the country I was born in or lived in at the time, but the images it conjured made my heart swell.

The history of the flag is as fascinating as America itself. The flag has survived battles, inspired songs, and evolved in response to the growth of the country, adding a star on the Fourth of July every time a new state enters the Union. It's like the country it represents: a work in progress. Historians believe it was designed by New Jersey Congressman Francis Hopkinson and sewn by Philadelphia seamstress Betsy Ross. The current flag consists of seven red and six white horizontal stripes, representing the original thirteen colonies, and fifty stars representing the states. The colors are symbolic as well: red for hardiness and valor, white for purity and innocence, and blue for vigilance, perseverance, and justice.

For my Stars and Stripes Pie, I wanted something that would be a show-stopper at any Fourth of July barbecue. I got fancy, using foil as a divider when filling the pie to mimic the color blocking of the flag and using two fillings—strawberry and blueberry—which breaks my personal rule of making sure everyone gets the same slice. Channeling my inner Betsy Ross, I cut the crust into lattice for the stripes, and pressed the stars out with a cookie cutter, "sewing" a flag of my own to kick off my journey through the fifty states.

STARS & STRIPES PIE

ACTIVE TIME: 1 HOUR — BAKE TIME: 1 HOUR — TOTAL TIME: 5 HOURS — MAKES ONE 10-INCH PIE

CRUST

All-Butter Crust (double, page 332), rolled out (see page 339); one for the base, one for the stars-and-stripes decorative work

½ teaspoon all-purpose flour

½ teaspoon granulated sugar

Egg wash (see page 346)

Finishing sugar (see page 346)

FILLINGS

Strawberry Filling

6 cups strawberries, stemmed and quartered

½ cup granulated sugar

2 tablespoons cornstarch

½ teaspoon kosher salt

2 teaspoons lemon juice

1 teaspoon vanilla extract

Blueberry Filling

1½ cups blueberries

¼ cup granulated sugar

2 teaspoons cornstarch

¼ teaspoon kosher salt

¾ teaspoon lemon juice

1 teaspoon vanilla extract

SPECIAL EQUIPMENT

Pizza cutter

Ruler

1½-inch star cookie cutter

MAKE THE CRUST: Fit one rolled-out crust in a greased 10-inch pie plate and crimp the edges. Place the other rolled-out crust on a baking sheet. Freeze both crusts for 30 minutes.

Remove the crust on the baking sheet from the freezer. Using a pizza cutter and a ruler, measure out 1-inch strips; cut three full-length strips and two half-length strips. Use the remainder of the crust dough to cut out the stars using a cookie cutter. Place stars and stripes back on to the baking sheet and freeze until ready to use.

MAKE THE FILLINGS: Preheat the oven to 375°F. In a large bowl, combine the strawberries, sugar, cornstarch, salt, lemon juice, and vanilla. In a separate smaller bowl, combine the blueberries, sugar, cornstarch, salt, lemon juice, and vanilla.

ASSEMBLE THE PIE: To keep your blueberry and strawberry fillings separate, make a barrier: Cut a strip of aluminum foil about 2 inches wide and fold it in half lengthwise so you have an inch-wide strip. Then crease it in half widthwise to create an "L" shape.

Remove the crimped crust from the freezer. Place the L-shaped foil piece in the top left corner of the pie crust, creating a compartment that is a quarter of the whole pie in size. Sprinkle the ½ teaspoons flour and sugar on the crust base; this will help prevent a soggy bottom. Pour the blueberry filling into the smaller section and the strawberry filling into the larger section. Remove the foil and adjust the berries if some rolled out of place.

Recipe continues ★★★

Remove the 1-inch dough strips and stars from the freezer. Place the stars and stripes to resemble a flag, being sure to press the ends of the stripes into the edge of the bottom crust.

Brush the entire crust with egg wash, making sure not to pull the berries' sugary syrup onto the crust, as it will burn. Sprinkle finishing sugar over the whole thing for a sparkly finish. Freeze entire pie for 30 minutes before baking.

BAKE THE PIE: Preheat the oven to 375°F. Place the pie on a baking sheet and then on the center rack of the oven. Bake for 1 hour to 1 hour and 15 minutes, rotating the pie 90 degrees every 15 minutes. The pie is done when it is golden brown and sparkling from sea to shining sea. Let the pie cool for at least 3 hours and enjoy à la mode!

Savannah

am so unequivocally in love with Savannah, Georgia: its tree-lined streets draped in Spanish moss, its beautiful historical homes, all the food that sticks to your bones. The grits and the gravy! I have been blessed to experience many places around this incredible country, but Savannah is the only place other than New York that has such an intense hold on me.

I left the comforts of Hong Kong for college here. My big life move was prompted by an episode of *One Tree Hill*: Season 3, episode 19, to be exact. Peyton visits Jake in "Savannah, Georgia" (though they actually shot it in Wilmington, North Carolina) and he tells her that she could move there to be with him and go to the Savannah College of Art and Design. To quote Peyton: "That place is awesome."

Okay, that's not the most convincing argument to apply to a college, but it resonated with me. I knew I wanted to study design, although I didn't know at the time what my focus might be,

and if Peyton could leave her hometown of Tree Hill and move to a new place, couldn't I? Did I want to go to America? Or did I want to follow my friends to England? I was wondering if it was time to forge my own path, shake things up, and throw caution to the wind. Why not? But before I applied, I had to google where Savannah was because I had no idea. An application, a portfolio review, an acceptance letter, a long flight away from home for a campus visit, and that's where I ended up.

Going to SCAD was one of the best decisions I have ever made. While there, I made lasting and cherished friendships that led me to many adventures and all of my personal growth since.

The SCAD mascot is the bee, which symbolizes hope. That's what the school gave me. For my first home in the United States, here's a honey peach pie. Savannah, you truly are the Hostess City of the South, forever my honey on a spoon.

HONEY PEACH PIE
WITH PECAN CRUMBLE TOPPING

ACTIVE TIME: 30 MINUTES — BAKE TIME: 1 HOUR — TOTAL TIME: 4 HOURS 30 MINUTES — MAKES ONE 10-INCH PIE

CRUST

All-Butter Crust (single, page 332), rolled out, fit into a greased 10-inch pie pan, crimped, and frozen (see page 339)

½ teaspoon all-purpose flour

½ teaspoon granulated sugar

FILLING

1 cup honey (preferably Savannah Bee Company's Savannah Honey)

½ to 1 cup warm water

4 cups sliced peeled peaches (from 7 to 9 medium peaches)

½ cup all-purpose flour

¼ teaspoon ground cinnamon

CRUMBLE TOPPING

¾ cup all-purpose flour

½ cup packed dark brown sugar

1 teaspoon ground cinnamon

½ cup pecans, chopped

⅓ cup (⅔ stick) unsalted butter, softened

MAKE THE FILLING: Preheat the oven to 375°F. In a medium saucepan, stir together the honey and ½ cup of the warm water to form a light syrup that coats the back of a spoon. If it's too thick, stir in up to ½ cup more water. If it's *still* too thick, stir the honey mixture in a pan over low heat until it coats the back of a spoon.

In a large mixing bowl, stir together the honey syrup, peaches, flour, and cinnamon.

MAKE THE TOPPING: In a medium mixing bowl, combine the flour, brown sugar, cinnamon, and pecans and mix well. Add the butter and mix until the consistency of wet sand.

ASSEMBLE THE PIE: Place the frozen pie crust on a baking sheet. Sprinkle the ½ teaspoons flour and sugar on the bottom. With a slotted spoon, fill the crust with the peach filling, leaving the liquid behind. Top evenly with the crumble topping.

BAKE THE PIE: Bake the pie on the center rack for 1 hour, rotating the pan 90 degrees every 15 minutes, until the crust and crumble are golden brown. Allow to cool for at least 3 hours before serving à la mode while listening to "Georgia on My Mind," the Willie Nelson version.

have lived in New York for a total of thirteen years, as of this writing, and for twelve of those years I have been in the same apartment in South Brooklyn. It is the longest I have lived in one abode in my entire life, and I couldn't be more attached to my apartment, the surrounding neighborhood, and Prospect Park right across the street.

One of my most favorite things to do is grab a bagel and sit in the park on a blanket and stare at the sky while I eat it in four pieces. I order the same bagel every time I have a little cash: a poppy seed bagel (really, a flagel if they have it), toasted hard, with scallion cream cheese, onions, and fresh lox. If I am penny pinching, then it's a poppy seed bagel toasted hard with lox spread. What can I say? I've got fresh lox taste on a lox spread budget.

My lovely BFF Lauren taught me to add thinly sliced lemon to my fresh lox bagel when I got home, and I never looked back. The acidity and slight bitterness of the rind of the lemon cuts through the fat of the cream cheese and the lox, making the whole experience oh so satisfying.

To the borough I call my home: a pie inspired by my bagel order. Is there anything more grand than eating a bagel plein air with bare feet in the sun? Doubt it.

SCALLION BAGEL PIE
WITH LOX, ONION, AND THINLY SLICED LEMON

ACTIVE TIME: 15 MINUTES — BAKE TIME: 1 HOUR 30 MINUTES — TOTAL TIME: 2 HOURS 45 MINUTES — MAKES ONE 10-INCH PIE

CRUST

Poppy Seed All-Butter Crust (single, page 333), rolled out, fit into a greased 10-inch pie pan, crimped, and fully blind baked (see page 339)

FILLING

6 large eggs

¾ cup heavy cream

6 ounces (¾ cup) cream cheese, softened

2 teaspoons kosher salt

¾ teaspoon freshly ground black pepper

8 whole scallions, thinly sliced, both greens and whites

TOPPINGS

10 ounces smoked salmon

½ small red onion, thinly sliced

1 medium lemon, thinly sliced

Freshly ground black pepper

MAKE THE FILLING: Preheat the oven to 300°F. In a large mixing bowl, whisk the eggs, cream, cream cheese, salt, and pepper to combine. Add the scallions and whisk to incorporate.

ASSEMBLE AND BAKE THE PIE: Place the fully baked pie crust on a baking sheet and pour in the filling. Bake on the center rack for 80 to 90 minutes, until the filling is just set. Let cool for at least 1 hour.

TOP THE PIE: Top the cooled pie with ribbons of the smoked salmon, the red onion, lemon, and a little fresh cracked black pepper. Slice and enjoy in your favorite park by your abode!

This pie is my dedication to the bakery that made me fall in love with pie. Their cookbook brought me out of a deep sadness and into my first job in the food world. You never know where a cold email will take you!

Four & Twenty Blackbirds, I will always love you. I will display my oven scars and butterscotch burns with pride, and to be honest I don't think my body will ever truly fully recover from baking and assembling 300 pies during each Thanksgiving overnight shift. I learned a lot about what I was capable of during my time there. I found out I am really strong, like hauling-50-pound-bags-of-flour strong, but also mentally pretty sharp. During my time at the bakery, I made mistakes, tried harder, learned, and always left feeling accomplished.

After every fistful of ibuprofen I've taken for my aching bones, I always wanted to get up and do it all again because I love pie, and I love the people I met and worked with there.

I have to give a special shout-out to Rica Borich, who gave a lady with no bakery experience a chance and trained me to be the best pie crust crimper and baker I could be.

This pie is a little riff on Four & Twenty Blackbirds' Salty Honey Pie. It's a combo: a little of me and a lot of them. Golden syrup is a common ingredient in Hong Kong desserts, so I swapped it in for the honey. I recommend eating this pie while listening to Ebo Taylor or Marc Anthony radio on Spotify, something we frequently did during my bakery shifts.

SALTY GOLDEN SYRUP PIE

ACTIVE TIME: 30 MINUTES — BAKE TIME: 1 HOUR — TOTAL TIME: 4 HOURS 30 MINUTES — MAKES ONE 10-INCH PIE

CRUST

All-Butter Crust (single, page 332), rolled out, fit into a greased 10-inch pie pan, crimped, and frozen (see page 339)

FILLING

¾ cup granulated sugar

½ cup (1 stick) unsalted butter, melted

1 tablespoon cornmeal

1 teaspoon vanilla paste (preferably Nielsen-Massey)

½ teaspoon kosher salt

¾ cup golden syrup (preferably Lyle's)

3 large eggs

½ cup heavy cream

2 teaspoons white vinegar

TOPPING

Flaky sea salt (preferably Maldon)

MAKE THE FILLING: Preheat the oven to 375°F. In a medium bowl, combine the sugar, melted butter, cornmeal, vanilla, and salt. Stir in the golden syrup, then incorporate the eggs one at a time. Stir in the cream and vinegar. Strain the filling through a fine-mesh sieve into a large bowl.

ASSEMBLE AND BAKE THE PIE: Place the frozen crust on a baking sheet. and add the strained filling.

Bake on the center rack for 1 hour, rotating the pie 90 degrees every 15 minutes. The pie is done when the edges are set, the filling has puffed up, and the overall appearance is golden brown. Let cool for at least 3 hours before finishing with flaky sea salt, slicing, and enjoying!

Alabama

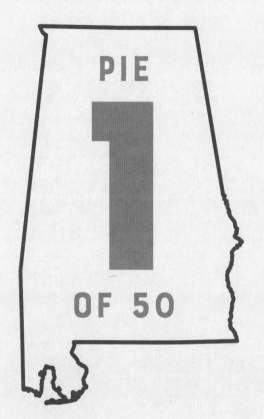

PIE
1
OF 50

THE STARS FELL ON ALABAMA

STATE FRUIT: BLACKBERRY ★ STATE TREE FRUIT: PEACH ★ STATE NUT: PECAN

THE STATE!

Alabama is number one in my alphabetical pie journey but was the twenty-second state to join the Union. I had heard stereotypes about the state that gave it a bad rap—a place that was socially backwards. But when I visited, my assumptions were totally proven wrong.

The first time I set foot in Alabama was when my college roommate Jessica Chavez took me to her hometown. Jess, like almost everyone that I know from Alabama, grew up in Madison, a suburb of Huntsville in the northern part of the state (shout-out to Bob Jones High School). Huntsville is nicknamed the Rocket City because it is where the Saturn V rocket was built, which sent the first Americans to the moon. But the thing I remember most is its miles and miles of churches—I once counted eight churches on just one street!

Another trip to Madison fell on the Fourth of July, and it brought to life a scene I had conjured in my head many a time about the perfect night in America: We spent the Fourth sitting in the back of a pickup truck in a Kroger parking lot, drinking beers out of Solo cups and listening to country music while fireworks went off. It was incredible—a different kind of religious experience.

You know what Lynyrd Skynyrd says: "Sweet home Alabama, where the skies are so blue. Sweet home Alabama, Lord I'm comin' home to you." Roll Tide!

THE PIE!

Alabama designated the blackberry as the official state fruit in 2004 after a campaign led by the third graders at Fairhope Elementary School, guided by their teachers, Susan Sims and Amy Jones. The peach was recognized as the state tree fruit in 2006. Once I learned these two facts, this pie practically built itself. The star ingredients complement each other, with peaches, soft and luscious as they cook down, that are set off by pops of bright and tart blackberry. Plus, they just look so darn beautiful together when they cook, the deep warm orange and the luxurious dark purple intermingling in the jammy filling. The crumble topping adds texture that dances on your tongue. This bad boy is best eaten in the back of a pickup with Merle Haggard blasting under a sky filled with fireworks. Wash it down with a cold light beer!

BLACKBERRY AND PEACH PIE
WITH PECAN CRUMBLE

ACTIVE TIME: 30 MINUTES — BAKE TIME: 1 HOUR — TOTAL TIME: 2 HOURS 30 MINUTES — MAKES ONE 10-INCH PIE

CRUST

All-Butter Crust (single, page 332), rolled out, fit into a greased 10-inch pie pan, crimped, and frozen (see page 339)

½ teaspoon all-purpose flour

½ teaspoon granulated sugar

FILLING

3 cups blackberries

2 cups sliced peaches (about 3 medium)

¾ cup granulated sugar

3 tablespoons cornstarch

1 teaspoon ground cinnamon

½ teaspoon ground nutmeg

CRUMBLE TOPPING

½ cup all-purpose flour

¼ cup lightly packed light brown sugar

½ teaspoon kosher salt

¼ teaspoon ground cinnamon

½ cup chopped pecan pieces

5 tablespoons unsalted butter, softened at room temperature

MAKE THE FILLING: In a large bowl, mix all the filling ingredients together. Make sure that the cornstarch is thoroughly incorporated. Set it aside for 30 minutes for the fruit to macerate.

MAKE THE CRUMBLE TOPPING: In a medium bowl, mix together the flour, brown sugar, salt, cinnamon, and pecans. Using your fingers, slowly incorporate the softened butter in small amounts into the dry ingredients until the consistency resembles wet sand. Put in the fridge until ready to use to keep the butter cool. The crumble can be made ahead and refrigerated for up to a week.

ASSEMBLE THE PIE: Preheat the oven to 375°F. Sprinkle the ½ teaspoons sugar and flour on the frozen crust base and swirl around with your fingers. Using a slotted spoon, fill the crust with the filling, leaving the juices behind. Top the filling with the crumble topping, making sure to cover all the fruit.

BAKE THE PIE: Bake the pie on a baking sheet on the center rack for 1 hour, rotating the pie clockwise every 15 minutes to make sure it cooks evenly. Cover the crust with foil for the last 15 minutes if the edges are getting too brown. Cool for at least 1 hour before serving and enjoying with a Miller Lite while country music blasts.

THE DEDICATION!

This pie is dedicated to Adam Zachary Porter, the first person I met from Alabama and one of the first friends I made in college. It's a celebration of our seventeen years of friendship so far, which honestly started with our mutual love of the same early '00s emo bands. Our friendship is kind of like when peaches and blackberries intermingle, and the crumble on top is all the fun adventures we've been on. I couldn't imagine my life in America or in general without Adam. From sunup to sundown, I'm probably talking to Adam about nothing important but very important at the same time. I hope everyone in life is blessed to find a friend as wonderful as Adam is to me.

The first pie of the 50! What a wonderful place to start.

Alaska

PIE

2

OF 50

BEYOND YOUR DREAMS, WITHIN YOUR REACH

NO STATE FOODS

THE STATE!

Alaska's name comes from the native Aleut word alyeska, which roughly translates as "great land." Ever since people settled in this region, they have hunted moose, caribou, bear, whale, walrus, and seals and fished salmon and halibut. Though the winters are harsh, the summers are bountiful.

Though we now couldn't imagine America without Alaska, it didn't become the forty-ninth state until 1959. In 1867, the United States purchased the land from Russia for two cents an acre. At first they thought they had made a bad investment due to Alaska's harsh terrain, but then they struck gold, literally, in 1872. Interestingly enough, during the ensuing gold rush, potatoes were practically worth their weight in gold, being valued for their high vitamin C content, which miners craved.

Gold might have been found in Alaska but the true treasure here is the state's natural wonders. Before I die, I would like to see the aurora borealis. Also known as the Northern Lights, the bands of brightly colored light that dance across the night sky are caused by electrically charged particles colliding with gasses in the atmosphere. My best friend growing up and I made a pact that we would see it together before we turn 50, and we still have time! The lights shine big and bright in Alaska.

Take it from Johnny Horton, who said Alaska is "where the river is windin', big nuggets they're findin', North to Alaska, go north the rush is on."

THE PIE!

The forty-ninth state has a state animal that inspired this savory pie: the king (aka Chinook) salmon. Alaska is the largest supplier of salmon, crab, halibut, and herring in the United States and the seafood industry is the largest private employer in Alaska. I am deeply in love with all things seafood: Give it to me raw, fried, or canned any day of the week and most especially in the form of a tower on my birthday.

King salmon can grow up to 3 feet long and weigh 25 to 60 pounds. Big bois! The largest on record is 125 pounds—a Very Big Boi! Their peak season is in June and it's often the most expensive fish in any store, with prices ranging from $30 to $50 a pound. The oily red flesh of the fish is tender and melts in your mouth, but its flavor is strong, so I pair it with another Alaskan favorite, halibut, which is light and flaky with a mild but distinct flavor. I also had to include that gold rush staple, the potato! Smooth and luxurious, this pie is made for eating while you bask in the summer sun of Alaska, dipping your toes in a river while writing postcards to someone you love: "Wish You Were Here!"

WILD ALASKAN SALMON AND HALIBUT PIE
WITH MASHED POTATO TOP

ACTIVE TIME: 1 HOUR — BAKE TIME: 30 MINUTES — TOTAL TIME: 1 HOUR 45 MINUTES — MAKES ONE 10-INCH PIE

CRUST

All-Butter Crust (single, page 332), rolled out, fit into a greased 10-inch pie pan, crimped, and partially blind baked (see page 339)

TOPPING AND FILLING

1½ pounds Yukon Gold potatoes, peeled and cut into 1-inch pieces

12 ounces wild Alaskan halibut, skin removed

12 ounces wild Alaskan salmon, skin removed

1 cup vegetable stock

1 bay leaf

2 tablespoons unsalted butter

¼ cup dry white wine

3 tablespoons cornstarch

7 tablespoons whole milk

½ cup frozen green peas, thawed

1 tablespoon chopped fresh dill

Flaky sea salt and freshly ground black pepper to taste

MAKE THE FILLING AND TOPPING: Cook the potatoes in lightly salted boiling water for about 20 minutes, until fork tender. Drain the potatoes well and set aside.

Place the halibut and salmon in a shallow saucepan and add the stock, bay leaf, and 1 tablespoon of the butter. Bring to a gentle simmer, partially cover, and poach for 5 to 6 minutes, until the fish is cooked through, opaque, and flakes easily. Using a slotted spoon, lift the fillets out and place in a medium mixing bowl. Don't discard the poaching liquid.

Remove the bay leaf from the poaching liquid and add the wine to the liquid. In a small bowl, mix the cornstarch and 3 tablespoons of the milk together, creating a slurry. Whisk the slurry into the poaching liquid. Place the pan over medium heat and cook, stirring constantly, until thickened and smooth, about 5 minutes. Stir in the peas and dill and season to taste with salt and pepper. Transfer to the bowl with the fish and fold to combine.

In a large mixing bowl, mash the drained potatoes with the remaining 1 tablespoon butter and remaining 4 tablespoons milk. Season with salt and pepper to taste.

ASSEMBLE THE PIE: Preheat the oven to 375°F. Fill the partially baked crust with the fish filling. Spoon the mashed potatoes on top, spreading them to cover the entire surface. With the back of a large spoon, make swooshing shapes on the potatoes to resemble the aurora borealis. Sprinkle with flaky sea salt and pepper.

BAKE THE PIE: Bake on a baking sheet on the center rack, rotating the pie clockwise after 15 minutes for even baking, for 30 minutes, or until the top is golden brown. Before serving, place under the broiler for a few minutes to brown top for crisp potato edges. Best served warm while basking in the Alaskan summer sun.

THE DEDICATION!

This pie is dedicated to Alex Miller of New Boston, New Hampshire, who spent a summer in Alaska bartending on a train that traveled between Anchorage and Denali National Park. I met Miller when I was three sheets to the wind on the Fourth of July, 2015, and we've been friends and sometimes a little more ever since. We have spent many an evening together listening to *The Freewheelin' Bob Dylan*, my favorite Dylan album, on vinyl. Whenever I listen to "Oxford Town" I hear the song in Miller's voice.

While Miller was in Alaska he would FaceTime me from the train. I couldn't hear a dang word, but I enjoyed the views of the sprawling mountains. Like Alaska, Miller will always be a little mysterious to me and a great adventure I continue to pursue. Alaska, you are beyond my wildest dreams but within my reach.

Arizona

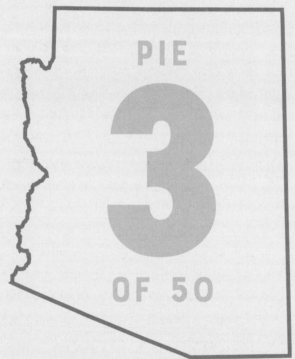

PIE

3

OF 50

THE GRAND CANYON STATE

NO STATE FOODS

THE STATE!

There are two tales about how the forty-eighth state got its name. The first is that it was named by an early explorer of Spanish descent named Juan Bautista de Anza and comes from a Basque word meaning "the good oak tree." The second is that it came from a Papago word that translates as "place of the young spring." Indigenous people have inhabited Arizona for at least 20,000 years, well before written history. The Hopi, Zuni, Navajo, and Apache tribes still live there today. In 1863 Arizona became a U.S. territory, then the forty-eighth state in 1912.

Arizona is home to the Grand Canyon, one of the Seven Natural Wonders of the world, and the only one in the continental United States. As a girl in Hong Kong, I dreamed about going to the Grand Canyon. I wanted to sit with my feet dangling on the edge at sunrise, again at sunset, and all the time in between. I wanted to listen to the playlist I had been curating for that moment for the better half of my life. I wanted to take it all in.

I basically wanted to be in front of something that would make me feel so small, yet fill me up with so much beauty that it would make me feel so whole and big. I finally got the opportunity to do that on my 30th birthday. I spent the four days leading up to that birthday hiking and exploring the North Rim of the Grand Canyon. When I first laid eyes on it, I was overcome and the tears wouldn't stop. It was so beautiful, so overwhelming, so much more than I had dreamed.

On the first day of my next rotation around the sun I woke up alone on the edge of the North Rim of the Grand Canyon and said a fond farewell to my 20s. Arizona, you're as grand as your state motto promises.

THE PIE!

Arizona has no official state foods, so I did a deep dive into foods that are commonly found and eaten in Arizona. I struck gold with the prickly pear. This sweet, pink-purply fruit is gorgeous, soft, and tender, and similar in texture and taste to dragon fruit, which I ate copious amounts of growing up. I had never tasted a prickly pear before developing this pie, and now I'm hooked. (Fun fact: The fruit is not actually a pear but a berry!) The trick with a prickly pear is making sure to remove the microscopic, clear spines that cover its outer skin.

Blushing apples and candied ginger meld perfectly with the prickly pear: The ginger delivers a lot of sass and a little heat and the apple serves as a neutral filler and texture builder to enhance and balance the sweetness of the pear. As the candied ginger cooks down it gives the fruit in the filling a beautiful sheen. The best time to bake this pie is late summer through early winter, as that's the peak season for prickly pears in the Northern Hemisphere.

The crust sets a Southwest scene: a little coyote howling at the moon. The coyote cookie cutter I used was a souvenir my friend Patrick picked up for me while he was visiting his parents in Arizona. For the pink hues, I used a little of the natural dye knowledge I had from being a Fibers major at SCAD and painted the crust with beet juice that I reduced to make a thick syrup—an attempt to capture an Arizona sunset in look and in taste.

BLUSHING PRICKLY PEAR AND APPLE PIE

ACTIVE TIME: 30 MINUTES — BAKE TIME: 1 HOUR — TOTAL TIME: 3 HOURS 30 MINUTES — MAKES ONE 10-INCH PIE

CRUST

All-Butter Crust (double or triple, page 332), rolled out (see page 339); one for the base, one for the top, and an optional third one for extra decorations

½ teaspoon all-purpose flour

½ teaspoon granulated sugar

1 cup beet juice, reduced to one-third its volume (optional)

Egg wash (see page 346)

Finishing sugar (see page 346)

FILLING

4 medium prickly pears

¼ cup granulated sugar

¼ cup cornstarch

1 teaspoon ground cinnamon

½ teaspoon ground nutmeg

1 tablespoon lemon juice

2 medium Granny Smith apples, cored and shredded

2 tablespoons chopped candied ginger

SPECIAL EQUIPMENT

Coyote and crescent moon cookie cutters (optional)

Paintbrush

MAKE THE FILLING: Preheat the oven to 375°F. Wearing rubber gloves, rinse the prickly pears, removing the fine spines by scrubbing the surface lightly with a sponge. Cut them in half and remove the seeds.

Scrape the flesh of the prickly pears into a medium saucepan and add the sugar, cornstarch, cinnamon, nutmeg, and lemon juice. Place over medium-high heat and reduce, stirring occasionally, until the mixture has the consistency of a thick puree. Transfer to a large mixing bowl and let cool completely. Mix in the apple and candied ginger.

ASSEMBLE THE PIE: Fit the bottom crust into a greased 10-inch pie plate. Sprinkle the ½ teaspoons flour and sugar on the bottom of the crust and swirl around with your fingers. Using a spoon, fill the crust with the cooled filling. Top with top crust and roll and crimp the edges to seal tightly (see page 343).

If making the optional decorations, use the third pie crust to cut out a coyote and moon with cookie cutters. With the reduced beet juice, paint an Arizona sunset on the top crust. Place the coyote and moon on the top of the pie to create dimension. Brush the whole pie with the egg wash, avoiding any areas painted with beet juice. Sprinkle liberally with finishing sugar.

BAKE THE PIE: Place the pie on a baking sheet and bake on the center rack for 1 hour, rotating the pie clockwise every 15 minutes to make sure the pie cooks evenly, until golden brown. Cover the crust for the last 15 minutes if the edges are getting too brown. Cool for at least 2 hours before slicing and serving. Best enjoyed while watching a gorgeous sunset!

THE DEDICATION!

Arizona belongs to Sierra Seip, who hails from Paradise Valley in the Scottsdale area. I met Sierra when she interned at a fashion company I worked for. She was one of the best interns I have ever known, and we bonded over our love for aquatic animals and cocktails. Sierra has carved her way through the design industry with skill and tact. She is talented and beautiful and has a heart of gold. The world is a tough place to navigate sometimes but it helps to have friends like her—ones you know are always in your court and a beacon of light at the end of a dark night.

Arizona: Thank you for the canyons, the sunsets, and especially the friendships.

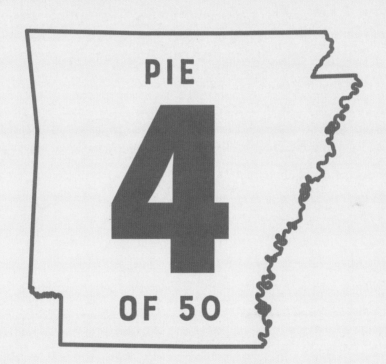

PIE

4

OF 50

THE NATURAL STATE

STATE BEVERAGE: COW'S MILK ★ STATE GRAIN: RICE

STATE GRAPE: CYNTHIANA ★ STATE NUT: PECAN

STATE FRUIT/VEGETABLE: SOUTH ARKANSAS VINE RIPE PINK TOMATO

THE STATE!

Arkansas's name comes from the Quapaw Nation by the way of early French explorers. At the time of early French exploration, the Quapaws lived west of the Mississippi and north of the Arkansas River. The Algonkian-speaking tribes of the Ohio Valley called them the "Arkansas," or "south wind." The state's name went through several spellings, from Akansea in French explorers Marquette and Joliet's *Journal of 1673*, to Acansa on a map a few years later. A map based on the journey of Jean-Baptiste Bénard de la Harpe in 1718–1722 refers to the river as the Arkansas and to the Native Americans of the area as les Akansas. In about 1811, Captain Zebulon Pike, a noted explorer, spelled it Arkansaw.

In the early days of statehood, two U.S. senators from the state of Arkansas were divided on the spelling and pronunciation. In 1881 the state's General Assembly passed a resolution declaring that the state's name should be spelled "Arkansas," but pronounced "Arkansaw."

Arkansas is nicknamed the Natural State because of its beautiful lakes, rivers, mountains, and wildlife. It is home to natural resources such as gold and diamonds and has bountiful fertile soil and fresh water that flows down from the springs in the Ozark Mountains to grow the freshest of foods. The Natural State became the twenty-fifth state on June 15, 1836, and it's the only state that has an official state cooking vessel: the Dutch oven, a nod to the early Arkansans who buried Dutch ovens in coals to cook campfire meals.

I bought my own Dutch oven with my first big-girl job paycheck when I moved to New York in 2010.

I have never been to Arkansas but when I go, I will visit the town of Atkins, where the fried pickle was invented in 1963. I will of course have ranch dressing in tow, for research purposes (and dipping).

Arkansas, I cannot wait to experience your abundance.

THE PIE!

Arkansas's state foods left me spoiled for choice! I knew I wanted to go a savory route. I thought about sitting on a blanket by Lake Ouachita, the state's largest lake and one of the cleanest in the nation, a breeze blowing through my hair, a Miller Lite in hand. What pie would I want to eat in that moment? It would have to travel well and be sturdy, nourishing, and the perfect thing after a refreshing lake swim. It also was essential that it pair well with the beverages my friend and I like to call "crispy bois."

The main inspiration came from the South Arkansas Vine Ripe Pink Tomato. Tomatoes are not native to Arkansas, but in the 1920s a commercial grower began to cultivate them in the southern part of the state. The pink tomato officially became both the state fruit *and* vegetable in 1987 because it is botanically a fruit but used as a vegetable. You might even say this state has a "ripe" history. The pie is an heirloom tomato and cow's milk cheese pie—all your summer picnic essentials in one. And with a sturdy herbed crust, it is portable enough for a little woodland exploration and bird watching. The best time of year to make this pie is in late summer, when tomatoes are at their peak. Bonus points if you can get your hands on the tomatoes sold at the Pink Tomato Festival in Warren.

HEIRLOOM TOMATO AND CHEESE PIE
WITH HERBED CRUST

ACTIVE TIME: 30 MINUTES — BAKE TIME: 30 MINUTES — TOTAL TIME: 1 HOUR 15 MINUTES — MAKES ONE 10-INCH PIE

CRUST

Herbed All-Butter Crust (single, page 333), rolled out, fit into a greased 10-inch pie pan, crimped, and partially blind baked (see page 339)

FILLING

2¼ pounds heirloom tomatoes (preferably South Arkansas Vine Ripe Tomatoes), sliced ¼ inch thick

Kosher salt and freshly ground black pepper

1 tablespoon extra-virgin olive oil

1 medium onion, chopped

½ cup shredded Gruyère cheese

½ cup grated Parmigiano Reggiano

¼ cup mayonnaise (preferably Duke's)

½ cup chopped mixed fresh herbs: chives, flat-leaf parsley, basil

MAKE THE FILLING: Preheat the oven to 350°F. Place the tomatoes on a clean dish towel in a single layer and sprinkle with about 2 teaspoons of salt, making sure all the tomatoes are covered in an even layer. Let them stand for 10 minutes, allowing the excess liquid to drain out.

While the tomatoes are draining, heat the oil in a medium skillet over medium heat. Add the onion and sauté for 3 to 4 minutes, until translucent and tender. Season with 1¼ teaspoons salt and 1¼ teaspoons pepper. Set aside. In a medium bowl, mix together the Gruyère, Parmesan, and mayonnaise.

ASSEMBLE THE PIE: Layer the ingredients in the partially baked pie crust, starting with about a quarter of the cheese mixture, then all the tomatoes, onions, and herbs, seasoning each layer with pepper. Sprinkle the remaining cheese mixture on top.

BAKE THE PIE: Place the pie on a baking sheet and bake on the center rack for 30 minutes, or until the cheese is bubbly. While it is still warm, wrap it up carefully in your favorite tea towel, take it to a park, and enjoy it outside in the sun on a blanket while you listen to the birds sing in the trees. It's a summertime dream to be enjoyed in the Natural State.

THE DEDICATION!

This pie is dedicated to a constant source of joy in my life: Olan (Kent) Reeves, who hails from Little Rock. Olan and I met in an Intro to Fibers class when we were 19—a hell of long time ago now. We spent countless hours in the studio listening to Ashlee Simpson, dyeing fabric, weaving, screen printing, and felting things together. Olan created a safe space for me. Whenever I was with him, I felt inspired and loved, and the creative vibes never stopped flowing. There is no one better to bounce ideas off than him, and he impresses me with art that fills the world with color and joy.

Arkansas, it's only natural that I've fallen for you.

California

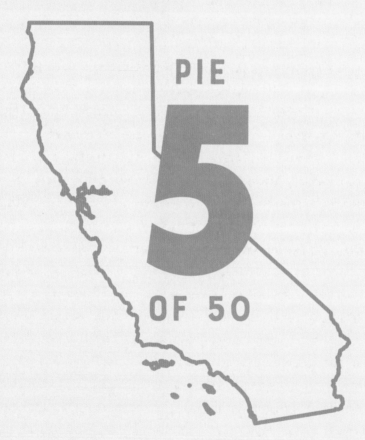

PIE

5

OF 50

THE GOLDEN STATE

STATE FRUIT: AVOCADO ★ STATE NUT: ALMOND
STATE GRAIN: RICE ★ STATE VEGETABLE: ARTICHOKE

THE STATE!

California, the Golden State! The name comes from a 16th-century Spanish novel that describes a mythical paradise called California. I don't like to play favorites, but dang, California is beautiful, from the southern tip of the state to the tippy top: filled with mountains, bordered by the ocean, and home to some of the freshest produce I have ever tasted. One of my dad's favorite songs is "San Francisco" by Scott McKenzie, and every time I think of California, that song plays in my head.

Gold was struck in 1848 at Sutter's Mill in Coloma and more than 100,000 people, nick-named the forty-niners, rushed to California the next year to seek their fortunes. Just a year later, California became the thirty-first state.

For my 21st birthday, I drove up Highway 1, the Pacific Coast Highway, slowly tracing the coastline, blasting tunes, and taking in the sights. I got to see Big Sur, grin from ear to ear watching seals lounge in the sun, hug a redwood tree, and tour some vineyards.

California is home to one of my favorite breakfast foods: Called the Rebel Within at Craftsman and Wolves in San Francisco, it is a savory muffin with a soft egg inside. How they do it boggles my mind. I always get one upon arrival and one on my way to the airport so I can have a luxurious snack on the plane home. The state is also home to the bakery I constantly dream about, Tartine, and their crusty bread with its custardy center. It is also home to Thomas Keller's fried chicken dinner at Ad Hoc; when I took my first bite, my life was forever changed.

A state full of some of the most delicious foods, perfect weather, and sprawling skies. I'll come back again and again. Stay Golden, California.

THE PIE!

The most obvious ingredient for a California pie is avocado. This state grows about 90 percent of all avocados grown in the United States, about 350 million pounds a year. There are hundreds of different varieties, but the Hass avocado is by far the most popular, and it also has a special relationship with the state. In the 1920s, Rudolph Hass, a mailman, purchased a seed from a grower and planted an avocado tree in his grove in La Habra Heights. The original "mother tree" died in 2002 at the age of 76, but all of today's Hass avocados in the world can be traced back to it. In 2013, California declared the avocado the state fruit.

However, here is where I abandon the avocado in favor of the road less travelled, choosing to go the long way up Highway 1. This is where the state vegetable—the artichoke—comes into the picture. California is responsible for 99 percent of the nation's artichoke crop. So with the artichokes decided upon, I wanted to give the pie more texture, which offered a perfect opportunity for the state nut, the almond, to join the party as part of a crumble. Fun fact: California grows eight out of every ten almonds eaten in the world! To tie all these elements together, we'll drizzle the whole thing with a wine reduction made from a classic California red.

ARTICHOKE PIE

WITH SAVORY ALMOND CRUMBLE AND RED WINE REDUCTION

ACTIVE TIME: 1 HOUR — BAKE TIME: 45 MINUTES — TOTAL TIME: 1 HOUR 45 MINUTES — MAKES ONE 10-INCH PIE

CRUST

All-Butter Crust (single, page 332),
    rolled out, fit into a greased
    10-inch pie pan, crimped, and
    partially blind baked (see page
    339)

Extra-virgin olive oil for brushing
    (California olive oil if you
    have it!)

TOPPINGS

Red Wine Reduction

1 tablespoon extra-virgin olive oil

½ cup chopped white onion

½ cup chopped celery

½ cup chopped carrot

1 clove garlic, minced

2¼ cups dry red wine

1½ cups ruby port

Kosher salt and freshly ground
    black pepper

Almond Crumble

½ cup unseasoned bread crumbs

½ cup grated Parmigiano Reggiano

6 tablespoons all-purpose flour

¼ cup chopped almonds

2 tablespoons chopped mixed fresh
    herbs (parsley, sage, thyme)

½ cup (1 stick) unsalted butter,
    softened

PRO TIP: *You can make the red wine reduction 2 days ahead. Make sure it's cooled completely before refrigerating in an airtight container.*

MAKE THE RED WINE REDUCTION: Heat the olive oil in a large saucepan over low heat. Add the onion, celery, carrot, and garlic and sauté until soft and translucent, 10 minutes. Add the wine and port, bring to a simmer, and reduce the heat. Simmer for 1 hour, or until the liquid has reduced by half in volume. Strain the mixture through a sieve and return the liquid to the saucepan. Continue to simmer to reduce the liquid to 1½ cups, about 10 minutes longer. Season with salt and pepper to taste. Set aside to cool.

MAKE THE ALMOND CRUMBLE: In a medium mixing bowl, mix the bread crumbs, Parmesan, flour, almonds, and herbs. With your fingers, incorporate the softened butter until the mixture looks like wet sand and everything is mixed well. Set aside in fridge until ready to use.

MAKE THE BÉCHAMEL: In a medium saucepan over medium heat, melt the butter. Add the flour and whisk until smooth. Continue to cook and whisk until the mixture turns golden brown, 6 to 7 minutes. Meanwhile, heat the milk in a separate saucepan until it's just about to boil.

Slowly add the hot milk to the flour mixture 1 cup at a time, continually whisking, until smooth. Bring to a boil, remove from the heat once the sauce has thickened, and season with the salt and nutmeg. Set aside to cool.

Recipe continues ★★★

BÉCHAMEL

5 tablespoons unsalted butter

¼ cup all-purpose flour

3 cups whole milk

2 teaspoons kosher salt

½ teaspoon grated nutmeg

FILLING

2 cups thawed frozen artichoke
hearts

½ cup extra-virgin olive oil

1 cup chopped white onion

Kosher salt and freshly ground
black pepper

¼ cup chopped fresh flat-leaf
parsley

MAKE THE FILLING: Cut the artichoke hearts into halves or quarters. Heat the olive oil in a large saucepan over medium heat. Add the artichoke pieces and onion, season with salt and pepper, and sauté until the onion is slightly caramelized, 6 to 8 minutes. Add just enough water to cover the bottom of the pan and cook over low heat for 15 minutes, until the artichokes are tender. Drain the artichoke mixture and transfer to a large mixing bowl. Add the parsley and béchamel, stir to combine, and season to taste.

ASSEMBLE AND BAKE THE PIE: Preheat the oven to 350°F. Place the partially baked crust on a baking sheet. Fill the crust with the artichoke filling and top with the almond crumble.

Bake the pie on the center rack for 35 minutes. Brush the crust with olive oil and bake for an additional 10 minutes, until the pie is golden brown.

While the pie finishes baking, warm the red wine reduction in a medium saucepan over medium heat. Serve the pie warm with red wine reduction drizzled on top and a big glass of your favorite California wine. Enjoy!

THE DEDICATION!

This pie is dedicated to Los Angeles native and my birthday twin, Lauren Vass! Lauren and I met at a party in college, found out that we were the same major, and the rest is a history filled with PBRs and dance parties. Lauren is as cool as a summer in San Francisco and as wonderful as eating a taco at sunset in Marina del Rey. She fills every room she enters with warmth and love.

California is home to so many people I love, it would take pages to name them all—but you know who you are and how much fun we had dancing at that flower shop in the Mission.

California: Eureka! You are the Golden State!

Colorado

PIE

6

OF 50

THE CENTENNIAL STATE

NO STATE FOODS

THE STATE!

Colorado: home of bluebird skies, sunshine, and the freshest air these lungs have ever had the opportunity to breathe. John Denver said it best: "friends around the campfire and everybody's high, Rocky Mountain high, Colorado."

Colorado is the thirty-eighth state and entered the Union in 1876, a hundred years after the Revolution began—making it the Centennial State. Before the state was filled with outdoor enthusiasts and tech moguls, the first settlements appeared thousands of years earlier in the southwest part of the state that was and is still inhabited by tribes including the Ute, Cheyenne, and Arapaho. In 1500, Spanish explorers arrived and named the region's largest river Rio Colorado, or "Colored River," due to the water's muddy red hue. The name would also come to refer to the state as we know it today.

Colorado is rectangular in shape and bordered by no less than six states: Utah, Wyoming, Nebraska, Kansas, Oklahoma, and New Mexico. The state's southwest corner is part of the Four Corners, where Colorado, Utah, New Mexico, and Arizona meet; it is the only place in the country where you can stand in four states at the same time. Colorado has the highest average elevation of any state, and its capital, Denver, is called the Mile High City because it sits at 5,280 feet above sea level, exactly one mile. I once heard the former governor of Colorado, John Hickenlooper, say on the NPR show *Wait Wait... Don't Tell Me* that if you took a piece of string and draped it across the state over every mountain and then laid the string flat, it would be as long as the width of Texas.

I was most recently in Colorado for my best friend's bachelor party: We rented a huge house in Salida, marveled at the nature surrounding us, and went white water rafting in Browns Canyon. Colorado makes its mark on your soul with every breath of air.

One of my favorite things about Colorado is that no matter where you turn, no matter where you look, there is always a mountain range in sight. How lucky is it to be enveloped by such beauty all the time? It feels like nature giving you a big hug.

THE PIE!

Colorado has no official state foods, but produces one of my favorite beverages, Coors beer. I'm not talking about Coors Light; I'm talking about that large butter-yellow can, the full Coors Banquet. A pie with just beer, though? Gross! Good thing the state's wide-open pastures make for the perfect environment to raise animals, supporting delicious beef, lamb, elk, and especially bison.

I love the deep, malty flavor that beer adds to a meat stew—the perfect filling for a pie. And while tucking into stew, I love to dip in some crusty bread, spread liberally with herbed butter. I wanted to translate that rich flavor and comforting feeling into a pie.

Here's a Coors-bison stew pie with an herbed crust and a fun decoration. I use a cookie cutter to cut out little bison, paint them with espresso, and arrange them in a "roaming" pattern too.

This pie is best after a long day on the slopes or white water rafting. It will stick to your bones. It's not just a meal: It's a whole dang banquet.

BISON AND COORS STEW PIE

ACTIVE TIME: 30 MINUTES — BAKE TIME: 1 HOUR — TOTAL TIME: 4 HOURS 30 MINUTES — MAKES ONE 10-INCH PIE

CRUST

Herbed All-Butter Crust (double, plus optional half portion, page 333), double crusts rolled out (see page 339) for top and bottom of pie; half crust rolled out for bison decorations if using

Egg wash (see page 346)

BISON STEW FILLING

1 pound bison stew meat, cubed

¼ cup all-purpose flour

2 tablespoons extra-virgin olive oil

1 tablespoon unsalted butter

1 medium onion, diced

2 cloves garlic, minced

1 tablespoon tomato paste

1 (12-ounce) can Coors Banquet

2 cups beef stock

1½ teaspoons Worcestershire sauce

½ teaspoon sugar

½ teaspoon paprika

½ teaspoon kosher salt

½ teaspoon freshly ground black pepper, plus more to finish

2 medium carrots, sliced

3 medium new potatoes, quartered with the skin left on

Finishing salt

SPECIAL EQUIPMENT

Dutch oven

2-inch bison cookie cutter (optional)

Instant espresso (optional)

Small paintbrush (optional)

MAKE THE FILLING: In a medium mixing bowl, toss the bison meat in the flour. Make sure the cubes are evenly coated in flour and shake off the excess. In a Dutch oven over medium heat, heat up the olive oil and butter. Add half of the bison cubes and cook, turning, until browned. Repeat with the remaining bison (I do this in batches so the pan doesn't get too crowded). Set the browned bison aside.

In the same pot, cook the onion for 2 to 3 minutes, then add the garlic and tomato paste and cook for an additional minute. Add the beer, stock, Worcestershire sauce, sugar, paprika, salt, and pepper and stir to combine. Return the bison to the pot, cover, and simmer for 1½ to 2 hours, until the liquid has reduced by a third. Add the carrots and potatoes and cook for an additional 30 minutes, until the carrots and potatoes are fork tender. Season to taste. Set aside to cool for at least an hour before filling the pie.

ASSEMBLE THE PIE: Preheat the oven to 375°F. Fit one rolled-out crust into a greased 10-inch pie pan. Fill the crust with the cooled bison filling and top with the top crust. Roll and crimp the edges to seal tightly (see page 343).

If decorating the crust with bison buddies: Roll out the half portion of herbed crust and cut out bison with the cookie

Recipe continues ★★★

cutter. Make one shot of instant espresso (2 tablespoons espresso powder mixed with 1 tablespoon water) and use to paint the little bison. Freeze for 15 minutes on a parchment-lined baking sheet.

BAKE THE PIE: Brush the top crust with the egg wash. If using, place your bison buddies as you wish on the top crust. Sprinkle the pie with finishing salt and pepper. Cut vents on top of pie crust.

Place the pie on a baking sheet. Bake the pie on the center rack, rotating it 90 degrees every 15 minutes, for 1 to 1½ hours, until the crust is golden brown. Let the pie rest for at least 15 minutes before cutting. Best enjoyed by a roaring fire, in your favorite hoodie and paired with an ice cold Coors Banquet. Enjoy!

THE DEDICATION!

This pie is dedicated to Emily Foelske of Boulder. She hired me to be a part of the handbag team at JCPenney in 2014 and we hit it off. We share the same humor, and we both appreciate a well-organized shelf and fresh stationery. Most importantly, we have the same taste in food and celebrity gossip. Nothing made me happier at work than when, right around 10:30 a.m., Emily would ask "So... what's for lunch?" I have Colorado and JCPenney to thank for a lifelong friend.

A special shout-out goes to Dan Gleason of Golden, my other desk buddy, with another special mention for Chuck and Kelsie's beautiful 15-year-young pup, Jackson Woodbury. I thought that Coors was my favorite thing to come out of Golden, but really, it's Jack Dog. He was the runt of the litter but couldn't hold a bigger place in my heart. I made Jack a mini version of this pie shaped like a buffalo, 'cause I love him so.

Colorado, you are the Centennial State. Any time I have spent with you has always been 100!

Connecticut

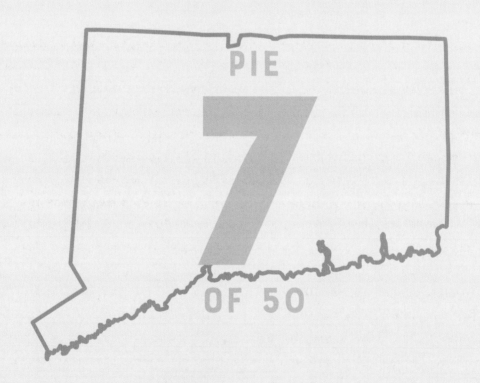

THE CONSTITUTION STATE

STATE COOKIE: SNICKERDOODLE ★ STATE DESSERT: ICE CREAM

THE STATE!

The name Connecticut comes from the Pequot word quinatucquet, which roughly translates as "beside the long tidal river," referring to the Connecticut River that cuts through the middle of the state. Its official nickname is the Constitution State because it is the birthplace to what some consider the first written constitution, the Fundamental Orders of Connecticut, adopted in 1639.

The first people to live in the area arrived more than 10,000 years ago. Thousands of years later, Native American tribes including the Mohegan, Pequot, and Niantic occupied the region and still occupy it today. It wasn't until the 1630s that the Dutch and English founded settlements in Connecticut, which became a British colony. In 1776, Connecticut's representatives signed the Declaration of Independence along with twelve other American colonies, and the American Revolution followed. The colonies won freedom from British rule in 1783 and five years later Connecticut became the fifth state.

I often feel like Connecticut is my home state. Some of my core memories from my teenage years are tied to the Nutmeg State: I spent two summers as a teenager in New Haven at Yale's summer camp, staying in the Yale dorms (I was a Vanderbilt Girl). I spent my days throwing video cameras at walls, making art from found objects, painting, writing, and falling in love with American boys. During those summers, I went to my first baseball game, had my first taste of "Chinese" food in takeout boxes, wore frosty lip gloss, and explored New England with awe.

Fairfield also holds a place in my heart. It is

where my second family, the Rinaldis, live. I know the place like the back of my hand. Sometimes I feel more comfortable in Fairfield than when I return home to Singapore. There is little that makes me happier than sitting around the Rinaldis' table, laughing my ass off and eating some of the delicious food my "mom" Joanne has cooked. Home is where the heart is, and I leave my heart in Connecticut every dang time.

THE PIE!

With both a state cookie and a state dessert for inspiration, this pie basically made itself! The snickerdoodle is an old-fashioned sugar cookie rolled in a mixture of cinnamon and white sugar; it's characterized by its soft texture, cracked surface, and buttery sweet flavor.

There is much debate about the cookie's origins. The most common story is that it came about in New England and is of German or Dutch origin. Some say that the name is simply a nonsensical word created from a New England naming tradition. In *The Book of New New England Cookery*, Judith Jones explains that "New England cooks had a penchant for giving odd names to their dishes—apparently for no other reason than the fun of saying them." Others believe that the name derives from the German schnecke knödel, or "snail dumpling." A rose by any other name would still taste as delicious.

I tried to translate the soft butter texture of the cookie into pie form with the addition of a little real nutmeg as a nod to the state's unofficial nickname, the Nutmeg State.

SNICKERDOODLE PIE

ACTIVE TIME: 30 MINUTES — BAKE TIME: 45 MINUTES — TOTAL TIME: 2 HOURS 15 MINUTES — MAKES ONE 10-INCH PIE

CRUST

All-Butter Crust (single, page 332), rolled out, fit into a greased 10-inch pie plate, crimped, and frozen (see page 339)

1 tablespoon granulated sugar

½ teaspoon ground cinnamon

2 teaspoons unsalted butter, softened

GLAZE

½ cup packed light brown sugar

¼ cup (½ stick) unsalted butter, softened at room temperature

3 tablespoons water

2 tablespoons light corn syrup

¼ teaspoon ground cinnamon

¼ teaspoon ground nutmeg

1 teaspoon vanilla extract

FILLING

¼ cup (½ stick) unsalted butter, softened at room temperature

½ cup granulated sugar

¼ cup confectioners' sugar

1 teaspoon baking powder

¼ teaspoon cream of tartar

½ teaspoon kosher salt

1 large egg

½ cup milk

1 teaspoon vanilla extract

1¼ cups all-purpose flour, sifted

SPECIAL EQUIPMENT

Stand mixer with paddle attachment or hand mixer

Pastry brush

COAT THE CRUST WITH CINNAMON SUGAR: In a small bowl, combine the granulated sugar and cinnamon. Brush the frozen crust with the soft butter, then sprinkle with the cinnamon sugar. Set the crust aside until ready to fill.

MAKE THE GLAZE: In a small saucepan, combine the brown sugar, butter, water, corn syrup, cinnamon, and nutmeg. Bring to a boil, stirring so the sugar dissolves. Boil for 2 minutes, then stir in the vanilla. Remove from the heat and set aside until ready to use.

MAKE THE FILLING: In a stand mixer with the paddle attachment, cream the room-temperature butter, granulated sugar, and confectioners' sugar until light and fluffy. Blend in the baking powder, cream of tartar, and salt. Add the egg, milk, and vanilla and blend until smooth. Blend in the sifted flour, making sure there are no streaks and the flour is fully incorporated.

ASSEMBLE AND BAKE THE PIE: Preheat the oven to 350°F. Place the coated pie crust on a baking sheet. Pour the filling into the crust and smooth. Pour the glaze on top but do not mix!

Bake on the center rack for 45 minutes, until browned or a toothpick inserted in the center comes out clean. Rotate pan clockwise every 15 minutes to make sure it bakes evenly. Let cool for at least 1 hour before serving. Enjoy à la mode!

THE DEDICATION!

The pie is dedicated to my best friend and sister, Lauren Rinaldi of Fairfield. I met Lauren my freshman year at SCAD and we cemented our friendship on a funny beach trip where we tagged along with our friends who were dating at the time. Now I pretty much run my every move through her.

We have the kind of friendship that is extremely annoying if you're the third person there, but we will never apologize. Some mornings Lauren and I FaceTime each other and set our phones so it looks like we are lying next to each other at a sleepover and chat about the day ahead. It's a special kind of friendship, a special kind of love.

Not only is Lauren a five-star friend, she is also a talented designer and illustrator, and her family has taken me in as one of their own. The Rinaldis have taught me so much about family, about communication, and most of all about my favorite holiday meal of all time, the Italian Christmas Eve Feast of the Seven Fishes. Feeling enveloped in love like theirs used to feel foreign to me, but with Joanne, Tony, Gianna, and Lauren, it's just a regular day.

Connecticut, you may be Full of Surprises, but I knew from the start I was going to fall for you.

Delaware

PIE

8

OF 50

IT'S GOOD BEING FIRST

STATE DESSERT: PEACH PIE

THE STATE!

It's always good being first! Delaware became the first state in 1787, when it was the first colony to ratify the Constitution.

At least 11,500 years ago, people were living in what we now know as Delaware. Thousands of years later, tribes including the Lenni Lenape and the Nanticoke occupied the region and still occupy it today. The first European to arrive is thought to be Henry Hudson, who reached the area's bay and river in 1609. The explorer Samuel Argall named the area in 1610 after the bay and river, which in turn were named after Virginia's then governor, Lord De La Warr. Dutch, English, and Swedish colonists settled in the land, and in 1674 the English gained control of the territory. Then in 1776 Delaware and the twelve other colonies declared their independence from England.

Delaware, the second smallest state, is full of personality and big draws, including a beautiful sandy coastline and some of the most delicious food I have ever eaten. The state gifted the world the sandwich known as the Bobbie, created at Capriotti's Sandwich Shop in Wilmington. It has all the best flavors of Thanksgiving: roast turkey, cranberry sauce, and stuffing served together on a roll all year long. I personally think it is best enjoyed while floating down the Delaware River, which I can attest to from personal experience.

THE PIE!

On May 9, 1895, the peach blossom was named the Delaware state flower, but for decades the state had already been a major peach producer. The first peach orchards were established in Delaware City in 1832 and spread to the southern regions of the state with the building of the railroads in the 1850s. The state was the country's leading producer of peaches for part of the 19th century, shipping 6 million baskets to market in 1875. Unfortunately, in the 1900s a disease changed everything. By the time the treatment was found for peach yellow, the crops had been decimated.

Today there are only three major peach orchards left in Delaware, but the state's love for the fruit hasn't wavered. Delaware designated the peach pie as its official dessert in 2009 as the result of a campaign started by fifth and sixth grade students at St. John's Lutheran School in Dover, the capital. The students suggested peach pie because of the historic and agricultural significance of the peach farming industry.

One of Delaware's nicknames is the Blue Hen State, a nod to the chickens that accompanied the state's soldiers in the American Revolution. So I took the peach pie one step further and made it a peach *custard* pie as an acknowledgment of the eggs laid by Blue Hens! Today, poultry farming is so big in the state that chickens outnumber people by more than 200 to 1.

A peach custard pie for a state that is in first place in the Union and ranks high up in my heart!

PEACH CUSTARD PIE

ACTIVE TIME: 30 MINUTES — BAKE TIME: 45 MINUTES — TOTAL TIME: 2 HOURS 15 MINUTES — MAKES ONE 10-INCH PIE

CRUST

All-Butter Crust (single, page 332), rolled out, fit into a greased 10-inch pie pan, crimped, and fully blind baked (see page 339)

FILLING

4 medium ripe but firm peaches (about 1⅓ pounds)

2 large eggs

¾ cup granulated sugar

¼ cup (½ stick) unsalted butter, melted

3 tablespoons all-purpose flour

Pinch of kosher salt

PREP THE PEACHES: Bring a large pot of water to a boil and prepare an ice bath. Cut a shallow "x" on the bottom of one peach, drop in the boiling water, and blanch for 1 minute. Immediately transfer to the ice water bath. Repeat for all the peaches. (This makes it easier to peel the peaches.) Let cool, then peel, pit, and cut into slices. Set aside until ready to fill the pie.

MAKE THE CUSTARD AND ASSEMBLE THE PIE: Preheat the oven to 375°F. In a medium bowl, whisk together the eggs, sugar, butter, flour, and salt.

Place the fully baked pie crust on a baking sheet. Pour the filling into the crust and arrange the peach slices in the custard as desired.

BAKE THE PIE: Bake the pie on the center rack for 45 minutes to 1 hour, rotating the pie clockwise every 15 minutes, until the edges are set but the center still jiggles like a soft thigh. Let the pie cool to room temperature for an hour then chill for an hour before serving. Enjoy à la mode or with whipped cream, maybe while floating down the Delaware River in the summer sun!

THE DEDICATION!

The pie is dedicated to one of Delaware's greatest exports, Stephani Stilwell of Middletown. I met Steph through our mutual friend Brian (Wisconsin pie recipient) and my pie project. Little did we know our collab on some illustration projects would lead to Steph becoming my roommate! Steph is a talented illustrator, author, and pattern pioneer but most of all she is the only person I know who knows as much useless *Top Chef* trivia as I do. Steph and I have a Thursday hangout date every week we dubbed Takeout Thursdays. We order a ton of takeout, sit on our couch in soft clothes, watch pure trash television, and air our woes. The comfort and safety I feel when I am with Steph is unparalleled.

A special shout-out goes to Steph's family: her mom Kathi and Mom Mom Jean. And last but not least this pie also goes out to my friend and twin flame, Becca Snyder of Wilmington.

Delaware: the first state in friendship!

florida

PIE

9

OF 50

THE SUNSHINE STATE

STATE BEVERAGE: ORANGE JUICE ★ **STATE FRUIT: ORANGE** ★ **STATE PIE: KEY LIME PIE**

THE STATE!

Florida gets a lot of flak for being the country's most whack-a-doo state, but I've only felt the warm rays of sunshine from the tail end of the East Coast.

Spanish conquistador Ponce de León sailed to Florida in 1513 searching for gold and silver. Instead, he found fertile farmland, endless coastlines, and some of the land's Indigenous inhabitants. In 1821, Spain gave Florida up to the United States in exchange for Spanish rule over Texas. Florida became the twenty-seventh state in 1845.

Florida's original Spanish name, La Florida, means "place of flowers." Some historians think Ponce de León chose the name to honor the blooming flowers he saw there, or as a tribute to Spain's Easter celebration, Pascua Florida, the Flowering Easter.

Many believe that de León was the first to plant orange seeds in Florida. Three centuries later, railroads connecting the states allowed for oranges to be shipped all over the country. Today the state produces 90 percent of America's oranges and a variety of other citrus including the key lime!

Growing up, I spent a couple summers in Miami when my dad was working on a hotel on Brickell Key. I remember vividly that it was when Britney Spears's "Hit Me Baby One More Time" came out, because I made my dad take me to a Tower Records to buy the CD. The bonus was that I got a taste of my first ever key lime pie. I have been hooked ever since. Florida, I love you right down to the tip.

THE PIE!

Whenever I think of Florida, these Bob Dylan lyrics come to mind: "She's still the one I want to see, I must find that Florida Key."

Key limes are smaller and more perishable than the Persian limes that are more common in U.S. grocery stores. The key lime tree, native to Malaysia, is said to have arrived in the Florida Keys in the 1500s with the Spanish.

Florida is proud of its key lime contribution to the pie world and aficionados argue endlessly about the proper way to make one. Should it be a graham or pastry crust? Should the topping be meringue or whipped cream? Should the filling be cooked or uncooked? The elements that everyone can agree on is that food coloring should never be added, the filling should be light yellow in hue, and sweetened condensed milk is essential to make the pie so smooth and delicious.

Who made the first key lime pie? The most likely story is that a woman known as Aunt Sally, cook for William Curry, a ship salvager and Florida's first self-made millionaire, was the first one to popularize it in the late 1800s. Some believe that she didn't create but perfected it, and that the delicacy was invented by area fishermen.

In 1994, the state legislature recognized the key lime pie as an important symbol of Florida, but passing legislation to designate a state dessert was not a piece of cake for Florida. Since the 1980s, north Florida lawmakers argued that a pie made of pecans also grown in Florida might better reflect the state's history. It wasn't until July 1, 2006, that key lime pie became the official pie.

KEY LIME PIE

ACTIVE TIME: 15 MINUTES — BAKE TIME: 15 MINUTES — TOTAL TIME: 4 HOURS 30 MINUTES — MAKES ONE 10-INCH PIE

CRUST

Graham Cracker Crust (page 336),
   blind baked as directed

FILLING

1 (14-ounce) can sweetened
   condensed milk

4 large egg yolks

2 teaspoons grated key lime zest

½ cup fresh key lime juice

TOPPING

1 cup heavy cream

2 to 3 key limes, sliced

SPECIAL EQUIPMENT

Stand mixer with whisk attachment
   or hand mixer

PRO TIP: *Make the pie from June to September when key limes are in season!*

MAKE THE FILLING: In a large mixing bowl, whisk the condensed milk and egg yolks until smooth and thick. Add the key lime zest and juice and whisk for 1 minute.

ASSEMBLE AND BAKE THE PIE: Preheat the oven to 350°F. Place the cooled graham cracker crust on a baking sheet and pour in the filling. Bake on the center rack for 15 minutes, until the edges are set but the center still jiggles like a soft thigh. Let the pie cool at room temperature for an hour before chilling for 3 hours to overnight in the fridge.

MAKE THE TOPPING: Whip the cream to stiff peaks with a stand mixer with the whisk attachment or a hand mixer, 8 to 9 minutes. Top the chilled pie with whipped cream and arrange sliced key limes on top as desired. Enjoy while basking in the warm sun pool side! Don't forget SPF!

THE DEDICATION!

This pie is dedicated to Haley Jordan Jones Phillips, who is more special than a Publix sub sandwich on a beach day. Haley hails from Orlando, the part of the state that gave us Disney World, but she is more magical. Haley also went to SCAD, but we didn't meet until we both lived in New York. I had the privilege of being co–maid of honor at her wedding, and we started a tradition where we send postcards of places we want to take each other. She is a designer, wife, mother, and superb friend. Whenever you're with her, the sun from the Sunshine State radiates from her.

A special shout-out also goes to my three favorite girls from West Palm Beach: Jaime Barker, Megan Balch, and Danielle LaMotte. Whenever I'm with the three of them it's like the first day at the beach on the first day of summer.

Florida, I can't wait until the next time my skin gets to bathe in your sunshine.

Georgia

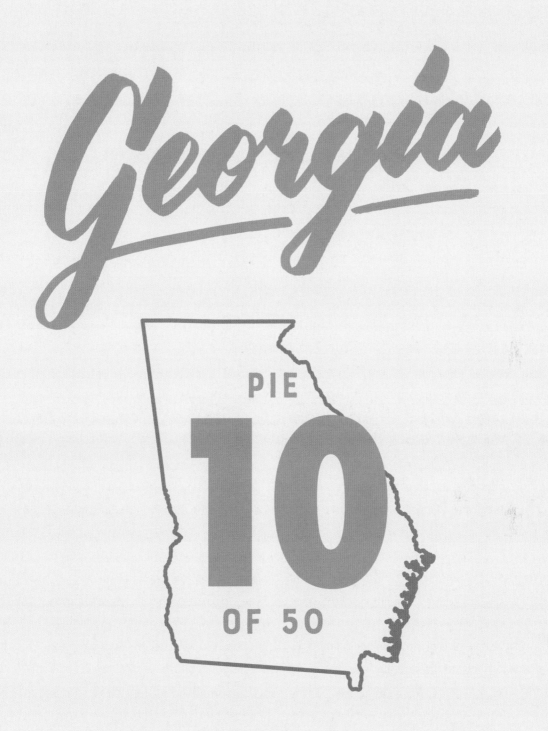

PIE

10

OF 50

GEORGIA ON MY MIND

STATE PREPARED FOOD: GRITS ★ STATE FRUIT: PEACH
STATE VEGETABLE: VIDALIA SWEET ONION

THE STATE!

Georgia is always on my mind. It's where I learned I could chug a beer wicked fast, where I first got my heart broken, and where I learned most of the wherewithal I have today. Georgia is a part of me, remembered with every peach I eat where the juice runs down my face.

Georgia was named after King George II, who approved the colony's charter in 1732. But the first people arrived in Georgia around 13,000 years ago and by 1,000 BCE, tribes including the Apalachee, Cherokee, and Choctaw lived there and still live there today. In 1732 Georgia was established as the thirteenth colony and in 1788 it became the fourth state.

I have experienced so much of the best this state has to offer. I've floated down the Chattahoochee River, which, just like Alan Jackson promised, was hotter than a hoochie coochie. I've explored all the corners of Savannah, swum at Tybee Beach, taken a nap under the trees in Forsyth Park, and gone to the last Riot Fest at the Masquerade in Atlanta.

And the food! I had never tried grits, biscuits and gravy, fried green tomatoes, or collard greens before moving to Savannah, but now I can't imagine my life without them. Some of my best food memories of the state are tied to Back in the Day Bakery in Savannah, run by Cheryl Day. Cheryl kept me fed, body and soul, all through college. Nothing made me happier than stopping in to get a big coffee and the best chicken salad sandwich.

I left Hong Kong to make a life for myself outside of what I was comfortable with. Georgia helped me shake it up, come out of my shell, and gave me so much more. Georgia, you're a real peach!

THE PIE!

The peach first made its way to the United States via Europe: Franciscan monks introduced the fruit to islands along Georgia's coast in 1571, where it flourished in Georgia's soil and produced the most detectably sweet strain. This fruit is also linked to the history of this state: During the Civil War, soldiers enticed by the fruit's deep flavor would pick peaches from the trees surrounding the battlefields, and the fruit grown in Georgia became renowned for its superior taste. The champagne of peaches!

The peach became the state fruit in 1995. But even though Georgia is the Peach State, Georgia's most valuable fruit crop is in fact the blueberry, and much of its land is dedicated to peanut farming. California now produces the most peaches in the United States, but nothing tastes as good as one from Georgia.

For this pie, I wanted to enhance the flavor of peaches with something extra. It had to be sweet tea, because almost every meal in the South is served with sweet tea. Georgia loves sweet tea so much that on April Fool's Day in 2003, John Noel, a Georgia state representative, and four co-sponsors tried to introduce House Bill 819, a proposal to require all Georgia restaurants that serve tea to offer *sweet* tea as an option. The bill was an attempt to bring humor to the legislature, but I wouldn't mind if it became law.

The pie for a state that has become one of my many homes is a stewed sweet-tea peach pie with a brown sugar–pecan crumble. It's delectably sweet and oh so charming.

SWEET TEA PEACH PIE
WITH PECAN CRUMBLE

ACTIVE TIME: 30 MINUTES — BAKE TIME: 1 HOUR — TOTAL TIME: 4 HOURS 30 MINUTES — MAKES ONE 10-INCH PIE

CRUST

All-Butter Crust (single, page 332), rolled out, fit into a greased 10-inch pie pan, crimped, and frozen (see page 339)

½ teaspoon all-purpose flour

½ teaspoon granulated sugar

SWEET TEA SYRUP

½ cup granulated sugar

½ cup water

2 black tea bags

½ lemon, zest removed with a vegetable peeler, then lemon juiced

PEACH FILLING

6 to 7 medium ripe peaches, peeled and sliced (about 5 cups)

½ cup all-purpose flour

¼ cup cornstarch

¼ teaspoon ground cinnamon

CRUMBLE TOPPING

¾ cup all-purpose flour

½ cup pecan pieces

¼ cup packed dark brown sugar

1 teaspoon ground cinnamon

⅓ cup (⅔ stick) unsalted butter, softened

MAKE THE SWEET TEA SYRUP: In a large saucepan, bring the sugar and water to a boil over medium heat. Reduce the heat and simmer, uncovered and stirring occasionally, until the sugar is dissolved, 3 to 5 minutes. Remove from the heat and add the tea bags and lemon zest strips. Cover and steep for 15 minutes. Strain the mixture then stir in the lemon juice. Set aside to cool to room temperature.

MAKE THE FILLING: In a large bowl, combine the sweet tea syrup, peaches, flour, cornstarch, and cinnamon. Set aside until ready to fill the pie.

MAKE THE CRUMBLE TOPPING: In a medium bowl, combine the flour, pecans, brown sugar, and cinnamon. Mix well and incorporate the butter until the mixture resembles coarse sand.

ASSEMBLE AND BAKE THE PIE: Preheat the oven to 375°F. Place the frozen crust on a baking sheet. Sprinkle the ½ teaspoons flour and sugar on the crust base and swirl around with your fingers. Fill with the filling and top with the crumble topping.

Bake for 1 hour on the center rack, rotating the pie clockwise every 15 minutes, until golden brown and you can hear the filling bubbling. Let cool for at least 3 hours before slicing and enjoying. Best served à la mode or with whipped cream and enjoyed on the front porch as the breeze blows through the magnolia trees!

THE DEDICATION!

The pie for Georgia is dedicated to my roommate of seven years, my friend since 2008, and the brother I always wanted, Patrick Racheff. Patrick and I met in college, and we grew close sitting in Gallery Espresso in Savannah, drinking tea and shooting the shit.

Weeks after graduation, Patrick and I packed up a truck and made the big move to New York together. He knows of all my secrets, and I await the nights out when we hit the sauce a little hard and end up at a karaoke bar where we will no doubt do a duet of "Love in This Club" by Usher. He is a talented filmmaker but most of all he is the best brother a lady could ask for. He's a real peach!

The pie is also dedicated to everyone I went to college with. Thank y'all for making me the woman I am today. Thank you to the Savannah College of Art and Design. I owe my greatest knowledge, my greatest loves, and my greatest friendships to you.

Georgia, you are always on my mind…and I carry you in my heart.

Hawai'i

THE ISLANDS OF ALOHA

NO STATE FOODS

THE STATE!

I was 7 years old in 1995 when my father was hired as a project manager to rebuild a resort on the Hawaiian island of O'ahu. We travelled 24 hours to get there from Hong Kong, and my life changed. That year I lived in the empty hotel with my family and the hotel staff while they renovated everything. The resort had a private beach, a dolphin lagoon, and a staff full of the kindest people, some of whom I am still in contact with. I spent my days exploring the resort and its surrounding areas in a swimsuit with my hair in braids, barefoot, with a Spam musubi in hand. I fed the dolphins and learned everything I could about them, stole the luggage carts with my sisters to race down the hallways, and consumed an insane amount of poke, pineapples, and coconut drinks. It was magical: every sunrise, every sunset. I didn't fathom how lucky I was then, but looking back I know now.

Before my sojourn to Hawai'i, I would watch *South Pacific* on repeat and sing "I'm Gonna Wash That Man Right Outa My Hair" without really a clue as to what it meant. (I have since found out.) Another favorite song is "Can't Help Falling in Love," which Elvis sang in the movie *Blue Hawaii*—it never fails to transport me back to this beautiful island state.

Hawai'i is said to be named for Hawai'i Loa, a legendary figure who discovered the islands. It is the world's largest island chain and the only U.S. state that is made up of only islands: a total of 137, only seven of which are inhabited. About

1,500 years ago, a group of canoes landed on one of the islands' shores, having rowed approximately 2,000 miles from what are now known as the Marquesas Islands in French Polynesia. Then 500 years later, people from what is now known as Tahiti rowed over 2,500 miles and joined them. These people brought cultures and traditions of their own, and over time created new traditions that are specifically Hawaiian. These traditions include but are not limited to surfing, hula, and the exchange of leis, or flower garlands.

Kamehameha became Hawai'i's first king in 1810 and the islands were ruled by royals for the majority of the 1800s, until they became a U.S. territory in 1898 and the fiftieth state in 1959.

To the Islands of Aloha: Elvis says only fools rush in, but I can't help falling in love with you.

THE PIE!

When I think of Hawai'i, I think of coconut trees softly swaying above white beaches with big blue waves crashing against the shore, and I think of the many days I spent swimming and drying off in the sun while eating pineapple. I have tried to capture these feelings with this pie.

Coconuts are not indigenous to the island; they were brought by Polynesian voyagers with other crops called "canoe plants," to grow wherever they found land. Besides providing vital nutrition for the Kānaka Maoli (Native Hawaiians), every part of the niu (coconut) was used in traditional Hawaiian culture. Now the coconut has woven itself into the landscape of the island and the food and the hearts of the people.

Pineapple, too, is closely linked with Hawai'i but not native, most likely originating in the Brazilian rainforest. In Hawaiian, a pineapple is called hala kahiki; from hala ("fruit") and kahiki ("foreign"). I think "Foreign Halas in Hawai'i" would make a great title for a sitcom featuring two transplants moving to Hawai'i to find a new lease on life...and possible romance.

Pineapples most likely debuted in Hawai'i when Spaniards set foot on the islands in the 16th century. Pineapples were taken on transatlantic voyages because they helped to curb scurvy. Later, the invention of ocean steamers and canning catapulted Hawai'i into the largest supplier of pineapples to the world. At its peak, Hawai'i was responsible for 80 percent of the world's canned pineapple.

So, the pie. A popular dessert in Hawai'i is haupia, or coconut custard, which is the main component of my pie, paired with pineapple to set it apart. So here's my coconut cream pie with a graham cracker crust and pineapple upside-down cake topping. A little '60s flair for my favorite state to get "lei'd" in.

COCONUT CREAM PIE
WITH PINEAPPLE UPSIDE-DOWN TOPPING

ACTIVE TIME: 1 HOUR — BAKE TIME: 30 MINUTES — TOTAL TIME: 4 HOURS 30 MINUTES — MAKES ONE 10-INCH PIE

CRUST

Graham Cracker Crust
(page 336), blind baked
as directed

FILLING

1 cup unsweetened coconut
flakes

1 (13.5-ounce) can coconut
milk

1½ cups heavy cream

3 large egg yolks

¾ cup granulated sugar

⅓ cup cornstarch

¼ teaspoon kosher salt

1 teaspoon vanilla extract

**PINEAPPLE UPSIDE-
DOWN TOPPING**

¼ cup (½ stick) unsalted
butter

1 cup packed light brown
sugar

1 (8-ounce) can sliced
pineapple in pineapple
juice

7 maraschino cherries

SPECIAL EQUIPMENT

10-inch cast-iron or other
circular oven-safe pan

PRO TIP: *This cold-set pie can be made a day in advance, but don't make the pineapple topping until you are ready to serve!*

MAKE THE FILLING: Preheat the oven to 350°F. Spread the coconut in an even layer on a rimmed baking sheet lined with parchment. Toast the coconut in the oven for 15 minutes, tossing every 5 minutes and making sure it doesn't burn, until the coconut is golden brown.

In a medium saucepan, combine the coconut milk, cream, egg yolks, granulated sugar, cornstarch, and salt. Bring the mixture to a boil over medium-low heat and cook, stirring constantly, until very thick, about 10 minutes. Remove from the heat and add the toasted coconut and vanilla. Let cool slightly before filling the pie.

FILL THE PIE: Pour the filling into the baked graham cracker crust and smooth the top with a spatula. Chill the pie in the fridge for 2 to 4 hours, until the filling is set.

MAKE THE TOPPING: Preheat the oven to 350°F. In a cast-iron or oven-safe 10-inch pan, melt the butter over medium-high heat. Add the brown sugar and blend. Arrange seven pineapple slices in the pan, covering the bottom. Place a cherry in the center of each ring. Bake for 30 minutes, until the pineapple is caramelized, checking every 10 minutes to make sure the pineapple caramelizes but does not burn.

FINISH THE PIE: This is tricky. Take the chilled pie, and place it upside down in the cast-iron skillet; the top of the pie should touch the pineapple mixture. Turn a plate upside down and place on the bottom of the pie, then flip everything over in one swift motion, setting the pie on the counter on the plate. Carefully remove the skillet; if a pineapple slice or cherry sticks to the skillet, just use a fork to move it to the top of the pie. Let the topping cool slightly and then slice and serve!

THE DEDICATION!

I dedicate Hawai'i to family. I hold these islands too close to my heart to give them to anyone else. This pie is for my family, especially my papa, Stephen Fong. Without him I would have never gotten the opportunity to live a year of my childhood in a way that most people can only dream of. Also, a big shout-out to the staff members of what was then the Kahala Mandarin Oriental Hotel, and a dolphin named Hoku, who baby Stacey spent many afternoons spilling all her hopes and dreams to.

A hui hou kakou. Until we meet again, Islands of Aloha!

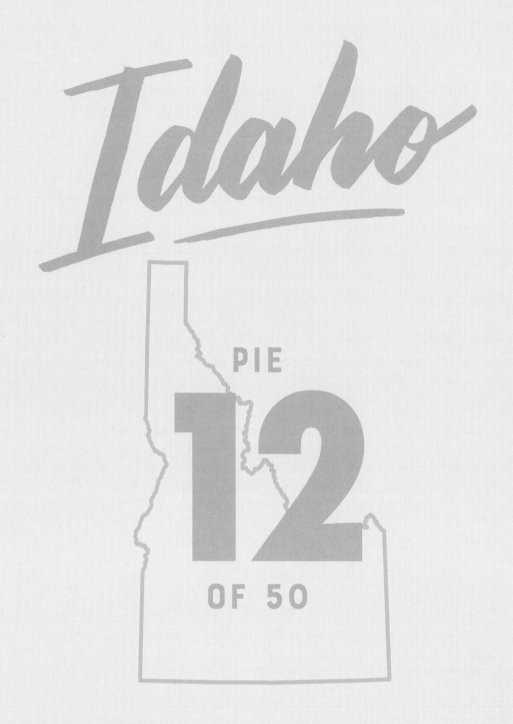

Idaho

PIE

12

OF 50

GREAT POTATOES.
TASTY DESTINATIONS

STATE VEGETABLE/FOOD: POTATO ★ STATE FRUIT: HUCKLEBERRY

THE STATE!

Idaho's name was completely made up! There are many tall tales about how the state got its name including one that says it is derived from a Native American word meaning "gem of the mountains," but it simply is not true. The state's name was made up in the mid-1800s at a time during which making up names was common practice.

The first people in this area made it their home 16,000 years ago. Thousands of years after that, other tribes, including the Nez Perce, Coeur d'Alene, Kootenai, Shoshone, Bannock, and Blackfeet, lived on its lands and still do today. The first non-Native people to reach what is now Idaho were American explorers Meriwether Lewis and William Clark in 1805. Both the United States and Great Britain claimed the region until 1846. In 1863 Idaho became its own territory. Seventeen years later, Idaho joined the Union as the forty-third state.

During the gold rush many Chinese immigrants moved there to work as gold miners, eventually making up a quarter of the state's population. The immigration led to the Chinese people planting some of the first gardens in the new towns, opening restaurants and grocery stores that introduced locals to rice, noodles, and dumplings, and widening the culinary landscape in the state.

As for me, I can't wait to set foot on Idaho's Craters of the Moon National Monument. This area was carved by ancient lava rivers and has terrain with large craters that seem to go on for miles and miles. It's the closest I might get to tippy-tapping my feet on the moon.

Idaho may be known as the Gem State, but we know the true gem of the state: the potato!

THE PIE!

The potato is native to the Americas and originated in what is now southern Peru. It gets its name from the Spanish word patata, derived from a combination of the Taino batata and the Quechua papa.

The potato became the official state vegetable of Idaho in 2002. The average American eats more than one hundred pounds of potatoes each year. That's a whole lot of spuds, my buds. Idaho's rich volcanic soil coupled with water from melting snow, fresh air, long sunny days, and cool nights combine to produce the perfect potato.

Idaho produces about one-third of the potatoes grown in the United States, almost 10 billion pounds a year. But the first potato in America was planted in New Hampshire in 1719. The potato wasn't brought to Idaho until 1836, by Henry Harmon Spalding.

Whether a potato is mashed, baked, boiled, steamed, french-fried, chipped, scalloped, home-fried, hash-browned, pancaked, or made into bread, I love it.

My Idaho offering is a mashed potato pie with a hash brown crush and a scalloped potato topper! Potatoes three ways for a state whose slogan was formerly "Famous Potatoes." The crispy edges of the hash brown crust, the creamy mashed filling, and the layers of the scalloped potatoes with their crispity crunchity bits dance all over your tongue. The only thing better than potatoes on their own is a pie made of them!

MASHED POTATO PIE

WITH HASH BROWN CRUST AND SCALLOPED POTATO TOPPING

ACTIVE TIME: 1 HOUR — BAKE TIME: 1 HOUR — TOTAL TIME: 2 HOURS 15 MINUTES — MAKES ONE 9-INCH PIE

CRUST

Hash Brown Crust (page 338), blind
  baked as directed

MASHED POTATO FILLING

4 medium potatoes, peeled and
  chopped into 1-inch pieces
2 sprigs fresh rosemary
2 sprigs fresh sage
1 cup heavy cream
1½ tablespoons unsalted butter
1 bay leaf
Kosher salt and freshly ground black
  pepper to taste
2 tablespoons chopped fresh chives

SCALLOPED POTATO TOPPING

1 teaspoon kosher salt
1 teaspoon freshly ground black pepper
¼ teaspoon grated nutmeg
3 to 4 small red and purple potatoes,
  peeled and thinly sliced (with
  mandoline if available)
1½ tablespoons unsalted butter, cubed
¾ cup heavy cream
¼ cup whole milk

SPECIAL EQUIPMENT

Mandoline
Potato masher, hand mixer, or stand
  mixer with paddle attachment

MAKE THE FILLING: Add the potatoes, rosemary, and
sage to a large pot filled with cold water and bring to a
boil over medium-high heat. Cook for about 20 minutes,
until the potatoes are fork tender. Drain the potatoes and
discard the herbs. Transfer the potatoes to a large bowl.

In a medium saucepan, heat the cream, butter, and
bay leaf until almost at a rolling boil. Remove and discard
the bay leaf. Mash the potatoes with a potato masher
or mixer, making sure not to overmix. Continue mashing
the potatoes, adding the hot cream mixture a little bit
at a time, until it is fully incorporated. Season with salt
and pepper to taste and mix in the chives. Set aside until
ready to fill the pie.

MAKE THE TOPPING: Preheat the oven to 350°F. Mix
the salt, pepper, and nutmeg together. In a greased 9-inch
pie pan, arrange about one-third of the sliced potatoes in
a single layer. Sprinkle about 1 teaspoon of the salt-spice
mixture and ½ tablespoon of the cubed butter on top.
Continue layering to make three layers. Pour the cream
and milk all over the potatoes, making sure the potatoes
are submerged in liquid. Cover the pan with foil and bake
for 1 hour, until the edges are crispy and the center is fork
tender.

Recipe continues ★★★

ASSEMBLE THE PIE: Heat the broiler. Place the hash brown crust on a baking sheet and fill with the mashed potatoes, smoothing the top as best possible. Place the cooked scalloped potatoes on top. You can do this by using a spoon or by quickly inverting the pie and placing it, mashed potato side down, onto the scalloped potatoes. Then in a swift motion, flip so the potatoes end up on top. Remove the scalloped potato pan. Place the pie on an oven rack 2 inches under the broiler and broil for 3 to 5 minutes, until golden brown. Watch it carefully to make sure it doesn't burn. Let the pie sit for 10 minutes before serving. Best served in a hot tub while it snows and you're drinking a chilled white wine. Enjoy!

THE DEDICATION!

When I first baked this pie, I didn't know anyone from Idaho. And I still don't know anyone from Idaho! Guess I need to change that.

The pie was consumed by my friend Katie Libutti, formerly of Rochester, New York, and myself. We may not be Idahoans but we eat more potatoes than the average American. I have spent many nights putting tequila to the face with Katie, dancing to a perfectly curated '90s playlist that includes Alanis Morissette and my personal favorite, Jewel, and consuming some sort of fried potato product to end the night. This final act is always in an effort to make sure that the sins we sit with the next day aren't too harsh. In typical fashion, we start the next day with a large pile of home fries to soak it all up, too.

Idaho, I will breathe your fresh air and see your sprawling lands one day. Thank you for giving us "Great Potatoes. Tasty Destinations."

Illinois

PIE
13
OF 50

LAND OF LINCOLN

STATE SNACK FOOD: POPCORN ★ STATE FRUIT: GOLD RUSH APPLE
STATE VEGETABLE: SWEET CORN ★ STATE GRAIN: CORN ★ STATE PIE: PUMPKIN PIE

THE STATE!

Illinois is a study in contradictions. You might even say a microcosm of everything this country has to offer: It's one of our leading producers of corn and soybeans, but also home to one of the world's busiest airports and to towering skyscrapers. It has the greatest concentration of land, water, and air transportation facilities in the world. Much of Illinois was once covered in grass, earning its nickname, the Prairie State.

The first Europeans to reach the area, in 1673, were the French explorers Jacques Marquette and Louis Jolliet. In 1717, Illinois became part of the Louisiana territory, a French colony. In 1763, at the end of the French and Indian War, the French gave up the region to Britain. After the American Revolution, Illinois became a U.S. territory and in 1818 the twenty-first state.

Its slogan, Land of Lincoln, refers to a pivotal moment in Abraham Lincoln's career. Though Lincoln was born in Kentucky and lived in Indiana before moving to Illinois, he began his political career with an unsuccessful run for the Illinois General Assembly in 1832. Lincoln eventually was elected to four terms in the state's General Assembly and served from 1834 to 1842. Illinois was also where Lincoln lived when he became President of the United States in 1861.

In 1871 a huge fire swept through Chicago; the reconstruction that followed was the beginning of the modern city that it is today. The first skyscraper to appear in the city was built in 1885, and the city is now home to North America's third tallest building, the Willis Tower.

Growing up in Hong Kong, whenever anyone mentioned Illinois or Chicago, all I could think about was Michael Jordan. Like everyone during that time, I was entranced by the Chicago Bulls. I still have my Jordan jersey from then…it just fits a whole lot tighter. And yet, I have never been to Illinois!

Until I make it over to eat a Chicago dog at Wrigley Field, this pie will have to do.

THE PIE!

The Illinois food landscape is rich with German, Polish, and Greek flavors, but after much research into its state foods, I decided its pie could only be one thing: pumpkin, my arch nemesis in the pie world. I have never met a pumpkin pie I liked, but hey, I'm doing this project for the people. So I accepted the challenge.

In 2015, Illinois State Representative Keith Sommer of Morton sponsored legislation to name pumpkin pie as the state pie to pay tribute to how much pumpkin is produced in Illinois: about 85 percent of canned pumpkin consumed in the United States comes from the Prairie State.

But I couldn't make a regular ol' pumpkin pie! I had to think outside the box. Then it hit me: I could make the love child of a pumpkin pie and a deep-dish pizza, which is thick and baked in a skillet and requires a fork and knife to eat 'cause it's too dang hard to pick up! Like one of Chicago's skyscrapers, this deep-dish pumpkin pie was an engineering feat.

If possible, it's best to make the filling a day in advance.

DEEP-DISH PUMPKIN PIE

ACTIVE TIME: 1 HOUR — BAKE TIME: 50 MINUTES — TOTAL TIME: 6 HOURS — MAKES ONE 9-INCH PIE

CRUST

All-Butter Crust (double, page
332), do not separate into two
portions; entire quantity of crust
rolled out and blind baked in
a 9-inch springform pan (see
below for detailed instructions)

Egg wash (see page 346)

PUMPKIN FILLING

1 cup granulated sugar

1 cup packed light brown sugar

2 tablespoons cornstarch

2 teaspoons ground ginger

2 teaspoons ground cinnamon

1 teaspoon ground nutmeg

¼ teaspoon ground cloves

1 teaspoon kosher salt

¼ teaspoon freshly ground black
pepper

2 (15-ounce) cans pumpkin puree
(I prefer Libby's)

2½ cups heavy cream

6 large eggs, beaten

SPECIAL EQUIPMENT

9-inch springform pan that is at
least 2½ inches deep

Parchment paper

PRO TIP: *Just a pep talk before you start baking this pie.
The deep-dish crust is the hardest part of this recipe. Don't be
stressed, and take your time. After all, Chicago wasn't rebuilt in
a day after the fire. You got this!*

MAKE THE FILLING: In a medium bowl, whisk together the
dry ingredients: sugars, cornstarch, ginger, cinnamon, nutmeg,
cloves, salt, and pepper. In a separate medium bowl, mix the
pumpkin, cream, and eggs together until well incorporated.
Mix in the dry ingredients and make sure everything is well
incorporated. Refrigerate for at least 2 hours, or up to overnight.

BLIND BAKE THE CRUST: Preheat the oven to 425°F. Roll
out the double portion of dough so that there will be at least a
1-inch overhang beyond the edge of the springform pan. Spray
the 9-inch springform pan liberally with nonstick cooking spray.
Line the bottom with parchment paper. Fit the rolled-out crust in
the pan, making sure to push the dough into all corners on the
bottom and that all the sides are covered. Leave about ½ inch of
dough hanging over the edge of the pan. Freeze for 1 hour.

Prick the dough with a fork on the base and sides. Line the
entire crust with foil, making sure it is tight around the edges.
Fill to the brim with pie weights or beans. Bake for 30 minutes,
until the crust is lightly golden at the edges. Let the crust cool
completely with the weights still in the crust; it may take 2 to 3
hours to cool completely.

Recipe continues ★★★

FILL AND BAKE THE PIE: Preheat the oven to 400°F. Remove the foil and weights from the baked crust and brush the entire crust with egg wash to seal. Keep the crust in the springform pan.

Place the baked crust on a baking sheet and fill with the chilled pumpkin filling. Bake the pie on the center rack, rotating the baking sheet 90 degrees every 15 minutes to make sure the filling is cooking evenly, for 45 to 50 minutes, until the center has a slight jiggle but is mostly set. Check the edge of the crust at 30 minutes; if it is getting too brown, tent with foil. Let the pie cool for at least 4 hours before removing from the springform pan.

Serve with whipped cream if desired. Best enjoyed while watching *The Last Dance* documentary series about Michael Jordan and the 1997 Chicago Bulls.

THE DEDICATION!

This Illinois pie is dedicated to my fine friend Taryn Haas, from Palatine, a suburb of Chicago. Soon after meeting, we bonded over the subtle nuances of late '90s teen sitcoms and Disney Channel original movies. And she threw a party with the best theme I have ever heard: "Britney Through the Ages." Taryn and I have ripped plenty of dance floors to shreds and giggled until the sun comes up. Life is better with a Taryn in your life and I have the Prairie State to thank for that.

I pine for the day I am neck deep in a deep-dish pizza in Illinois!

Indiana

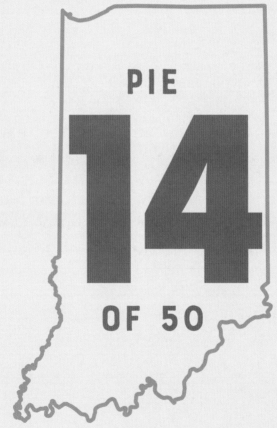

PIE

14

OF 50

HONEST TO GOODNESS

UNOFFICIAL STATE PIE: SUGAR CREAM PIE/HOOSIER PIE

THE STATE!

The British named the territory Indiana, in attempted recognition of its original inhabitants, after winning it from France in 1763 after the French and Indian War. At the end of the American Revolution, in 1783, Britain ceded Indiana to the United States, and in 1816 it became the nineteenth state to join the Union.

The state is affectionately known as the Hoosier State, but what is a Hoosier? There isn't a clear-cut answer. The earliest known use of the word was in a letter from 1827 that said, "There is a yankee trick for you—done up by a Hoosier." In 1848, Hoosier was defined as "a nickname given at the west to natives of Indiana." In a poem by John Finley, the term is used to encapsulate the qualities they possess, like self-reliance and bravery. Without a clear story of how the name came to be, the mystery lives on!

The state is home to the Indianapolis 500, a car race going back more than one hundred years. I would love to attend the Indy 500 while munching on one of my favorite snack foods, popcorn. But although corn is king in the Midwest and Indiana ranks second only to Nebraska in popcorn production, for dessert it couldn't be anything other than sugar cream pie!

THE PIE!

Sugar cream pie, also known as Hoosier pie, has been the unofficial pie of Indiana ever since the Indiana Senate adopted a special nonbinding resolution in 2009. The pie is said to have originated in eastern Indiana Shaker communities, dating back to 1816. The oldest recipe on record is in *The Hoosier Cookbook* published in 1976 by Elaine Lumbra and Jacqueline Lacy. Its recipe for Sugar Cream Pie was contributed by Mrs. Kenneth D. Hahn of Miami County, Indiana.

This kind of pie is known as a "desperation pie" since you can make it even when supplies are tight and apple bins are empty: It takes only six ingredients and needs no eggs. It is also affectionately known as "finger pie" because you stir the pie with your finger during baking to avoid breaking the crust.

This pie is full of thick vanilla custard cradled by a flaky, buttery crust dusted with a thin veil of spicy nutmeg. There is nothing desperate about this baby. It's straight up delectable!

SUGAR CREAM PIE

ACTIVE TIME: 15 MINUTES — BAKE TIME: 45 MINUTES — TOTAL TIME: 3 HOURS — MAKES ONE 10-INCH PIE

CRUST

All-Butter Crust (single, page 332), rolled out, fit into a greased 10-inch pie pan, crimped, and frozen (see page 339)

FILLING

1½ cups heavy cream

½ cup half-and-half

1 teaspoon vanilla extract

6 ounces granulated sugar (just under 1 cup)

½ cup all-purpose flour

½ teaspoon kosher salt

Fresh nutmeg, for grating

1 tablespoon unsalted butter, cubed small

SPECIAL EQUIPMENT

Fine grater or Microplane

MAKE THE FILLING: In a medium bowl, whisk together the cream, half-and-half, and vanilla. In a separate medium bowl, whisk together the sugar, flour, and salt. Mix the dries with the wets and set aside until ready to fill the pie.

ASSEMBLE THE PIE: Preheat the oven to 425°F. Place the frozen crust on a baking sheet and grate an even layer of nutmeg over the bottom. Scatter the butter over the base of the crust and slowly pour in the filling.

BAKE THE PIE: Bake the pie on the center rack for 10 minutes. Stir the filling in the center shallowly, using either a finger (as it was traditionally done) or a spoon. Turn the heat down to 325°F and bake, shaking the baking sheet every 8 minutes (to prevent the sugar from settling and to give you a thick creamy filling), for an additional 30 to 35 minutes. The pie is done when the edges are set but the center of the pie jiggles like a soft thigh. While the pie is still hot, grate nutmeg over the whole pie. Let cool for at least 2 hours before slicing; enjoy while watching the Indy 500!

THE DEDICATION!

The Indiana pie belongs to my friend Kathryn Irizarry, who hails from Carmel, a suburb north of Indianapolis. Kathryn and I found friendship like the Rihanna song says, "in a hopeless place"—smack dab in the middle of the pandemic in 2020. We met when I took my first kitchen job at the Brooklyn bakery Four & Twenty Blackbirds. I was a lost little soul fresh from the fashion world and soft from quarantine. We have since continued our quest to find the most delicious food and drink by checking off a list of restaurants called Eatey Places with Stacey. We even found out during a photoshoot at the bakery that we have twin hands, now littered with small burns from working in a kitchen.

Honest to Goodness Indiana, thank you for Kathryn!

A special shout-out also goes to friend, ceramic artist, and the Latch Key founder Whitney Sharpe who grew up in Elkhart County and is my Virgo sister from college.

Iowa

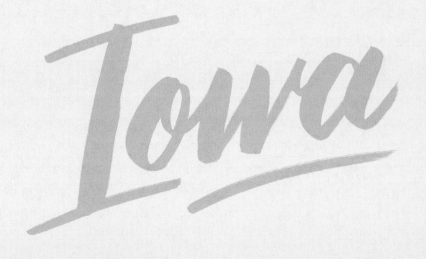

PIE

15

OF 50

LIFE CHANGING;
FIELDS OF OPPORTUNITY

NO STATE FOODS

THE STATE!

Whenever I hear the phrase "corn-fed American man" I imagine someone from this state of sprawling corn fields and farmlands. I think about riding around with said man in an old Ford pickup and then drinking beers in the truck bed under the stars. Basically, I think about the kind of life Taylor Swift describes in "Our Song."

Iowa (the only state name that starts with two vowels) is named for the Iowa River, which itself was named for the Native American tribe who lived in the territory. Tribes including the Ioway, Dakota Sioux, Illini, Missouria, and Otoe have called this state home for thousands of years.

Iowa is the only state whose east and west borders are formed by water, from the Missouri and Mississippi Rivers. In 1803 the United States acquired the territory from France through the Louisiana Purchase, and Iowa became the twenty-ninth state to join the Union in 1846.

Iowa's greatest natural resource is its rich soil, and it produces the most corn in the nation—so much that it converts some into ethanol, making it the top producer of this energy source as well. Iowa is home to many of America's favorite things like Quaker Oats, based in Cedar Rapids and the largest cereal company in the world. And the house that inspired artist Grant Wood's famous painting *American Gothic* stands in Eldon. I would love to one day make the trek to see the house and re-create the painting for myself. But when I finally get to Iowa, I plan to first run through cornfields, climb bales of hay, and enjoy an ear of corn slathered with butter…and drink a lot of beer.

THE PIE!

The sour cream raisin pie is a traditional American pie that is especially popular at the Iowa State Fair, which has a baking contest devoted to it. Some say the pie is German in origin, while others say it originated in America's heartland or is a Mennonite recipe. Maybe it is a mish-mosh of all these things. Whatever its origins, this creamy, delectable pie with a fluffy meringue top blew me away. Admittedly, when first I heard about this "Sour Cream Raisin Pie," I had my reservations, but boy, I've changed my tune.

From my own research, I have come to believe the pie's origins must be tied to the funeral pie, also known as raisin pie (or rosine pie, which is German for "raisin"). Funeral pie was traditionally served with a meal prepared for the family or friends following a funeral. Before the invention of refrigeration, fresh fruits were not always readily available, but most homes had raisins on hand. This pie became a favorite of Mennonite cooks because its ingredients were always in the pantry and it kept well. Unlike other dishes, it could be made a day or two ahead of the funeral supper and stored safely without refrigeration.

The original raisin pie is a double-crust pie. My guess is that Iowa's sour cream raisin pie was an evolution of that. The main differences between the two are that the latter includes sour cream and eggs and is baked before it's chilled.

SOUR CREAM AND RAISIN PIE

ACTIVE TIME: 30 MINUTES — BAKE TIME: 15 MINUTES — TOTAL TIME: 4 HOURS 45 MINUTES — MAKES ONE 10-INCH PIE

CRUST

All-Butter Crust (single, page 332), rolled out, fit into a greased 10-inch pie pan, crimped, and fully blind baked (see page 339)

FILLING

1 cup raisins

2/3 cup granulated sugar

2 tablespoons cornstarch

1/2 teaspoon ground cinnamon

1/4 teaspoon ground cloves

1/4 teaspoon kosher salt

1 cup sour cream

1/2 cup 2-percent milk

3 large egg yolks, at room temperature, beaten

MERINGUE TOPPING

3 large egg whites, at room temperature

1/4 teaspoon kosher salt

1/8 teaspoon cream of tartar

6 tablespoons granulated sugar

SPECIAL EQUIPMENT

Stand mixer with whisk attachment or hand mixer

PRO TIP: *For a fluffier meringue, separate your eggs while they are cold and then let them come to room temperature. Also make sure the bowl you are using for your meringue is spotless!*

MAKE THE FILLING: In a small saucepan, combine the raisins with enough water to just cover and bring to a boil. Remove the pan from the heat and set aside. In a large saucepan, combine the sugar, cornstarch, cinnamon, cloves, and salt. Stir in the sour cream and milk until the mixture is smooth. Cook the mixture over medium-high heat until it thickens and is bubbly. Reduce the heat to low and cook and stir continuously for an additional 2 minutes, until the bubbles subside and the mixture can coat the back of a spoon. Remove from the heat. Stir a small amount of the hot mixture into the egg yolks to temper, then add the egg yolk mixture to the pan, stirring constantly. Bring the mixture back up to a gentle boil and boil for 2 minutes, then remove from the heat. While the mixture cools slightly, drain the raisins, reserving 1/2 cup of the liquid. Gently stir the liquid into the filling and then add the raisins. Set the filling aside until ready to fill the pie.

MAKE THE MERINGUE: In the bowl of the stand mixer or in a small bowl if using a hand mixer, beat the egg whites and salt until soft peaks form. Add the cream of tartar. Gradually beat in the sugar on high speed, 1 tablespoon at a time, making sure that the sugar is fully incorporated before adding more. Beat until stiff peaks form.

Recipe continues ★★★

ASSEMBLE AND BAKE THE PIE: Preheat the oven to 350°F and position the top rack about 4 inches from the top of the oven. Place the baked pie crust on a baking sheet and fill with the filling, smoothing the top. Spread the meringue over the filling, making sure to seal the edge of the meringue to the crust. Bake on the top rack for 15 minutes, or until golden brown. Let the pie cool on a wire rack for 1 hour before refrigerating for 1 to 2 hours. The pie is best served chilled after eating a large meal consisting of meat, potatoes, and corn on the cob. Enjoy!

THE DEDICATION!

This pie is for Saranden Seip, sister of Arizona pie recipient Sierra. Though Saranden and Sierra did not grow up in Iowa, their father hails from this great state and their brother and sister live there now. Saranden even got married in Iowa City; this pie was my wedding present to the happy couple. I hope that, like this pie, their marriage has a long legacy with a little mystery to keep things spicy.

Iowa, thank you for your Life Changing; Fields of Opportunity in both a literal and physical sense. I can't wait to run through your cornfields!

Kansas

PIE

16

OF 50

KANSAS, AS BIG AS YOU THINK

NO STATE FOODS

THE STATE!

The Wizard of Oz, one of my dad's favorite movies, was my only point of reference for Kansas when I was young. All I knew about the state was Dorothy grew up there, the tornadoes that rolled through would run amok, and that there truly is no place like home even after a long trip down the Yellow Brick Road to the Emerald City.

I have since come to learn that Smith County, Kansas, is truly the "heart" of America's heartland: the exact geographical center of the forty-eight contiguous states. Kansas gets its name from the Kaw Nation word meaning People of the South Wind. The first people settled here roughly 12,200 years ago, and thousands of years later Native American tribes including the Kansa, Osage, Pawnee, Kiowa, and Comanche lived on the land. It became a U.S. territory in 1803, when the United States bought the land from France as part of the Louisiana Purchase. In 1861, Kansas joined the Union and became the thirty-fourth state.

One of the state's top natural resources is its fertile farmland. The state, though abundant in a variety of crops, is largely a producer of wheat and Sumner County is known as the Wheat Capital of the World. In 1997, Kansas produced a record 492.2 million bushels of wheat—enough to make 35.9 billion loaves of bread!

Yet when people think about Kansas, we should really think about sunflowers: Fields of these towering beauties cover the state and are grown not only for their flowers but for their seeds and oil. When the fields are in full bloom it must be a true sight to behold, all the faces of these massive flowers worshiping the sun above.

THE PIE!

This pie nods to all that Kansas has to offer, including cows, corn, and wheat. The perfect jumping off point for the pie was a bierock, a meaty, hand-sized Russian bread roll with a thin layer of dough swaddling a filling of ground beef, cabbage (often sauerkraut), onion (usually yellow), spices, and brown mustard. From its Russian origins, it was originally called pirok, from the Russian word pirog. Its popularity spread throughout Eastern Europe, constant in its form but forever changing in name. German settlers called it bierock and brought it to the Great Plains of Kansas in the 1870s along with red wheat seeds. These pioneer farming families came to be known for preparing bierocks throughout the years, solidifying the roll's place in Kansas history.

After doing countless hours of research and printing out photos of bierocks, Dorothy from *The Wizard of Oz*, and corn to tack up on a wall, then stringing the images together with red yarn like a detective trying to solve a murder, I decided to make a beef stew pie that has the flavors of a bierock. It's rich and hearty but sweetened with a little corn, which gives the filling bright pops of juicy kernels amid the thick gravy. As a nod to the wheat industry, a whole wheat crust swaddles this stew, and for texture a savory bread crumb crumble tops it off. It's my ode to a state that's as big as you think!

BIEROCK-INSPIRED BEEF STEW PIE
WITH SAVORY CRUMBLE

ACTIVE TIME: 1 HOUR — BAKE TIME: 45 MINUTES — TOTAL TIME: 3 HOURS 50 MINUTES — MAKES ONE 10-INCH PIE

CRUST

Whole Wheat All-Butter Crust
(single, page 334), rolled out, fit
into a greased 10-inch pie pan,
crimped, and frozen (page 339)

Egg wash (see page 346)

FILLING

3 tablespoons all-purpose flour

1½ teaspoons kosher salt

½ teaspoon freshly ground black
pepper

1 pound boneless beef round steak,
cut into 1-inch pieces

2 tablespoons olive oil

½ cup chopped yellow onion

2 cloves garlic, minced

2 cups water

½ cup fresh yellow corn kernels
(drained canned corn or thawed
frozen corn also works)

½ cup sauerkraut with brine

1 tablespoon spicy brown mustard

1 bay leaf

3 tablespoons cornstarch

SAVORY CRUMBLE TOPPING

2 cups crushed Ritz crackers (about 2 sleeves
of crackers)

½ cup finely shredded white cheddar cheese

2 teaspoons roughly chopped fresh parsley

½ teaspoon freshly ground black pepper

½ cup (1 stick) unsalted butter, softened

MAKE THE FILLING: In a large mixing bowl, combine the
flour, salt, and pepper. Add the cubed beef in batches and
toss to coat evenly with flour. Heat the oil in a Dutch oven
or heavy-bottomed pot over medium-high heat. In batches,
add the beef and brown on all sides until golden brown.
Return all the beef to the pan, add the onion and garlic, and
cook until the onion is translucent. Add ¼ cup of the water
to the pot and stir to scrape up all the wonderful brown bits
on the bottom of the pot. Add 1½ cups water, then the corn,
sauerkraut, mustard, and bay leaf. Stir to combine and bring
to a boil. Once at a boil, cover, reduce the heat, and simmer
for 1 hour and 30 minutes, until the meat is tender. Combine
the remaining ¼ cup water and the cornstarch until smooth;
gradually stir into the stew. Bring the stew to a boil and cook
for an additional 10 minutes, until thickened and bubbly.
Discard the bay leaf and allow the stew to cool for at least
1 hour before filling the pie.

MAKE THE SAVORY CRUMBLE: In a medium bowl,
combine the crushed crackers, cheese, parsley, and pepper

Recipe continues ★★★

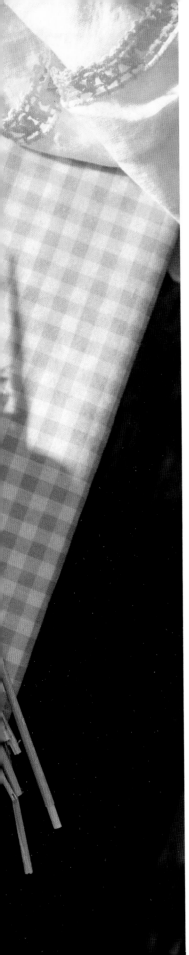

and mix until incorporated. Add the softened butter in pieces and rub and mix with your hands until the mixture resembles wet sand. Set aside until ready to assemble the pie.

ASSEMBLE AND BAKE THE PIE: Preheat the oven to 425°F. Place the frozen whole wheat crust on a baking sheet. Fill with the cooled filling and top with the crumble, making sure to pack the crumble into an even layer. Brush the crimps of crust with the egg wash. Bake on the center rack for 45 minutes, or until the crust and crumble are golden brown. Let it rest for at least 10 to 20 minutes before slicing and serving. Best enjoyed sitting at a table with a wonderful sunflower arrangement! Enjoy!

THE DEDICATION!

This pie is dedicated to the sweetest American boy made of meat and potatoes I know, Michael Palm, who hails from the city of Olathe. Olathe is the Shawnee word for "beautiful," and part of the Kansas City major metropolitan area. I met Mike Palm—you have to say Mike Palm's first and last name together or it just doesn't feel right—through Alabama pie recipient Adam Porter at an end-of-quarter party in college. At those parties we would fill a bathtub with ice and Pabst Blue Ribbon, and no one could leave the party until all the beers were gone. We continued throwing that party all through college. Thursday night was the night to go out at SCAD, which often resulted in us drinking the night away at a bar called Murphy's that no longer exists, yell-singing "Sex on Fire" by the Kings of Leon.

Kansas, you are the Sunflower State and it's always sunny when I'm with Mike Palm!

Kentucky

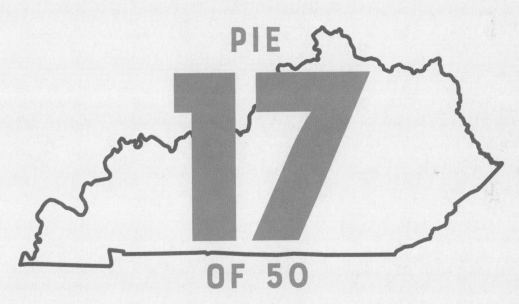

PIE

17

OF 50

UNBRIDLED SPIRIT

STATE FRUIT: BLACKBERRY

THE STATE!

The name Kentucky likely comes from the Wyandot name for the area, kah-ten-tah-the, which translates as "land of tomorrow," or the Shawnee name, kain-tuck-ee, which means "at the head of the river"—or it could also derive from the Iroquoian or Mohawk word kentucke, which means "among the meadows." Kentucky officially entered statehood in 1792, becoming the fifteenth state to join the Union.

Kentucky is lush and beautiful. I spent a lovely week during college in Lancaster, just outside of Lexington, at my friend Katie's mum's lake house, where we rode jet skis, drank PBRs, and got burnt while sitting in the sun eating coconut shrimp.

The state is home to Mammoth Cave—the world's longest cave—and caves with the shortest and deepest underground rivers in the world, the Lost River Cave. I was fascinated to find out why Kentucky bluegrass is called blue even though it's green: In the spring, bluegrass produces bluish purple buds that give the vast fields a blue cast.

The state is famously home to the Kentucky Derby, the oldest continuously held horse race in the country, which takes place at Churchill Downs in Louisville on the first Saturday in May, when the mint juleps flow free. Kentucky also gave us the song "Happy Birthday to You," written by Louisville sisters Mildred and Patty Hill in 1893.

In terms of food, Kentucky did not just give us the Colonel's fried chicken. It also gave us a pie that could only come from somewhere with as much unbridled spirit as Kentucky: the Derby!

THE PIE!

Kentucky's derby pie is a thick and gooey chocolate and walnut treat similar to pecan pie. It was created in 1950 at the Melrose Inn in Prospect, Kentucky, as a specialty pastry by Walter and Leaudra Kern and their son George. They spent years researching and testing the optimal recipe. How did the pie get its name? Out of a hat! The family put the various names they each wanted to call it in a hat, and pulled out "derby pie."

The family left the Melrose Inn in 1960 to open Kern's Kitchen. Derby-Pie is a registered trademark of Kern's Kitchen and the original recipe of the pie is kept secret, known only to a small group of family members and a single Kern's Kitchen employee (who mixes the recipe today). Kern's Kitchen guards the trademark and has filed more than twenty-five lawsuits to protect the use of "Derby-Pie" over the years. Because of this trademark, makers of similar pies have had to use different names.

No matter how intimidating it would be, I had to make my own version of derby pie. I also wanted to pay homage to the blackberry, which was designated the state fruit in 2004 in a bill proposed by Senator R. J. Palmer. The passing of this bill took precedence over a budget proposal. It led a television journalist to report that, "The blackberry bill gets passed while the governor's budget proposal gets caught in a jam."

In the end we have a wonderfully sweet pie with a smooth center and added crunch from walnuts. The richness of the chocolate is balanced out by the tartness of blackberry sauce, which brightens it all up. It's lovely on the first Saturday in May, but really this is a pie for all seasons.

KENTUCKY DERBY-STYLE PIE
WITH BLACKBERRY SAUCE

ACTIVE TIME: 30 MINUTES — BAKE TIME: 1 HOUR — TOTAL TIME: 2 HOURS 30 MINUTES — MAKES ONE 10-INCH PIE

CRUST

All-Butter Crust (single, page 332),
    rolled out, fit into a greased
    10-inch pie pan, crimped, and
    frozen (see page 339)
Egg wash (see page 346)
Finishing sugar (see page 346)

FILLING

4 large eggs
½ cup all-purpose flour
¾ cup packed light brown sugar
¼ cup granulated sugar
¾ cup light corn syrup
½ cup (1 stick) unsalted butter,
    melted and cooled
2 tablespoons Kentucky bourbon
1½ teaspoons vanilla extract
1¼ cups chopped walnuts, toasted
¾ cup semisweet chocolate chips

BLACKBERRY SAUCE

2 cups blackberries
½ cup granulated sugar
½ cup water

MAKE THE FILLING: In a large mixing bowl, whisk the eggs, flour, brown sugar, granulated sugar, corn syrup, melted butter, bourbon, and vanilla until smooth. Fold in the walnuts and chocolate chips. Set aside until ready to fill the pie.

ASSEMBLE AND BAKE THE PIE: Preheat the oven to 350°F. Place the frozen pie crust on a baking sheet and fill with the filling. Bake on the center rack for 50 to 60 minutes, until a hard crust forms on the top of the pie. Cool for at least 1 hour.

MAKE THE BLACKBERRY SAUCE: Combine the blackberries, granulated sugar, and water in a medium saucepan and cook over medium-high heat until the berries cook down and halve in volume, about 10 minutes. Strain the sauce through a sieve so it is smooth.

Slice the pie and drizzle the sauce over the slices, serving with a mint julep if your heart desires. Either way you're gonna be coming first in the race! Enjoy!

THE DEDICATION!

This pie is dedicated to Mark Dorf, who grew up in Kentucky's largest city, Louisville, which sits on the Ohio River along the Indiana border and is home to Churchill Downs, site of the Kentucky Derby. Mark taught me about the derby pie, its history, and why it could be the only choice for a pie for his home state. Mark is a talented visual artist who has had solo shows in New York and had his pieces featured in galleries all over the world.

I have only the fondest feelings for the state of Kentucky. You truly are full of Unbridled Spirit!

Louisiana

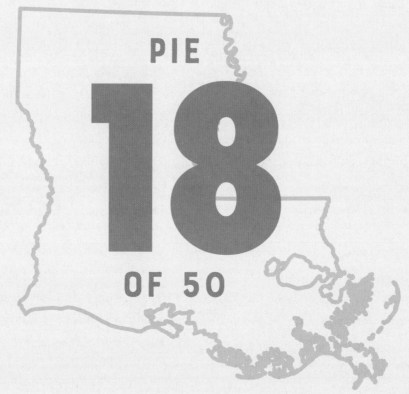

PIE

18

OF 50

COME AS YOU ARE. LEAVE DIFFERENT!

STATE FRUIT: STRAWBERRY ★ STATE JELLIES: MAYHAW JELLY &
LOUISIANA SUGAR CANE JELLY ★ STATE MEAT PIE: NATCHITOCHES MEAT PIE
STATE DOUGHNUT: BEIGNET ★ STATE VEGETABLE: SWEET POTATO ★ STATE DISH: GUMBO

THE STATE!

Oh boy, do I love Louisiana and New Orleans. If you've learned anything about me from this book, you know that I love to eat and I love to party—and this state provides plentifully on both those fronts. The first time I went to New Orleans, it was because my college roommate Jess called me to tell me that we were driving to New Orleans to crash her parents' vacation. It was the most fun, spontaneous ten-hour road trip. Once we got to New Orleans the eating and the drinking did not stop! I drank approximately one million hurricanes and ate too many po' boys and oysters on saltines with hot sauce, and even tried alligator for the first time!

On another trip to New Orleans my friends and I danced to a live jazz band for a solid eight hours, so long that we couldn't get our butts out of bed the next day...At least not until we knew beignets were on the agenda.

Louisiana, the eighteenth state, was named for King Louis XIV when France claimed the land in 1682. This state is a beautiful mix of cultures and people, and it has gifted us some of the most delicious regional dishes—think gumbo, red beans and rice, and muffulettas. Louisiana may be best known for New Orleans but it's so much more than that. It is home to sprawling swamps waiting to be explored by air boat, and no matter how high your expectations are entering the state, each one will be met, and you'll leave with a full soul and the top button of your jeans buckling under the tension.

THE PIE!

Louisiana has two state jellies! Jelly, fresh strawberries, and fried dough are a dream menage à trois.

Mayhaw trees are native to the swamps of most southern Gulf Coast states and produce yellow to bright red fruits the size of cherries that taste similar to a tart crab apple. The fruit itself isn't really eaten out of hand, but turned into jellies, syrups, and fresh pressed juices. Louisiana designated mayhaw jelly an official jelly in 2003.

But the pie couldn't just be jelly; we need a little freshness, a little texture. Here comes the official state fruit, the strawberry! It became the state fruit twice, first in 1980, then after a few years of fruit flip-flopping, for the second time in 2001. Louisiana is among the top-ten strawberry-producing states in the nation.

To root the pie not only in Louisiana but also in the beloved traditions of New Orleans (and my fried-dough hangover cure), I top the pie with beignets in the shape of fleurs de lis and dust the whole thing with king cake–inspired sanding sugars. Beignets, the official state doughnut of Louisiana, made their way from Rome and Paris to the Great White North and found their final home in the Big Easy: French settlers brought them as they migrated to the eastern coasts of Canada to a region called Acadia. In the 17th century, because of forced migration, many Acadians settled in Louisiana, where their descendants became known as Cajun. Today, beignets reign supreme in their powdered-sugar-dusted glory in the French Quarter of New Orleans.

A pie worthy of the Big Easy: a strawberry mayhaw jelly pie with a fleur de lis beignet topper—and king cake decor!

STRAWBERRY MAYHAW JELLY PIE
WITH BEIGNET TOPPERS

ACTIVE TIME: 1 HOUR — BAKE TIME: 30 MINUTES — TOTAL TIME: 3 HOURS 30 MINUTES — MAKES ONE 10-INCH PIE

CRUST

All-Butter Crust (single, page 332), rolled out, fit into a greased 10-inch pie pan, crimped, and fully blind baked (see page 339)

BEIGNET TOPPING

¾ cup lukewarm water

¼ cup granulated sugar

¾ teaspoon active dry yeast

½ cup evaporated milk

1 large egg, beaten

⅝ teaspoon kosher salt

3½ cups bread flour

2 tablespoons shortening

2 quarts neutral oil for frying (canola or vegetable oil will work)

1½ cups confectioners' sugar

Purple, green, and yellow sanding sugars

FILLING

3 cups sliced fresh strawberries

½ cup granulated sugar

½ cup mayhaw jelly (or strawberry jam if mayhaw jelly is unavailable)

¾ cup water

3 tablespoons cornstarch

MAKE THE BEIGNET DOUGH: In a large bowl, mix the lukewarm water, granulated sugar, and yeast and let sit for 10 minutes to give the yeast time to bloom. In the mixing bowl of stand mixer, beat the evaporated milk, egg, and salt on medium speed. Add the yeast mixture to the egg mixture along with 1½ cups of the flour and combine. Add the shortening and continue to mix while adding the remaining flour. Remember to scrape the sides of the bowl down. Once all the ingredients are combined, remove the dough from the bowl and knead on a lightly floured surface until smooth. Spray a large bowl with nonstick spray, place the dough in the bowl, and cover with plastic wrap. Let it rise in a warm place for 2 hours.

MAKE THE FILLING: In a medium saucepan over medium-high heat, combine 2 cups of the strawberries, the granulated sugar, and jelly. Bring the mixture to a boil, stirring frequently. In a separate bowl, whisk together the water and cornstarch, making a slurry. Slowly incorporate the slurry into the jelly mixture, then reduce the heat to low and simmer, stirring constantly, until the mixture thickens, about 10 minutes. Remove from the heat and set aside until ready to fill the pie.

FILL THE PIE: Arrange the remaining 1 cup fresh strawberries in an even layer on the bottom of the baked crust. Pour the filling into the crust. Chill in fridge for at least 30 minutes.

MAKE THE BEIGNETS: Roll out the beignet dough to ¼ inch thick and cut out five or six fleur de lis shapes using a cookie cutter.

Recipe continues ★★★

Stand mixer with paddle attachment

Nonstick cooking spray

3-inch-wide fleur de lis cookie cutter

Dutch oven or deep cast-iron pan
  for frying

Deep-fry thermometer

Chopsticks (optional)

Heat the oil in a Dutch oven over medium-high heat until it reaches 350°F. While the oil is heating, pour the confectioners' sugar into a large bowl for tossing the fried beignets. Once the oil comes to temperature, add two or three beignets at a time (so that the temperature of the oil doesn't drop too much). Fry the beignets for 2 to 3 minutes, until they are golden brown, flipping constantly. I love to use chopsticks for this! Drain each beignet on paper towels for a few seconds before tossing in the confectioners' sugar. Continue frying until all the dough is used up.

ASSEMBLE THE PIE: Arrange the beignets on top of the chilled pie and sprinkle liberally with sanding sugars. Toss some beads in the air, drink a hurricane, and laissez les bons temps rouler!

THE DEDICATION!

This pie is for Zachery James Kohler, better known as Moses. Moses was born and raised in New Orleans and resides there now in Bayou St. John with his sweet pup Kosch Dog. His house is a stone's throw from one of the best bars ever, Pal's. Moses and I went to college together but didn't meet until the wedding of our friends Chuck and Kelsie in Hebron, New Hampshire. If I remember correctly, Moses wore a three-piece suit in the middle of a sweltering hot July. We locked eyes and our friendship was sealed as we ripped apart that dance floor for the rest of the evening. I would later visit him in New Orleans and we would continue the dance party in his kitchen while we made and ate red beans and rice and then again the next night for eight hours until we couldn't walk or dance anymore.

New Orleans, laissez les bon temps rouler!

Maine

PIE

19

OF 50

VACATIONLAND

STATE DESSERT: WILD BLUEBERRY PIE ★ STATE FRUIT: WILD BLUEBERRY
STATE SOFT DRINK: MOXIE ★ STATE TREAT: WHOOPIE PIE

THE STATE!

When I was in elementary school in Hong Kong, all I wanted was a red L.L. Bean backpack with my name on it. One birthday I saw that an L.L. Bean package had arrived all the way from Maine to Hong Kong. The stoke level was HIGH! I opened it, and found that my dad had gotten the backpack for me! But instead of STACEY, it said FONG... so my sisters and I could share it. In hindsight, it was very resourceful, but at the moment it was a blow of disappointment. My sorrow was eventually softened by the fact he also got me the space-themed sleeping bag I requested.

L.L. Bean is based in Maine, up at the tippy top of the East Coast and on the tippy top of my list of places I want to visit. Maine entered the Union in 1820 as the twenty-third state. Some historians think that Maine got its name from the nautical term "mainland" or "the main," which is how colony founders differentiated Maine from the islands off its coast. A less romantic theory states it might have been named after an English village of the same name. It is the largest state in New England and it's said that Eastport is the first place on the East Coast to get sunlight in the morning.

All I wish is for one summer to be in a seaside abode on the coast of Maine, catching the sunrise in a cardigan, staring out onto the ocean like some forlorn widow reminiscing about a love that once was. Doesn't that just sound like an absolute dream?

It honestly feels like Maine could be my ideal place to rest my bones: It's famous for its lobster and clams—two of my favorite foods—and is home to the potato doughnut! Made with buttermilk and potatoes, the potato donut is an ode to Maine's biggest crop for 200 years. What's not to love?

But for a Pine Tree State pie, with its plethora of state foods on offer and even a state dessert that is a pie, I knew I had to turn on the charm. I wanted to make a pie that would be the perfect complement to any clam bake.

THE PIE!

The state designated the wild blueberry the official berry in 1991 and recognized the blueberry pie made with the wild blueberries as the official dessert in 2011. I had to follow that lead.

The Maine wild blueberry is a tough cookie of a fruit whose journey started 10,000 years ago—a scrappy survivor in the sandy, nutrient-deficient plains left behind from receding glaciers. Its survival paid off as it became a signature Maine product that grows bountifully in fields and barrens that stretch along the coast of the state. Not only is it a survivor, it is adaptable and has adjusted to Maine's acidic soils and relentless winters, needing only minimal care. These sweet tiny berries grow in jewel tones of magenta and purple, their skin gleaming as the bright sun hits them. Until recently, all of the state's native berries were harvested by hand using a special rake, unlike the commercial highbush blueberry. In one year Maine produces 99 percent of all wild blueberries for the nation.

But I couldn't bake a simple wild blueberry pie! To add another layer of flavor, I turned to the state soft drink, Moxie. It's a regional soda whose popularity has largely remained exclusive to the Northeast. Like most sodas we have come to know, it started as a concentrated medicine; it was invented by Maine-born Dr. Augustin Thompson in 1876 and likely named after Somerset County's Moxie Falls or Moxie Pond. The original ingredients included gentian root, wintergreen, sassafras, and possibly even cocaine. In 1884, carbonation was added and it was branded as Moxie Nerve Food, which was intended to cure drunkenness, make homes more happy, and remedy all forms of anxiety, which would lead to less crime and

suffering in New England. It became the nation's favorite soft drink, outselling even Coca-Cola when Coke first hit the market in 1886, and was renamed Moxie in 1906. With such a decorated history, it is no surprise that it became the official soft drink of Maine in 2005. But how to incorporate it into my pie? Since you can't just dump soda in a pie, I boiled it down and made a syrup to complement and sweeten the wild blueberries!

So the pie for Vacationland is a wild blueberry–Moxie pie, with an added bonus of a lobster decorated crust. An ode to a state where I hope to have a future abode!

WILD BLUEBERRY AND MOXIE PIE

ACTIVE TIME: 30 MINUTES — BAKE TIME: 1 HOUR — TOTAL TIME: 3 HOUR 35 MINUTES — MAKES ONE 10-INCH PIE

CRUST

All-Butter Crust (double, page 332),
   rolled out (see page 339)
½ teaspoon all-purpose flour
½ teaspoon granulated sugar
Egg wash (see page 346)
Finishing sugar (see page 346)

MOXIE SYRUP

1 cup Moxie soda

FILLING

5 cups wild blueberries, frozen
   or fresh (use regular blueberries
   if wild are unavailable)
¼ cup cornstarch
½ cup granulated sugar
1 teaspoon lemon juice

SPECIAL EQUIPMENT

X-Acto knife
Red food coloring
Paintbrush

FOR MAINE LOBSTER CRUST
DESIGN TEMPLATE, SCAN CODE

PRO TIP: *The pie is best made between early July and late September when wild Maine blueberries flourish!*

MAKE THE MOXIE SYRUP: In a small saucepan over medium-low heat, reduce the Moxie until it is half its volume, 10 to 15 minutes, stirring occasionally to make sure it doesn't burn. Set aside to cool.

MAKE THE FILLING: In a large mixing bowl, combine 2 tablespoons of the Moxie syrup, the blueberries, cornstarch, sugar, and lemon juice and stir to mix.

ASSEMBLE AND BAKE THE PIE: Fit the bottom crust into a 10-inch greased pie pan. Sprinkle the ½ teaspoons sugar and flour onto the base of the crust and fill with the blueberry filling. Place the second crust on a flour-dusted sheet pan.

If painting lobsters, create a stencil with the template, and mix 6 to 8 drops of food coloring into 1 tablespoon water. Place the stencil on top of the crust and use a small brush to paint on lobsters. Place the crust on top of the pie, roll and crimp to seal edges (see page 343), and freeze for at least 30 minutes. Once frozen, cut four vents in between your painted lobsters to let steam escape.

Preheat the oven to 375°F. Brush the top crust with the egg wash (avoiding lobsters so that the food coloring doesn't run). Sprinkle liberally with finishing sugar. Bake for 1 hour on a sheet pan, rotating 90 degrees clockwise every 15 minutes, until the crust is golden brown and the filling is bubbling up. Cool for at least 2 hours before serving. Best enjoyed with a large glass of Moxie on ice after eating a big basket of fried clams!

THE DEDICATION!

Maine is dedicated to my jewel of a friend, Aaron Ruff. Aaron is from Dresden (Maine!), but now lives in Brooklyn with his family. He is a talented jewelry designer, founder of Digby & Iona, and makes the most beautiful fine jewelry that is delicate yet sturdy enough to weather a storm. Three out of the four pieces of jewelry I wear every day are of his making. One of the most special pieces he has made for me is a signet pinky ring with my grandfather's initials on it. The gold we used was melted down from a baby bracelet my grandparents gave me when I was born. Gold baby bracelets are often given in Chinese tradition to symbolize good fortune and health for the baby.

Aaron and I met almost a decade ago when I won a giveaway on his Instagram. The Internet can be a beautiful place. Aaron may make the finest jewelry in the Northeast but his friendship is the true gem.

Maine, the way life should be. You truly are Vacationland, postcard perfection.

Maryland

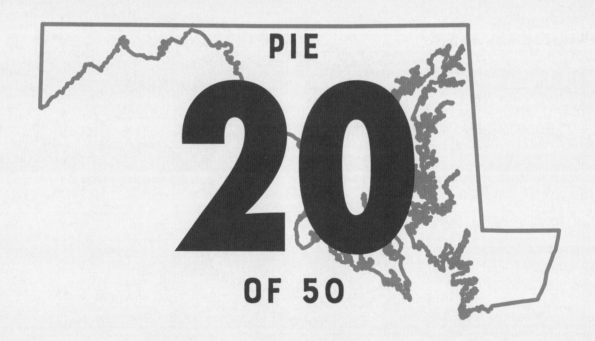

PIE

20

OF 50

MORE THAN YOU CAN IMAGINE

STATE FOOD: BLUE CRAB ★ STATE DESSERT: SMITH ISLAND CAKE

THE STATE!

When I think of Maryland, I think of three things: blue crabs, John Waters, and *The Wire*. I'm a crab over lobster lady, *Cry Baby* is one of my most favorite movies, and, well, I like to take every chance I get to quote Omar Little.

Maryland became the seventh state in 1788, and two years after that contributed part of its land to form Washington, DC. Later, a Maryland attorney named Francis Scott Key wrote what would become the national anthem, "The Star-Spangled Banner," on September 14, 1814. Pretty wild that this state gave up the land for the nation's capital and also gave the country its national anthem.

The state is named for Queen Henrietta Maria of England, whose husband, King Charles I, granted permission for Maryland to become a colony. Now, Maryland is often referred to as America in Miniature since it has such a wide variety of terrains, from mountains and farmland to beaches and sand dunes.

I have had nothing but fun in the state of Maryland. I ate the largest oyster ever at Fells Point in Baltimore. I danced the night away at my friend Peirce's wedding in Salisbury. That night we slept in Jess and Darren's RV that was parked in Peirce's driveway and spent the evening playing card games after ordering Domino's to the RV front steps. What's better than late-night Domino's in an RV? To this day, we still talk and think about Michael the delivery guy.

Every time I return to Baltimore, I fall in love with it more and more. It's a wonderful city but most of all it is home to some of my most wonderful friends.

THE PIE!

Henrietta Maria was queen consort to King Charles I, but in this state, crab is the real king. The blue crab from the Chesapeake Bay is the state's most famous food. Maryland's miles and miles of coastline are the perfect habitat for the blue crab, which was designated the state crustacean in 1989. Its scientific name, *Callinectes sapidus* Rathbun, translates as "beautiful swimmer that is savory." Its flavor is often compared to the sweetness of lobster meat and is best appreciated when it is steamed or during its soft-shell stage. Its short season typically starts around April and lasts until Memorial Day.

I immediately knew the flavor I had to incorporate into my crab-based pie: Old Bay! The spice blend was invented by Gustav Brunn, a German refugee who came to Maryland in 1939 and named the blend after the ship line on the Chesapeake Bay. In 1990, McCormick & Company bought the spice blend. The company doesn't publicly disclose all of its eighteen herbs and spices, but the recipe has remained unchanged since its conception over seventy-five years ago. Traditionally used for seafood, it is now used in everything from ice cream topping to summer ales.

I wanted to get it into as many components of the pie as possible so here we have an Old Bay blue crab dip pie with spicy Old Bay crust! It's spicy, it's creamy, it's rich, and what you really wanna do is eat it and drink a cold ass beer!

BLUE-CRAB-DIP PIE
WITH HOT-OLD-BAY CRUST

ACTIVE TIME: 15 MINUTES — BAKE TIME: 40 MINUTES — TOTAL TIME: 1 HOUR 15 MINUTES — MAKES ONE 10-INCH PIE

CRUST

Hot-Old-Bay All-Butter Crust (single, page 333), rolled out, fit into a greased 10-inch pie pan, crimped, and partially blind baked (see page 339)

FILLING

2 large eggs, beaten

½ cup mayonnaise (preferably Duke's)

½ cup whole milk

4 ounces Swiss cheese, shredded

4 ounces cheddar cheese, shredded

¼ cup chopped green bell pepper

¼ cup chopped red bell pepper

¼ cup chopped white onion

1 tablespoon all-purpose flour

1 tablespoon Old Bay seasoning, plus more for sprinkling

½ pound crab meat (preferably blue crab from the Chesapeake Bay)

MAKE THE FILLING: In a large mixing bowl, combine the eggs, mayonnaise, and milk and mix well. Fold in the Swiss, cheddar, peppers, onion, flour, and Old Bay and mix well. Fold in the crab meat, making sure not to break up the crab meat too much.

ASSEMBLE AND BAKE THE PIE: Preheat the oven to 350°F. Place the partially baked crust on a baking sheet and fill with the filling. Sprinkle the filling with additional Old Bay and bake on the center rack for 40 to 50 minutes, until bubbly. Let cool for 10 minutes before serving with a Spaghett cocktail! (Add an ounce of both Aperol and lemon juice to a glass bottle of Miller High Life. The drink was made famous by Wet City Brewing in Baltimore.) It's the perfect summertime pie and drink!

THE DEDICATION!

America in Miniature is dedicated to my beautiful friend, Peirce Kea of Salisbury. I met Peirce sophomore year in college, and since then she and I have spent countless nights dancing at the best dive bar in the country, the Rail Pub, in her kitchen in Savannah, and at as many house parties as we could cram into one night with a PBR in hand. We have spent many a day-after sitting on her sofa watching hours of "What Not to Wear" and eating ceviche—and then doing it all over again. Nothing is better than a friend you want to spend all night Saturday partying with and then all day Sunday sitting in your sins with.

If you are looking for merry land, go to Maryland!

Massachusetts

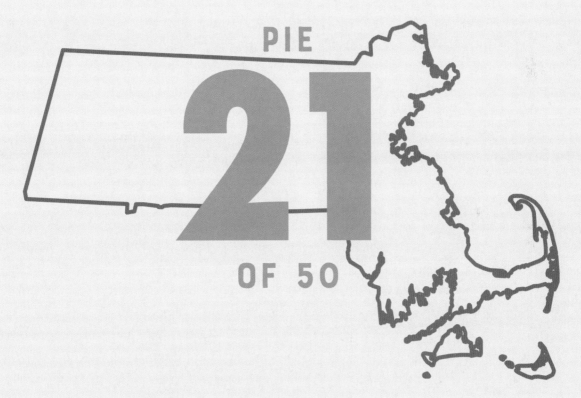

PIE

21

OF 50

MAKE IT YOURS,
THE SPIRIT OF AMERICA

STATE BERRY: CRANBERRY ★ **STATE MUFFIN: CORN MUFFIN**
STATE BEAN: BAKED NAVY BEAN ★ **STATE DESSERT: BOSTON CREAM PIE**
STATE DOUGHNUT: BOSTON CREAM DOUGHNUT

THE STATE!

In 1788, Massachusetts became the sixth state to enter the Union. The state was most likely named after the Massachusett tribe, whose name translates as "near the great hill" or "near the range of hills," which pays homage to the Blue Hills south of Boston.

I deeply love New England and Massachusetts, and I have the Bee Gees to thank for starting me on that path. Growing up, I listened to a lot of the Bee Gees with my father and I loved their song "Massachusetts"; it still conjures good feelings. I finally got to visit when I was at summer camp at Yale the summer before my junior year of high school. We could pick weekend excursions to go on, and I chose a visit to Harvard. I wanted to see for myself the halls that Elle Woods's heels clicked and clacked through in *Legally Blonde*. I didn't end up at Harvard or Yale for a degree, but my sisters went to college in Boston, at Emerson and Northeastern, so there have been many Fong family visits to that wonderful city.

Massachusetts has been the scene of many historical events. In 1639, America's first post office opened in Boston. Boston is also home to the first public park in America, the Boston Common, which opened in 1634.

I am happy to report that I have spent several summer days and evenings with fine friends cracking lobsters, eating steamers, and dancing the night away on Cape Cod. I have very proudly driven through the town of Sandwich and eaten the best lobster roll of my life at Sesuit Harbor Cafe in Dennis.

I am so happy to have visited and made so many good memories in a state where you can truly make it yours, the Spirit of America!

THE PIE!

The state dessert is the Boston cream pie—which isn't actually a pie but a layered sponge cake filled with pastry cream and glazed with chocolate. Cooks in New England and Pennsylvania Dutch regions were known for creating wonderful cakes and pies, and the line between them was very thin. These cakes were most likely called pies because pie tins were more common than cake pans in the 19th century and these first versions might have been baked in pie tins. The original Boston cream pie was created by French chef Sanzian at Boston's Parker House Hotel. It was called the Parker House "chocolate cream pie" and was created to celebrate the opening of the hotel in 1856. It is said to be a remake of the early American "pudding cake pie."

The Boston cream pie became the official state dessert on December 12, 1996. A civics class from Norton High School sponsored the bill. The pie beat out other candidates including the famous Toll House chocolate chip cookie.

So here we have a Boston Cream Pie Pie: a buttery crust filled with chocolate ganache and pastry cream, topped with cubes of pound cake and a chocolate drizzle. All your favorite parts of biting into a Boston cream pie doughnut or cake... finally in true pie form.

BOSTON CREAM PIE PIE

ACTIVE TIME: 1 HOUR — BAKE TIME: 1 HOUR 30 MINUTES — TOTAL TIME: 6 HOURS 30 MINUTES — MAKES ONE 10-INCH PIE

CRUST

All-Butter Crust (single, page 332),
    rolled out, fit into a greased
    10-inch pie pan, crimped, and
    fully blind baked (see page 339)

POUND CAKE TOPPING

1½ cups all-purpose flour

¼ teaspoon kosher salt

½ cup (1 stick) unsalted butter,
    softened

1½ cups granulated sugar

4 large eggs, at room temperature

1 teaspoon vanilla extract

½ cup heavy whipping cream

FILLING

Chocolate Layer

4 ounces bittersweet chocolate,
    chopped or in chips

½ cup heavy whipping cream

1 large egg, beaten

½ teaspoon vanilla extract

½ teaspoon kosher salt

Pastry Cream

½ cup granulated sugar

⅓ cup all-purpose flour, sifted

1 teaspoon kosher salt

2 cups whole milk

2 large egg yolks

½ teaspoon vanilla extract

MAKE THE POUND CAKE TOPPING: Position an oven rack in the middle of the oven but do not preheat the oven. Grease the loaf pan with softened butter and coat with a light dusting of flour.

In a large mixing bowl, sift together the flour and salt; sift three more times. In the bowl of the stand mixer with the paddle attachment, beat the butter and sugar on medium speed for about 5 minutes, until pale, light, and fluffy. Add one egg at a time, beating well after each addition, then add the vanilla. Reduce the speed to low and add half of the flour mixture. Add the cream and mix well, then add the remaining flour mixture. Remember to scrape down the sides of the bowl, then beat at medium-high speed for 5 minutes, until the mixture is pale yellow.

Spoon the batter into the greased loaf pan and tap the pan against the counter to eliminate air bubbles. Place the pan in the cold oven, then turn the oven to 350°F. Bake the cake for 1 to 1½ hours, until a cake tester or toothpick inserted in the center comes out clean. Let it cool for at least 30 minutes. Unmold and cut the cake into ½-inch cubes. Cover and set aside until ready to assemble pie.

MAKE AND BAKE THE CHOCOLATE LAYER: Preheat the oven to 350°F. Put the chocolate in a medium bowl. In a separate, microwave-safe bowl, microwave the cream, uncovered, for 30 seconds. Pour the cream over the chocolate and stir until smooth. Reserve 2 tablespoons of the chocolate mixture for topping. To the remaining mixture, stir in the beaten egg, vanilla, and salt.

Pastry brush

Standard loaf pan, 8½ by 4½
    inches wide, 2½ inches deep

Stand mixer or hand mixer

Pour into the fully baked pie crust, place on a baking sheet, and bake on the center rack for 10 minutes, until the edges are set and the center still has a slight jiggle. Let cool for at least 15 minutes while you make the cream layer.

MAKE THE PASTRY CREAM: Set up a double boiler: Place a heat-safe mixing bowl on top of a medium saucepan. In the saucepan, bring water—just enough so the bottom of the bowl does not touch the water—to a simmer.

In a separate medium bowl, combine the sugar, flour, and salt. In the heat-safe mixing bowl, beat the milk and egg yolks together. Add the sugar mixture and cook over the simmering water in the double boiler, stirring constantly, for 10 to 12 minutes, until the mixture coats the back of a spoon. Stir in the vanilla.

Pour the cream over the chocolate layer in the pie crust. Cover with plastic wrap touching the cream layer so that a skin doesn't form. Refrigerate for a minimum of 4 hours.

FINISH THE PIE: Top the chilled pie with the cubed pound cake, melt the reserved chocolate, and drizzle on top. Best enjoyed by a fire with a cold Sam Adams beer in the other hand!

THE DEDICATION!

This Boston cream pie pie is dedicated to Matthew McInerney of Deerfield. At first, I thought he hated me. When my friend Susannah started dating him, I said, "He is really cute, but kind of an asshole." The description still stands—but many beers and scream-singalongs to Taking Back Sunday later we are the finest friends. Such fine friends that I had the honor of being one of his groomspeople when he married Susannah.

Matt is always there for me when I need to discuss a new Midwest emo band or some internet rapper beef, or when I need to talk through an existential life problem that he will no doubt make an infographic about. His home state has blessed me with not just a wonderful friend but the brother I always wanted.

Massachusetts, you are the Spirit of America.

Michigan

PIE

22

OF 50

PURE MICHIGAN

NO STATE FOODS

THE STATE!

Michigan, the twenty-sixth state, joined the Union in 1837. The state was likely named after Lake Michigan, which got its name from an Ojibwe word, mishigami, that roughly translates to "big lake." Four Great Lakes border Michigan—Superior, Huron, Michigan, and Erie—which is why it's known as the Great Lakes State. I remember the commercials from the tourism board that hammered in the slogan, "Pure Michigan": Visit the Great Lakes, fresh air, family! They got me hook, line, and sinker, and I've wanted to swim in those crisp lakes ever since.

Over 40 percent of Michigan is covered in water, the most of any state. It is said that from anywhere you stand in the state you are no more than 85 miles from a body of water. Michigan is also the only state that is split into two big pieces: the Upper Peninsula and the Lower Peninsula (affectionately known as "the mitten"), connected by the five-mile-long Mackinac Bridge.

Some of the first cars were built in Michigan by automakers Ransom E. Olds and Henry Ford just before 1900, and Detroit, the Motor City, became the car capital of the world. When Ford cars made it over to Singapore, my grandfather saved up to get himself one. It was shiny and black and he took my grandmother on rides to get snacks at local street stalls. Now that's what I call romance.

THE PIE!

The Kellogg Company of Battle Creek is the leading American producer of cereal, and its Corn Flakes were one of the first and still most popular breakfast cereals. It is said that when Kellogg's burns the Corn Flakes today the whole town can smell it. When I learned this, I knew that Michigan's pie crust had to be made of cereal.

John Harvey Kellogg and his younger brother Will Keith revolutionized the way America ate breakfast in 1895 with the invention of their crispy, golden flakes of corn. What a lot of people don't know is that cereal was born not only because of their brotherly ingenuity but because of the Seventh-day Adventist Church. The church is a homegrown American faith, first established in Battle Creek, and its emphasis on spiritual and physical health became a pillar in Kellogg family life—and led to the invention.

Meanwhile, Traverse City is the cherry capital of the world. Cherries were brought to America by ship with early settlers in the 1600s, flourishing first in the Northwest. In 1852, Peter Dougherty, a Presbyterian missionary, planted the first cherry orchard in the Grand Traverse area of Michigan. Cherry trees can grow just about anywhere, but the conditions in which they reach their full potential are very specific, and Traverse City has it all. Lake Michigan tempers arctic winds in the winter and cools the orchards in the summer!

My sweet and tart cherry pie has a jammy center that is offset by the crispy, crunchy cornflake crust and cereal crumb top. It's the perfect pie to enjoy on a sand dune overlooking Lake Michigan.

CHERRY PIE
WITH CEREAL CRUST AND CEREAL CRUMBLE TOPPING

ACTIVE TIME: 30 MINUTES — BAKE TIME: 55 MINUTES — TOTAL TIME: 2 HOURS 25 MINUTES — MAKES ONE 10-INCH PIE

CRUST

Cereal Crust (page 336), blind
    baked as directed

FILLING

3 cups frozen cherries

1 ¼ cups dried cherries

½ teaspoon grated lemon zest

1 tablespoon lemon juice

½ teaspoon almond extract

1 cup granulated sugar

½ cup cornstarch

CRUMBLE TOPPING

¾ cup cornflake cereal

½ cup all-purpose flour

½ cup packed light brown sugar

⅓ cup (⅔ stick) unsalted butter,
    softened

¼ teaspoon kosher salt

MAKE THE FILLING: Preheat the oven to 375°F. In a large mixing bowl, toss the frozen cherries and dried cherries with the lemon zest and juice and almond extract. Mix the sugar and cornstarch together and add to the cherry mixture. Set aside until ready to fill the pie.

MAKE THE CRUMBLE TOPPING: In medium bowl, mix all the crumble ingredients until the texture of wet sand. Set aside until ready to assemble the pie.

ASSEMBLE AND BAKE THE PIE: Place the cereal crust on a baking sheet, add the filling, and sprinkle the crumble over the filling. Bake on the center rack for 45 to 55 minutes, rotating the pie 90 degrees every 15 minutes, until the filling is bubbly and the edges of the crust are golden brown. Allow to cool for at least 1 hour before slicing. Enjoy with a cool lake breeze blowing through your hair!

THE DEDICATION!

This pie is dedicated to Anne Patterson; everyone calls her AP. She grew up in Grand Rapids, but now lives in Brooklyn with her lovely wife Cheryl and their son Cal.

    The first thing I noticed about AP when we met at a party was her megawatt smile. She is pure sunshine and a hug from her can cure all woes. I'm glad I got to dedicate this pie full of bright flavor and fun texture to her and the great state that brought us not only the sweetest cherries but my sweet friend.

    Michigan, you're Great Lakes, great times, and most importantly, great friends.

Minnesota

PIE

23

OF 50

LAND OF 10,000 LAKES

STATE FRUIT: HONEYCRISP APPLE ★ STATE GRAIN: WILD RICE
STATE MUFFIN: BLUEBERRY MUFFIN ★ STATE MUSHROOM: MOREL

THE STATE!

The thirty-second state entered statehood in 1858 and got its name from the Dakota tribe's word for the Minnesota River, mni sota, which means either "cloudy, muddy water" or "sky-tinted water." Minnesota is home to 11,842 lakes that run and weave through the state. Minneapolis is home to a nine-mile-long system of aboveground heated walkways that stretch between city buildings and that remind me of a long walkway in Hong Kong's Central District.

We have this wonderful state to thank for the dearly beloved musical icon Prince, bizarre foods adventurer Andrew Zimmern, 3M's masking and Scotch tapes, Wheaties, the Bundt cake pan, Bisquick…the list is endless.

But I thank the state most for Spam. In 1937 the Hormel company in Austin gave us the luncheon meat that defined my childhood. In Hong Kong, my favorite afterschool snack was fried Spam, eggs, and rice topped with sambal belacan (an Indonesian chili paste).

Spam has a complicated history. After the bombing of Pearl Harbor and the American military's deployment to the Pacific, wherever American troops went, Spam followed. Spam became a symbol of American generosity in helping feed people in need, and also a reminder of immense suffering.

Robert Ji-Song Ku, the author of *Dubious Gastronomy*, wrote, "There is something quirky yet meaningful to these Asian Americans, who by consuming Spam are really embracing their histories and experience and the legacy as Asian Americans."

I have dreams of entering a pie into the Minnesota State Fair, the second largest in the country. Who knows: There might be a little Spam in it. Spam and all the ways Asians and Asian Americans have adapted it into new dishes is, well, as American as apple pie.

THE PIE!

This pie is an ode to the fried foods of the state fair. Whenever my friend Rebecca talked about her summers at the Minnesota fair, her eyes lit up with joy and her mouth watered in anticipation of her annual trip home. The fair is the perfect meeting point for all Minnesotans to congregate and bask in the glory of their state's livestock, art, cooking, and the plethora of foods served on a stick. I wanted to capture that excitement in a pie.

Many of the foods at the fair are deep-fried, and two foods that Rebecca got most excited about eating during her many sojourns to the state fair were corndogs and funnel cake. I had to incorporate them both.

My Minnesota pie is a corn dog–hotdish pie with a cornmeal crust and savory funnel cake topper, served with mustard and ketchup of course! A pie that is all your state fair faves in one. Hopefully one that deserves a crown like the one that is worn by Princess Kay of the Milky Way, the ambassador of dairy farmers in Minnesota.

CORN DOG-HOTDISH PIE
WITH SAVORY FUNNEL-CAKE TOPPING

ACTIVE TIME: 1 HOUR — BAKE TIME: 35 MINUTES — TOTAL TIME: 1 HOUR 35 MINUTES — MAKES ONE 10-INCH PIE

CRUST

Cornmeal Crust (single, page 335),
  rolled out, fit into a greased
  10-inch pie pan, crimped, and
  partially blind baked (see page
  339)

FILLING

½ cup diced celery

½ cup diced onion

1 tablespoon unsalted butter

10 hot dogs, chopped into bite-size
  pieces

1 large egg

⅓ cup whole milk

2 tablespoons granulated sugar

½ teaspoon finely chopped fresh
  sage

¼ teaspoon freshly ground black
  pepper

1 cup shredded cheddar cheese

1 (8.5-ounce) package Jiffy brand
  corn muffin mix

**SAVORY FUNNEL CAKE
  TOPPING**

2 large eggs

1½ cups whole milk

2 cups all-purpose flour

1 tablespoon garlic powder

MAKE THE FILLING: In a large skillet over medium-high heat, sweat the celery and onions in the butter until translucent; this should take 5 to 8 minutes. Transfer to a large mixing bowl. Sauté the hot dog pieces in the same skillet until lightly browned, 5 minutes. Add to the bowl with the vegetables.

In a separate medium bowl, combine the egg, milk, sugar, sage, and pepper. Add half of the hotdog mixture, ¾ cup of the cheese, and all the corn muffin mix. Set aside until ready to fill the pie.

ASSEMBLE AND BAKE THE PIE: Preheat the oven to 400°F. Place the partially baked crust on a baking sheet. Pour the filling into the crust, top with remaining hot dog mixture, and sprinkle with the remaining cheese. Bake on the center rack for 35 minutes, until the surface of the pie is slightly puffy and golden brown.

MAKE THE SAVORY FUNNEL CAKE: In a large mixing bowl, combine the eggs, milk, flour, garlic powder, chili powder, baking powder, salt, and sugar and whisk to combine. Rest the batter for 10 minutes in the fridge before frying.

While the batter rests, fill a large heavy-bottomed pot such as a Dutch oven with vegetable oil and heat over medium heat until 350° to 375°F, using a thermometer to check the temperature.

Fill a squeeze bottle or ziplock bag with batter (and cut off a corner of the bag if using). When the oil comes to temperature, hold the bottle or bag about 10 inches over the oil and squeeze in a circular and zig zag motion to make a

Recipe continues ★★★

1 teaspoon chili powder

1¼ teaspoons baking powder

1 teaspoon kosher salt

1 teaspoon granulated sugar

4 to 6 cups vegetable oil

½ cup chopped scallions,
   for garnish

CONDIMENTS (OPTIONAL)

Ketchup

Mustard

Hot sauce

SPECIAL EQUIPMENT

Heavy-bottomed pot or Dutch oven

Deep-fry thermometer

Squeeze bottle or ziplock bag

rough round shape in the oil. Fry the funnel cake until golden brown on one size, flip, and fry until the other side is golden brown as well, about 5 minutes total. I love using a chopstick for the flipping portion. Remove from the oil and drain on paper towels. Repeat with the remaining batter to make about nine funnel cakes.

ASSEMBLE THE PIE: Arrange the funnel cakes on the baked pie and sprinkle with the scallions. Serve with condiments on the side and enjoy while listening to the ambient sounds of a state fair!

THE DEDICATION!

This pie is dedicated to my friend and former boss, Rebecca Schneider, my design director at JCPenney for five wonderful years. Rebecca was born in Minneapolis and goes back every ding dang year for the state fair. We started at JCPenney around the same time and shook things up in the handbag and accessories department as all good new hires do. We logged many hours together on planes, trains, and cars on long trips to China, Korea, and Hong Kong on factory visits. Though the days were grueling, we filled our evenings with what we loved most: eating and drinking.

Minnesota, I can't wait to explore your 10,000-plus lakes, eat everything on a stick, and fulfill my dream of winning a prize ribbon at your state fair. You may have the second largest state fair in the country, but you are the first in my heart!

Mississippi

PIE
24
OF 50

THE SOUTH'S WARMEST WELCOME

NO STATE FOODS

THE STATE!

Mississippi is known as the Magnolia State and the South's Warmest Welcome. The twentieth state entered statehood in 1817 and got its name from the Ojibwe word gichi-ziibi, meaning "a big river." The Ojibwe people lived in Northern Minnesota, where the river begins, not in the state named after it. The Mississippi River, or Old Man River, is the largest river in the United States and the nation's chief waterway.

Magnolias grow in bounty in Mississippi, catfish are caught in the muddy banks of the river and fried to perfection, and blues music howls through the wind to influence the music we listen to today.

Growing up I was barely ever allowed to have soda, but on those special occasions I always picked root beer. I loved its subtle bitter undertones. Barq's root beer was invented in 1898 by Edward Charles Edmond Barq in Biloxi and first bottled in 1906. He was a trained chemist who had worked on Louisiana sugar plantations in the winters and spent his summers in Biloxi, bottling artesian water and concocting "soda pop flavors." Of their many slogans my favorite has to be "Barq's Has Bite." We love a little play on words.

In 1902, Theodore Roosevelt refused to shoot a captured bear during a hunting expedition in the western part of the state, deeming it unsportsmanlike. Toymaker Morris Michtom saw a drawing of this incident in *The Washington Post*, created a soft bear-cub toy, and sent it to Roosevelt asking for permission to use his name. The teddy bear became an immediate success. Growing up

I hated dolls and lived for my plush teddy. Who knew a girl growing up on the other side of the world would have so many ties to the state?

THE PIE!

With a state so rich in history and with river banks overflowing with charm, what pie could capture all of its glory? There really could only be one: Mississippi mud pie!

The origins of this dessert are as muddy as the waters of the Mississippi. One thing we know for sure is that it must not be confused with dirt cake or mud cake. Some people believe that the pie is a 1970s interpretation of the mud cake, which appeared during World War II when pantries were bare and women developed desserts with cheap ingredients. But the most popular story is that in 1927 Jenny Meyer decided to bake a dense pie with simple ingredients. She melted chocolate and made a filling that resembled the muddy banks of the Mississippi River.

Mississippi mud pie is a rich chocolate dessert composed of some combination of pudding, cake, cookies, ice cream, whipped cream, marshmallows, and liquor. It is always in a cookie crust, built in layers, and finished with chocolate shavings.

My interpretation of the pie uses a chocolate graham cracker crust and a chocolate fudge filling with whipped cream and chocolate shavings. Best enjoyed while dipping your feet down in the mud of the river banks, the coolest place in Mississippi.

MISSISSIPPI MUD PIE

ACTIVE TIME: 30 MINUTES — BAKE TIME: 45 MINUTES — TOTAL TIME: 3 HOURS 15 MINUTES — MAKES ONE 10-INCH PIE

CRUST

Chocolate Graham Cracker Crust
(page 336), blind baked as
directed

FILLING

⅔ cup semisweet chocolate chips

¾ cup (1½ sticks) unsalted butter,
softened at room temperature

1¾ cups packed light brown sugar

4 large eggs

¼ cup unsweetened cocoa powder

1¼ cups heavy whipping cream

TOPPINGS

1 cup heavy whipping cream

3 tablespoons confectioners' sugar

1 teaspoon vanilla extract

½ cup chocolate shavings

SPECIAL EQUIPMENT

Stand mixer with paddle and whisk
attachments

MAKE THE FILLING: In a medium microwave-safe bowl, melt the chocolate chips in the microwave in 30-second intervals, stirring as you go to make sure the chocolate doesn't burn, until fully melted. In the bowl of the stand mixer using the paddle attachment, beat the butter and brown sugar on medium speed until creamed. On low speed, beat in the eggs one a time, scraping the sides between each addition. Mix in the melted chocolate, cocoa powder, and cream. Set aside until ready to fill the pie.

BAKE THE PIE: Preheat the oven to 325°F. Place baked crust on a baking sheet and pour in the filling. Bake the pie on the center rack for 45 minutes, rotating halfway through, until the edges are set and the center has a slight jiggle like a soft thigh. Cool until room temperature, 2 to 3 hours.

MAKE THE TOPPING AND FINISH THE PIE: While the pie is cooling, in a stand mixer with a whisk attachment, mix the cream, confectioners' sugar, and vanilla at medium-high speed until stiff peaks form.

When the pie is cool, top with the whipped cream and sprinkle chocolate shavings on top. Enjoy while cooling your feet in the mud on the banks of a river, preferably the Mississippi!

THE DEDICATION!

This pie is for Rachel Sevin. Rachel wasn't born in Mississippi but her mom sure was! Rachel and her family have spent many Christmases in Sebastopol and will continue to spend many more in Mississippi since her parents recently retired and moved to Biloxi.

I met Rachel the day I graduated from college while singing karaoke at McDonough's Restaurant & Lounge in Savannah, Georgia. The memories of that night are hazy but I remember one thing for sure: I had just an absolute blast with her and we have remained friends ever since.

Mississippi, you sure are the South's Warmest Welcome. The minute I set foot in you it will feel like coming home.

PIE

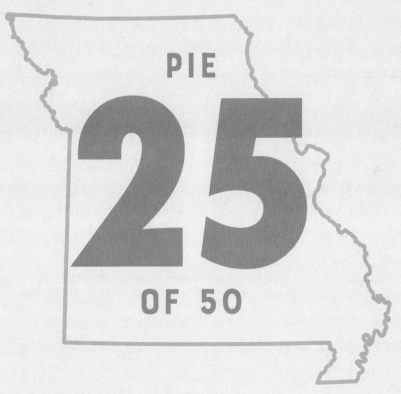

25

OF 50

THE SHOW ME STATE

STATE DESSERT: ICE CREAM CONE

THE STATE!

Missouri, land of fertile plains, rolling hills, prairies, and rivers, became the twenty-fourth state in 1821. The state was named after the Missouri tribe. It comes from ouemessourita, which roughly translates as "wooden canoe people" or "those who have dugout canoes."

Missouri's nickname is also the state slogan: The Show Me State came about around the 1890s. The most popular legend is that Congressman Willard Duncan Vandiver once questioned the accuracy of a speaker's remarks in Philadelphia by saying, "I come from a state that raises corn and cotton and cockleburs and Democrats, and frothy eloquence neither convinces nor satisfies me. I am from Missouri. You have got to show me." His statement meant that actions speak louder than words. Though this story has been told and retold and can't be proven conclusively, regardless of the nickname's origins, it is now emblazoned on Missouri license plates.

The ice cream cone was introduced at the 1904 World's Fair in St. Louis! An ice cream vendor ran out of cups so he teamed up with his neighbor at the fair, a waffle maker. They folded the waffles into cones, filled them with ice cream, and marketed the frozen treat as an "ice cream sandwich" or "ice cream cornucopia." The dessert was a hit and folks across the nation have been eating ice cream cones ever since.

St. Louis is home to Anheuser Busch, the largest beer producer in the nation. They do the lord's work that has fueled many nights that have turned into mornings, and given everyone the liquid courage they need to take the stage at a karaoke bar. I have drunk a serious amount of Bud Heavy and Bud Light in my life so far, and must toast the great state that gave me the sweet gift of a cold one after a long day.

THE PIE!

I wanted the pie for this state to be a frozen treat. The state gave us ice cream cones, but something that only Missouri has is Ted Drewes frozen custard. Ted Drewes is a family-owned business that has been selling frozen custard for over eighty years in St. Louis. Their signature item is the "concrete," a frozen custard so thick you can flip the cup upside down and the custard won't fall out.

Frozen custard deserves a little mix-in! For this pie, it could only be one thing: gooey butter cake, which consists of a dry, flat base covered in delicious goo. The cake is sticky, chewy, and oh-so toothsome. The cake was made by accident in the early 1940s when Johnny Hoffman of St. Louis Pastries Bakery messed up the butter proportion in one of his cakes. Rather than throwing out the batter, he sold the sugary, sticky confection and it was an instant hit.

My Missouri pie is a Ted Drewes copycat frozen custard pie with homemade gooey butter cake pieces folded in with rainbow sprinkles on top. The thick creamy custard cradles the soft gooey cake pieces and, well, the rainbow sprinkles are just for a little flair. It's best enjoyed while sitting in awe of St. Louis's Gateway Arch or on the road down Route 66.

TED DREWES-INSPIRED FROZEN CUSTARD PIE
WITH ST. LOUIS GOOEY BUTTER CAKE SWIRL

ACTIVE TIME: 1 HOUR — BAKE TIME: 35 MINUTES — TOTAL TIME: 10 HOURS 15 MINUTES — MAKES ONE 10-INCH PIE

CRUST

All-Butter Crust (single, page 332), rolled out, crimped, fit into a greased 10-inch pie pan, and fully blind baked (see page 339)

FILLING

Frozen Custard

1 tablespoon cornstarch

1¾ cups whole milk

¾ cup plus 1 tablespoon granulated sugar

3 tablespoons honey

Pinch of kosher salt

6 large egg yolks

1¾ cups heavy whipping cream

1 tablespoon vanilla extract

Butter Cake

1½ tablespoons whole milk, at room temperature

2 tablespoons warm water

⅞ teaspoon active dry yeast

3 tablespoons unsalted butter, softened at room temperature

1½ tablespoons granulated sugar

½ teaspoon kosher salt

1 large egg

¾ cup plus 2 tablespoons all-purpose flour

Confectioners' sugar for dusting

MAKE THE FROZEN CUSTARD: In a small bowl, whisk together the cornstarch and ½ cup of the milk until smooth. In a medium saucepan, whisk the remaining 1¼ cups milk with the granulated sugar, honey, and salt. Stir in the cornstarch mixture and cook over medium-high heat until it is bubbling but not boiling. In a separate large bowl, whisk the egg yolks. Whisking rapidly, pour ½ cup of the hot milk mixture slowly into the yolks to temper them, making sure they don't scramble. Pour the tempered egg mixture back into the pan and cook over medium heat for 5 minutes, stirring constantly to make sure it doesn't boil. Remove the saucepan from the heat and stir in the cream and vanilla. Pour into large bowl. Cover the bowl with plastic wrap, pressing the wrap against the custard so it doesn't form a film. Refrigerate for 4 hours.

Transfer the custard to an ice cream machine and churn for 30 minutes according to manufacturer's directions. Remove the custard from the ice cream machine and freeze for 2 hours.

MAKE THE BUTTER CAKE BATTER: In a small bowl, mix the milk and warm water, add the yeast, and whisk gently until the yeast dissolves. Set aside. Using a stand mixer with paddle attachment, cream the butter, granulated sugar, and salt until fluffy. Scrape down the sides of the bowl and add the egg. Alternately add portions of the flour and the yeast mixture, making sure to scrape down the sides of the bowl after each addition. Beat on medium speed until a smooth dough mass is formed, 7 to 10 minutes. Press the dough into an ungreased 9x13-inch baking dish and cover the dish with plastic wrap or a clean towel. Let it rise in a warm place until doubled in size, 2 to 3 hours.

Recipe continues ★★★

2 tablespoons water

1½ tablespoons light corn syrup

1½ teaspoons vanilla extract

6 tablespoons (¾ stick) unsalted
  butter, softened at room
  temperature

¾ cup granulated sugar

¼ teaspoon kosher salt

1 large egg

½ cup plus 1½ tablespoons
  all-purpose flour

Rainbow sprinkles for decoration

SPECIAL EQUIPMENT

Ice cream machine

Stand mixer with paddle attachment

9x13-inch baking dish, at least
  2 inches deep

MAKE THE GOOEY TOPPING: Preheat the oven to 350°F. In a small bowl, mix the water, corn syrup, and vanilla. Using the stand mixer with paddle attachment, cream the butter, granulated sugar, and salt until fluffy, 5 to 7 minutes. Scrape down the sides and add the egg. Alternately add the flour and corn syrup mixture, scraping down the bowl after each addition.

TOP AND BAKE THE CAKE: Spoon dollops of topping over the risen cake batter and use a spatula to gently spread over the top. Bake for 35 to 45 minutes, until the surface is golden brown and a toothpick inserted in the center comes out clean. Let the cake cool for at least 2 to 3 hours before dusting with confectioners' sugar and cutting into ½-inch cubes. Set aside until ready to mix into the frozen custard.

ASSEMBLE THE PIE: When the custard has been frozen for 2 hours, mix in the gooey butter cake pieces and return the custard to the freezer until ready to fill pie.

Take the custard out of the freezer and let sit at room temperature for 10 minutes, so it is spreadable. Fill the baked pie crust with the cake and custard mixture and smooth the top with a spatula. Sprinkle rainbow sprinkles on top if using. Freeze for 10 minutes before serving. Enjoy with an ice cold Budweiser from Anheuser-Busch and toast the Show Me State!

THE DEDICATION!

This pie is dedicated to my wonderful friend of seventeen-plus years, Katie Glenn. Katie was born in Hawai'i but moved to Columbia when she was 8 years old. Her mother, Barb, whom I adore, was born in St. Louis and her dad, Jeff, was born in Columbia. I love a wooded glen just as much as the next person but these are my favorite Glenns!

When Katie and I first met is a complete mystery. We do not remember a time when we weren't friends. Both of us moved to New York after college and continued to spend many nights drinking, dancing, and getting into all sorts of trouble together. Here's to many more nights of polishing off a bottle of whiskey and living to tell the tale.

Missouri, Show Me!

Montana

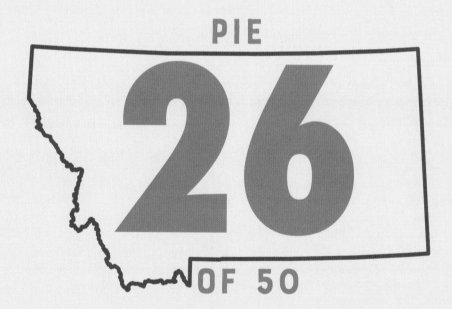

PIE

26

OF 50

BIG SKY COUNTRY

NO STATE FOODS

THE STATE!

The name of the forty-first state comes from the Spanish word montaña, meaning "mountain"—a nod to the state being home to at least 300 peaks that reach over 9,600 feet tall. Not only are the mountains tall but they are full of treasures. Gold and silver deposits have been mined from Montana's mountains going back as far as the 1800s, earning the state its nickname, the Treasure State. It got its other nickname, Big Sky Country, because of the many vantage points that offer an uninterrupted view of the horizon that spreads out under its panoramic skies.

Montana is home to the first-ever National Park, Yellowstone, as well as Glacier National Park. Within the boundaries of Glacier National Park are 7,000-year-old glaciers and 250 lakes. Glacier is also home to Triple Divide Peak, which allows water to flow into the Pacific, Atlantic, and Hudson Bay. Montana is the only state where this phenomenon occurs: the one place where the country's water intersects and intermingles before it branches off into different directions. Like Union Square in New York City!

Besides the mountains, the state is also known for its Great Plains region, which sprawls across its eastern three-fifths. This region includes the Great Plains Badlands and Makoshika State Park. The word Makoshika comes from a variant spelling of a Lakota phrase meaning "bad land" or "bad earth."

There are more cattle than humans in Montana. Not only is it an important hub for livestock farming but it is also home to buffalo, elk, deer, and antelope that also outnumber humans.

THE PIE!

Montana's pie is inspired by the pasty, which first arrived in Butte in the late 1800s with the gold, tin, and copper miners from Cornwall, England. The pasty is a hearty all-in-one dish that was a "letter from home," since wives would send their husbands into the mines with these homemade pastries as sustenance for the long work day.

A pasty is a half-moon shaped pie-crust pastry stuffed with meats and vegetables that can weigh up to 2 pounds. It was also common for pasties to include not only a savory lunch but also a sweet or fruity dessert "course" at the end. The savory filling filled the pastry at one end and the sweet at the other, with a marking on the crust to tell the miners what was what. At meal times, miners used their shovels to reheat the pasties over the candles they wore on their heads.

Pasties were sealed with a thick crimp, which was beautiful and practical: The crimp allowed for easy grasping and lowered the risk of getting sick from dirty working hands. This is because once the inner part of the pasty was eaten, the crimp was often tossed aside as an offering to the ghosts of the dead, a kind gesture with a whisper of superstition.

The act of leaving the crust as an offering to the dead reminds me of the Hungry Ghost Festival in Chinese culture. On the fifteenth day of the seventh month in the lunar calendar, it is believed the ghosts and spirits come out from the lower realms to visit the living. The day before this, a large feast is held for the ghosts. People bring samples of food and place them on an offering table to please the ghosts and to ward off bad luck. The offerings are also placed at empty place settings at tables to honor deceased family members, treating them as if they were still living.

Montana's pie is both dinner and dessert in one, with a buffalo and root vegetable savory filling, and cherry filling to finish. In Butte, the pasty is often served with a side of gravy or ketchup. So that's what I do too. The pie is served with a warm brown gravy and best enjoyed under the stars in Big Sky Country.

PASTY PIE

WITH BUFFALO STEW AND CHERRY FILLINGS

ACTIVE TIME: 1 HOUR — BAKE TIME: 1 HOUR — TOTAL TIME: 2 HOURS 30 MINUTES — MAKES ONE 10-INCH PIE

CRUST

All-Butter Crust (double, page 332),
  rolled out for top and bottom
  crust (see page 339)
Egg wash (see page 346)
Flaky salt and cracked black pepper
  to taste

FILLINGS

Buffalo Stew

1 tablespoon vegetable oil
1 pound buffalo meat, minced
½ medium rutabaga, diced
1 small turnip, diced
1 large carrot, diced
½ medium onion, diced
1 medium potato, diced
Kosher salt and freshly ground
  black pepper to taste

Cherry Filling

1 cup cherries, pitted and sliced
  in half
2 tablespoons granulated sugar
1 tablespoon cornstarch

BROWN GRAVY TOPPING

2 tablespoons unsalted butter
2 tablespoons all-purpose flour
1 cup beef stock
1 teaspoon dried thyme
1 teaspoon dried granulated onion

MAKE THE BUFFALO STEW: Heat the oil in a skillet over medium-high heat, add the buffalo meat, and cook until browned and cooked through. In a large bowl, mix the rutabaga, turnip, carrot, onion, and potato. Add the browned meat, season with kosher salt and pepper, and mix well. Set aside until ready to fill the pie.

MAKE THE CHERRY FILLING: In a small mixing bowl, mix together the cherries, sugar, and cornstarch. Set aside until ready to fill the pie.

ASSEMBLE THE PIE: Fit the bottom crust into a greased 10-inch pie pan. Use foil to make a ring that is 8 inches in diameter. Place the foil ring in the pie crust and fill the middle with the buffalo filling. Fill the outside of the ring with the cherry filling. Remove the foil ring. Top the pie with the second crust and roll and crimp edges to seal (see page 343). Cut vents into the top crust so that steam can escape. Freeze the pie for at least 15 minutes. Place the pie on a baking sheet.

BAKE THE PIE: Preheat the oven to 375°F. Brush the egg wash over the top of the pie and sprinkle with flaky salt and cracked pepper. Bake on the center rack for 1 hour, rotating the pie 90 degrees every 15 minutes, until the pie is golden brown.

MAKE THE BROWN GRAVY: In a small saucepan, melt the butter over medium-high heat. Whisk in the flour and cook for 2 minutes, or until golden brown. Whisk in the stock, thyme, and granulated onion and bring mixture to a boil. Stir well and season to taste.

Recipe continues ★★★

SERVE THE PIE: Let the pie cool for at least 30 minutes. Slice and serve, pouring brown gravy on top! Best enjoyed while listening to "Wide Open Spaces" by the Chicks and enjoying the views of Big Sky Country!

THE DEDICATION!

This pie is dedicated to my sweet friend John Frederick. John is not from Montana but has driven through the vast state many a time on his cross-country road trips from his hometown of Baltimore to Portland, Oregon, where he went to school at Reed College. He has set foot in Bozeman and Missoula and has captivated me with his descriptions of the vast and sprawling wonder this state holds in its mountains and skies.

I met John when I was 15 years old in New Haven, Connecticut, at a summer program at Yale. We met on the quad and have been friends ever since. Whenever we met up after class we would lie on the grass on the quad listening to Dispatch and Sublime. Many years later we reunited in New York and it felt like time didn't pass at all.

Big Sky Country, I am charmed by you and can't wait to experience the Triple Divide and all your treasures soon.

Nebraska

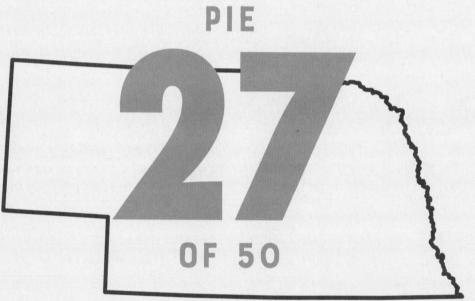

PIE

27

OF 50

THE CORNHUSKER STATE

NO STATE FOODS

THE STATE!

Nebraska, the thirty-seventh state, entered statehood in 1867. Its name comes from the Otoe words ñí brásge or the Omaha ní btháska, meaning "flat water," after the Platte river that flows through the state. Nebraska got its nickname of the Cornhusker State from the University of Nebraska's football team. In this state, football is not just a sport but a religion. On game day, the Cornhuskers' Memorial Stadium becomes the third largest city in the state.

The Great Plains spread across the western and northeastern parts of the state. This region is mostly flat but strewn with canyons, valleys, lakes, and wetlands. The state is home to Chimney Rock, which towers 300 feet into the sky. This beacon of natural beauty was a landmark for travelers throughout history on the Oregon, California, and Mormon Trails—letting them know that they were going the right way.

When Nebraska comes up, I think about Warren Buffett, the billionaire native son of Omaha, and his habit of drinking five Cherry Cokes a day. In 1930, a Lithuanian grocer in Omaha named Reuben Kulakofsky gave birth to one of my favorite deli specials, the Reuben sandwich. But none of these foods seems to say home to Nebraskans as much as a runza.

THE PIE!

The runza is a rectangular yeasted dough pocket sandwich with a filling of beef, cabbage or sauerkraut, and onions and is often called "as Nebraskan as Cornhusker football." It is said to have originated from the pirog, a Russian baked good. Volga Germans adapted the pirog to a yeasted pastry sandwich called the bierock that had similar ingredients. When the political climate turned against them in Russia, Volga Germans emigrated to the United States, creating communities across the Great Plains. Many who immigrated settled near Sutton, Nebraska.

Sarah "Sally" Everett, originally of Sutton, adapted her family's bierock recipe into the runza. She named it after the Low German word runsa, meaning "belly," which is the perfect description of the soft rounded shape of the pouch pastry. In 1949, Sally and her brother Alex opened the first Runza Drive Inn in Lincoln, which still serves the pastries today.

I love sauce and felt like the runza needed a dip complement. I went on a quest to find a regional sauce or dressing for a drizzle for the pie. I found her in Dorothy Lynch. In the late 1940s, Dorothy Lynch and her husband ran the restaurant at the Legion Club in St. Paul. This is where she first served her Dorothy Lynch Home Style dressing, a thick, sweet/spicy, tomato-based salad dressing with a creamy mouthfeel. The dressing was a smash hit and is now an essential ingredient in many Midwestern family recipes, and it is still bottled in Duncan, Nebraska.

Nebraska's pie, inspired by the runza, is a rectangular pie filled with ground beef, cabbage, onions, and sweet corn with a cornmeal crust. It is perfectly complemented by Dorothy Lynch's tangy, creamy dressing.

RUNZA PIE

WITH DOROTHY LYNCH DRESSING

ACTIVE TIME: 30 MINUTES — BAKE TIME: 1 HOUR — TOTAL TIME: 2 HOURS 30 MINUTES — MAKES ONE 9X13-INCH PIE

CRUST

All-Butter Crust (quadrupled,
    see below; page 332)

Egg wash (see page 346)

Flaky sea salt and freshly ground
    black pepper to taste

FILLING

1 pound ground beef

½ large head cabbage, shredded

½ medium onion, diced

1 cup sweet corn kernels (canned,
    fresh, or frozen)

Kosher salt and freshly ground black
    pepper to taste

FOR SERVING

Dorothy Lynch Home Style Dressing,
    found in grocery stores all over
    Nebraska (and online)

SPECIAL EQUIPMENT

9x13-inch baking dish

MAKE THE CRUST: Make four times the recipe for a single crust, but divide it into two. Roll one half into an approximate 14x10-inch rectangle (for the bottom crust), and the other to a 10x12-inch rectangle (for the top crust).

MAKE THE FILLING: In a large skillet over medium-high heat, cook the ground beef, stirring occasionally, until browned. Drain any excess liquid from the pan, then add the cabbage, onion, and corn. Cook until the onion is translucent, about 8 minutes. Season to taste. Let the filling cool for 30 minutes before filling the pie.

ASSEMBLE THE PIE: Preheat the oven to 425°F and arrange racks at the bottom and middle of the oven. Fit one crust into a greased 9x13-inch baking dish and fill with the filling. Place the second crust on top and roll and crimp edges to seal (see page 343). Brush egg wash over the entire pie and top with flaky sea salt and ground pepper.

BAKE THE PIE: Bake for 20 minutes on the bottom rack of the oven. Turn the oven down to 350°F, move the pie to the center rack, and bake for 45 minutes, until the crust is golden brown. Let cool for 30 minutes before serving with a drizzle of Dorothy Lynch dressing. Best enjoyed while watching the Cornhuskers play!

THE DEDICATION!

I have yet to meet anyone from the great state of Nebraska, but when I developed this pie, I gave it to my sweet and wonderful friend, Bryan Moreno. Why? Bryan grew up in New Jersey, but in college he did live on Lincoln Street in Savannah — and Lincoln is the capital of Nebraska. It's a stretch, I know. But Bryan does deserve the only rectangular pie I baked in the fifty states. Until I make this pie for my first Nebraskan friend, I will toast the state with a passion for corn, and revel in the glory that is the almost two-decade-long friendship between Bryan and me.

Nebraska, I know I'll love you like I love every kernel on an ear of corn.

Nevada

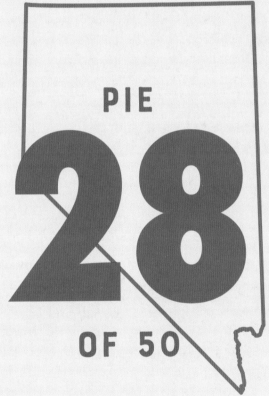

PIE

28

OF 50

BATTLE BORN

NO STATE FOODS

THE STATE!

Nevada was the thirty-sixth state to enter the Union in 1864, and its name comes from the Sierra Nevada ("snow-clad mountains" in Spanish) mountain range near Reno. But when I hear Nevada I think not of mountains but of slot machines and late nights full of sin.

The state produces about three-quarters of all the gold mined in the United States. In years past, prospectors found treasures including gold and silver, copper, and some of the world's best black opals. Now they have been replaced by fortune seekers hoping to strike it rich in casinos.

The first casino, the Pair-O-Dice Club, opened in 1931 on Highway 91, which would become the famous Las Vegas Strip. In 1960, there were 16,067 slot machines in Las Vegas; in 1999 there were 205,726. That's one slot machine for every ten residents! The state is also home to the largest state public works project, the Hoover Dam, which contains enough concrete to pave a two-lane highway from San Francisco to New York.

The first time I visited Las Vegas was with my dad and sisters, tagging along on a business trip. We went to M&M's World to pass the time and got bags of the candy. I chose only red, black, and white because that was my aesthetic as a teenager deep into her emo phase: wearing all black, listening to Brand New and Taking Back Sunday, writing in my LiveJournal, and not enjoying family time one bit.

My most recent experience was after a five-day solo sojourn to the North Rim of the Grand Canyon for my 30th birthday. After camping I just wanted to go to a hotel, take a shower, put on a robe, and eat a hamburger in bed. But how can you resist seeing Mariah Carey live and having a cocktail at Frankie's Tiki Room?

THE PIE!

For a state that is as good as gold, I threw caution to the wind. For me, an all-you-can-eat buffet is synonymous with Nevada, so that's where my pie began.

Growing up, I always viewed America as bigger, better—a land of excess. The perfect example of that excess is the buffet. The idea of a buffet originated in 12th-century France, and first touched American soil in 1939 at the New York World's Fair. In the 1940s it grew in popularity in Las Vegas, thanks to Herb McDonald. Herb created the Buckaroo Buffet, where diners chose from a selection of salads, seafood, and cold cuts. Intermingling the highbrow and lowbrow, his buffet's goal was to keep people inside the casino longer. They would be tempted by the food and stay to play the tables. An affordable meal left them more funds to spend on blackjack.

I started by looking up the menus at all the main casinos on the Strip to see what they served at their buffets, and made a spreadsheet to find the common denominators. I landed on four savory components and four sweet components. After all, Nevada is the state where you can have your cake and eat it too.

The savory half of the Nevada pie includes Caesar salad, shrimp cocktail, Alaskan king crab with herbed butter, and New York strip steak with caramelized onions and mashed potatoes, each served in an herbed crust compartment. The sweet side includes a fig jam–glazed fruit tart, chocolate mousse, cheesecake with strawberry glaze, and a cookies and cream sundae—all cradled in an all-butter crust.

It's extravagant, it's excessive, and, in all honesty, it's a little harebrained to put a tasting menu inside a single pie. But spin it like a roulette wheel and try your luck! Whichever compartment you land on, you've hit the jackpot. This all-you-can-eat buffet is a perfect solo adventure for one… or two, if you feel like sharing.

ALL-YOU-CAN-EAT BUFFET PIE!

ACTIVE TIME: 4 HOURS — BAKE TIME: 1 HOUR — TOTAL TIME: 5 HOURS — MAKES ONE 10-INCH PIE

CRUST

All-Butter Crust (single, page 332)
Herbed Crust (single, page 333)
Egg wash (see page 346)

SPECIAL EQUIPMENT

Cast-iron pan with eight
    compartments, or 10-inch pie
    pan with eight aluminum foil
    dividers (see below)
Stand mixer with whisk and paddle
    attachments

MAKE THE CRUST: For the crust, you are going to be making two halves of the pie (one half savory and one half sweet), using either a cast-iron pan with eight compartments or a regular pie pan divided with foil into two halves, Each with four compartments. Make one half at a time. Take your time, be patient—this is weird but worth it.

If using an eight-compartment cast-iron pan: Preheat the oven to 375°F. Grease one half of the pan. Roll out the herbed crust to ¼-inch thickness. Drape the dough over half of the pan (four of the compartments); it can drape over the other side a little while you are fitting the dough. Use your fingers to gently fit the dough into each compartment; take your time as to not rip the dough and make sure the crust is flush to each compartment. Trim the excess at the edge and crimp. Cut the excess that extends over the middle so that you have a half of a crust. Freeze for 10 minutes.

Line the four compartments with foil and fill with pie weights. Blind bake on a baking sheet for 30 minutes, until the crust is cooked through. Let cool and remove the crust from the pie pan. Repeat for other side of the pie with the all-butter crust.

If using a 10-inch pie pan and aluminum foil: Preheat the oven to 375°F. Using foil, make dividers within the pie pan to create eight "slices": Fold a strip of foil until it is 1 inch wide and stand it up vertically in the pan, dividing it in half and making a barrier. (Be sure to make the strip long enough so that you can wrap the end of the strip around the edge of the pie pan so it is secure and won't move.) Then place six smaller strips to divide the halves into four compartments each. Wrap the ends up and over the edge to secure. Grease the pie pan, including the dividers.

Recipe continues ★★★

FILLINGS

Savory Filling 1: Caesar Salad

3 leaves romaine lettuce, chopped

2 teaspoons grated Parmigiano Reggiano

2 tablespoons croutons

1 tablespoon Caesar salad dressing (store-bought is fine)

Savory Filling 2: Shrimp Cocktail

¼ cup shredded romaine lettuce

3 whole shrimp, poached and shelled

1 tablespoon cocktail sauce (store-bought is fine)

Savory Filling 3: Snow Crab with Garlic Butter

2 tablespoons unsalted butter

2 teaspoons minced garlic

2 teaspoons minced shallot

1 tablespoon chopped fresh flat-leaf parsley

2 teaspoons lemon juice

Kosher salt and freshly ground black pepper to taste

½ cup snow crab meat

Savory Filling 4: New York Strip with Caramelized Onions and Mashed Potatoes

4 ounces New York strip steak

Kosher salt and freshly ground black pepper

12 tablespoons unsalted butter (1½ sticks)

2 tablespoons extra-virgin olive oil

1 small yellow onion, sliced

¼ pound Yukon Gold potatoes, peeled and chopped into 1-inch pieces

Roll out the herbed crust to ¼-inch thickness. Drape it over half the pie pan and use your fingers to gently fit the dough into each compartment; take your time as to not rip the dough. Make sure the crust is flush to each compartment you've made, be gentle as to not disturb the foil dividers. Trim the excess at the edges and crimp. Cut the excess that extends over the middle so that you have a half of a crust. Freeze for 10 minutes. Line the compartments with foil and fill with pie weights. Blind bake on a baking sheet for 30 minutes, until the crust is cooked through. Let cool and carefully remove the crust from the pie pan. Repeat for other side of pie with the all-butter crust.

MAKE THE SAVORY FILLINGS: Tackle the savory fillings first (slices 1 to 4) to fill the savory herbed crust compartments.

Filling 1, Caesar Salad: Toss the chopped romaine, Parmesan, and croutons together. Just before serving, dress the salad and use to fill one pie compartment.

Filling 2, Shrimp Cocktail: Just before serving, lay a bed of shredded lettuce on the bottom of the pie compartment. Arrange the poached shrimp on top and drizzle with the cocktail sauce.

Filling 3, Snow Crab: In a medium saucepan over medium-low heat, melt the butter. Add the garlic and shallot and cook until fragrant and translucent, 3 to 5 minute. Stir in the parsley, lemon juice, salt, and pepper. Dress the crab with the butter mixture. Fill one pie crust compartment with the crab mixture.

Filling 4, New York Strip: Take the steak out of the fridge about an hour before cooking to let it come to room temperature. Season it generously with salt.

Start by making the caramelized onions: In a medium pan over medium heat, heat 4 tablespoons of the butter and 1 tablespoon of the olive oil. Add the onion and season with salt. Cook for 30 to 45 minutes, stirring occasionally to make sure the onions aren't sticking. You are cooking out all the liquid so that the sugars in the onion can start to caramelize.

1 bay leaf

¼ cup heavy cream

1 teaspoon chopped fresh chives

1 sprig fresh rosemary

Dessert Filling 5: Fruit Custard

1 cup whole milk

1 tablespoon cornstarch

½ teaspoon vanilla extract

1 large egg yolk

2 tablespoons confectioners' sugar

¼ cup fig jam

1 tablespoon water

2 strawberries, sliced

¼ kiwi, sliced

5 whole blueberries

Dessert Filling 6: Chocolate Mousse
with Whipped Cream and
Chocolate Shavings

¾ cup semisweet chocolate chips

¾ teaspoon vanilla extract

Pinch of kosher salt

6 tablespoons plus ¾ cup heavy
cream

2 ounces dark chocolate, shaved

Dessert Filling 7: Cheesecake with
Strawberry Glaze

4 ounces cream cheese, softened at
room temp

¼ teaspoon vanilla extract

¼ cup confectioners' sugar

1 tablespoon plus 1 teaspoon sour
cream

3 tablespoons cold heavy whipping
cream

1 tablespoon water

You will know the onions are ready when they are a beautiful brown and glossy. Set aside until ready to assemble the pie.

Make the mashed potatoes: In a medium pot, combine the potatoes, bay leaf, and 1½ teaspoons salt and cover with cold water. Bring to a boil over medium-high heat. Cook the potatoes for 20 minutes, or until fork tender. Drain the potatoes and remove the bay leaf. Heat the cream and 6 tablespoons butter in a separate pan until almost boiling. Mash the potatoes, then add the hot cream and butter mixture and continue to mash until smooth. Season to taste and stir in the chives. Set potatoes aside until ready to fill the pie.

Cook the steak: In a cast-iron pan, melt the remaining 2 tablespoons butter in the remaining 1 tablespoon olive oil. Add the sprig of rosemary, then the room-temperature steak and sear on each side, basting with melted butter, for 2 to 3 minutes, until medium-rare or to your desired doneness. Let rest for 10 minutes before slicing.

Fill one compartment with the mashed potatoes and top with the sliced steak and the onions.

MAKE THE DESSERT FILLINGS: Next make the sweet slices (slices 5 to 8) for the all-butter crust compartments.

Filling 5, Fruit Custard: In a medium bowl, whisk 1 tablespoon of the milk with the cornstarch until smooth; set aside. In a medium sauce pan, combine the remaining milk with the vanilla and warm gently over low heat. Add the egg yolk and confectioners' sugar to the cornstarch mixture and whisk to combine. Add a little of the warm milk to the egg mixture to temper it. Add all the egg mixture to the saucepan and whisk constantly until the mixture thickens, about 6 minutes. Pour into a bowl and cover the surface with plastic wrap so the pastry cream doesn't form a skin. Refrigerate until cool.

While the pastry cream is cooling, make the glaze by heating the jam and water in a small saucepan, stirring to melt and combine. Once it has come together, strain the mixture and set it aside. Once the pastry cream has cooled, fill one crust compartment with the pastry cream, top with the

Recipe continues ✳✳✳

¾ teaspoon cornstarch

¼ cup strawberry jelly

¾ teaspoon lemon juice

Red food coloring (optional)

Dessert Filling 8: Cookies and Cream Sundae

1 cup cookies and cream ice cream

1 tablespoon whipped cream

2 tablespoons crushed Oreo cookies (2 to 3 cookies)

1 maraschino cherry

strawberries, kiwi, and blueberries, and lightly brush the fruits with the glaze.

Filling 6, Chocolate Mousse: Combine the chocolate chips with the vanilla and salt in a large bowl. In a small saucepan, bring the 6 tablespoons cream to a bare simmer. Pour the cream over the chocolate and let it sit for 1 minute before whisking until smooth. Refrigerate for 30 minutes.

Using a stand mixer, whip the ¾ cup cream to stiff peaks, about 2 minutes. Whisk the chilled chocolate mixture to loosen, then fold into the whipped cream. Fill one crust compartment with the chocolate mousse, top with the whipped cream, and garnish with shaved chocolate pieces.

Filling 7, Cheesecake: In a stand mixer with paddle attachment, mix the cream cheese, vanilla, and confectioners' sugar until smooth and light, 2 to 3 minutes. Add the sour cream and cream and whip until creamy, 4 to 5 minutes. Refrigerate the mixture for at least 4 hours.

Make the strawberry glaze: In a saucepan combine the water and cornstarch. Add the jelly and cook over medium heat, stirring occasionally, until it thickens, about 5 minutes. Remove from the heat and stir in the lemon juice and food coloring if using. Cool until room temp. Fill one crust compartment with the cheesecake mixture and top with the strawberry glaze.

Filling 8, Cookies and Cream Sundae: Remove the ice cream from the freezer about 5 minutes before you plan to fill the pie; this will make the ice cream more scoopable and easier to fill the compartment. Fill the final compartment with the ice cream and top with the whipped cream, Oreos, and maraschino cherry.

When all the elements are assembled and all the crust compartments of both sides are filled, put the halves of the pie together to form your all you can eat buffet pie!

You have climbed the all-you-can-eat buffet pie mountain. Put your soft clothes on, sit your butt down, search for "casino sounds" on YouTube to play on blast, close your eyes, and eat your way around the pie, pretending you're in Las Vegas.

THE DEDICATION!

This Nevada pie is for Mark Johnson, who was born and raised in Las Vegas. His inside knowledge led to me to all the right places on my most recent visit, like my now-favorite tiki bar, Frankie's. He even bought me a souvenir mug for my birthday from Frankie's to celebrate the occasion.

Mark and I both went to SCAD but never met there; we never heard of each other until our buddy Matt introduced us when we were all living in NYC. We have taken many a road trip together to lake houses and weddings. We always make a fresh playlist, but he always puts "Thank You for Being a Friend" by Andrew Gold on it. The song always comes on at a really funny time during the car ride and we sing it to each other. I rolled the dice and hit the jackpot with this friendship.

New Hampshire

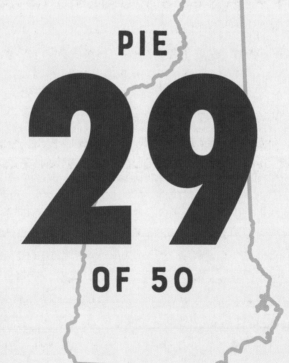

PIE

29

OF 50

LIVE FREE OR DIE

STATE FRUIT: PUMPKIN ★ STATE VEGETABLE: WHITE POTATO

THE STATE!

I love New Hampshire! So many of my closest friends hail from this great state. It was the first colony to create a constitution and declare its independence from Great Britain, but didn't officially become the ninth state until 1788.

New Hampshire was named by Englishman John Mason, who named it after Hampshire County in England where he had grown up. He invested in building on the land but never actually left England to see it. New Hampshire's White Mountains are home to Mount Washington, towering over the land at 6,288 feet—New England's highest point. The Whites used to be home to the Old Man of the Mountain, a granite formation that looked like a man's face. While the stones collapsed in 2003, his story and memory live on.

My first visit to New Hampshire was in the tiny town of Hebron in the western part of the state at the peak of the summer and mosquito season for the wedding of my friends Kelsie and Charles. I had a grand old time, dancing barefoot in the grass, swimming in Newfound Lake, jumping off cliffs, wading through swimming holes, and soaking in the sun with all my favorite people.

The state motto is Live Free or Die. It comes from a toast that General John Stark sent on July 21, 1809, when he declined an invitation to head up a 32nd anniversary reunion of the 1777 Battle of Bennington in Vermont due to poor health. In full, he said: "Live free or die; death is not the worst of evils." It became the official motto only 136 years later, in 1945.

I have been dreaming of climbing Mount Washington and chugging a beer when I get to the top. The only thing left to say really is, Live Free or Die.

THE PIE!

The pumpkin became New Hampshire's official state fruit in 2006 as the result of a quest by fifteen third- and fourth-graders, affectionately nicknamed the Pumpkin Kids, at Wells Memorial School in Harrisville, close to Keene. The seed for the idea was planted in a civics class by now-retired teacher Kathy Frick, who talked about the kids in Florida who had lobbied their governor to make the orange their official fruit. The kids asked if New Hampshire had a fruit and, when they found out it didn't, lobbied and testified in front of state legislators to make it happen. They petitioned for a bill and saw it signed into law. They picked the pumpkin because of the festival held in Keene that showcases thousands of carved pumpkins and holds the world record for the largest number of lit jack-o'-lanterns.

For this pumpkin-loving state, I had to make something truly special. My friend Heather runs Middle Branch Farm in New Boston, and once sent me the best maple syrup I have ever had, so I knew I had to infuse the pumpkin pie with a little bit of that maple flavor.

After Kelsie and Chuck's wedding, Kelsie saved a birch branch for me as a memento and I have kept it ever since. The white birch, native to New Hampshire and the state tree, graces the wooded slopes along the borders of lakes and streams and is a staple of the postcard-perfect scenery in the state. I wanted to capture this tree's beauty in a pie crust with details painted in strong espresso.

This maple-pumpkin pie is best enjoyed in the shadow of Mount Washington with a cool fall breeze whispering through the birches.

MAPLE PUMPKIN PIE
WITH PAINTED BIRCH TREE CRUST

ACTIVE TIME: 2 HOURS — BAKE TIME: 1 HOUR 30 MINUTES — TOTAL TIME: 3 HOURS 30 MINUTES — MAKES ONE 10-INCH PIE

CRUST

All-Butter Crust (double, page 332), one for bottom of pie, rolled out, fit into a 10-inch pie pan, and crimped (see page 339), one for birch tree crust design

FILLING

1 cup maple syrup
1 (15-ounce) can (1⅞ cups) pumpkin (preferably Libby's brand)
1 cup heavy whipping cream
⅔ cup whole milk
2 large eggs
1 teaspoon ground cinnamon
1 teaspoon ground ginger
½ teaspoon kosher salt

SPECIAL EQUIPMENT

X-Acto knife to cut birch tree design (see template below)
Instant espresso (for painting details)
Paintbrush

MAKE THE FILLING: In a medium saucepan over medium heat, gently bring the maple syrup to a boil. Turn the heat off and let the maple syrup cool slightly. In a large mixing bowl, whisk the cooled maple syrup, pumpkin, cream, milk, eggs, cinnamon, ginger, and salt. Set aside until ready to fill the pie.

ASSEMBLE AND BAKE THE PIE: Preheat the oven to 375°F. Place the prepared crust on a baking sheet and pour the filling into the crust. Bake on the center rack for 1 hour, until the filling is set but has a slight jiggle. Cool completely.

MAKE THE BIRCH TREE DECORATIONS: While the pie is cooling, use the birch tree template to cut trees out of rolled-out top crust. Place the cut-out trees onto a flour-dusted baking sheet. Mix 2 teaspoons ground instant espresso with 1 tablespoon water and use a clean paintbrush to paint on birch tree details. Freeze the finished trees for 20 minutes. Bake in the 375°F oven, rotating 180 degrees halfway through, for 20 to 30 minutes, until golden brown.

FINISH THE PIE: Place the birch trees on the cooled pie. Enjoy with whipped cream and a view of the White Mountains!

FOR BIRCH TREE CRUST DESIGN
TEMPLATE, SCAN CODE

THE DEDICATION!

New Hampshire is for a couple of my two favorite people in America if not on planet Earth: Charles and Kelsie Woodbury, who both grew up in New Boston. I have spent countless holidays with them, days on the beach and nights laughing on their sofa watching movies. One of my favorite moments was when the three of us were hanging out drinking and chatting and the song "Fast Car" by Tracy Chapman came on and we all yelled at the same time, "I LOVE THIS SONG!" We yell-sang, we laughed, we enjoyed each other's company.

Kelsie is my favorite person to listen to sad cowgirl songs with and Chuck is my favorite person to shoot the shit with on a Sunday afternoon over a really good sandwich. It's nice in life to have people that you can sit in silence with and just enjoy the air. All that's left to be said is, *Live Free or Die.*

new Jersey

PIE

30

OF 50

THE GARDEN STATE

STATE FRUIT: NORTHERN HIGHBUSH BLUEBERRY

THE STATE!

I deeply love New Jersey. The state gets an undeserved bad rap from its neighbor New York—and even I admit to giving my best friend Patrick shit for moving to Jersey City from Brooklyn. But who could disdain the state that gave us Bruce Springsteen, is home to the most diners in the country, and is the site of the first drive-in movie theater? All of these things were on my list of why I wanted to move to the United States in the first place: to eat at a diner and to be romanced in the back seat of a car during a movie while the Boss's "I'm on Fire" softly plays on the car radio.

New Jersey was the third state to enter the Union, in 1787, and was named in honor of George Carteret, who had been the governor of the Isle of Jersey in the English Channel. The state's nickname, the Garden State, can be quite puzzling if you have ever gotten lost in Newark among a tangle of highways with nary a tree or other plant in sight. But it received the nickname on New Jersey Day (August 24, 1876) from Abraham Browning of Camden at the Philadelphia Centennial exhibition. Browning said that the Garden State is an immense barrel, filled with good things to eat and open at both ends, with Pennsylvanians grabbing from one end and New Yorkers from the other. The name has stuck ever since. However, Benjamin Franklin is also credited with a similar comparison of New Jersey to a barrel tapped at both ends.

I feel the state's natural beauty is too often overlooked. I have had the pleasure of hiking the 20 miles of the Appalachian Trail that cross the northwestern corner of the state. I visited my friend Dave one summer while he was doing caricatures on the boardwalk at the shore and I've spent many wonderful weekends at my friend Jill's parents' house on Lake Hopatcong, where she fed me my first ever meatloaf.

This state gave us *The Sopranos*, the Gaslight Anthem, and the light bulb, but for me its charm is in the lakes and the trees. My heart is always in full bloom for the Garden State.

THE PIE!

The state fruit, the Northern highbush blueberry, is a cultivated blueberry developed by Elizabeth Coleman White. It was bred for a bountiful yield and easy harvest in comparison to the traditional wild blueberry, which grows on low bushes and is more difficult to pick. In 2003, a class of fourth-graders at Veterans Memorial Elementary School in Brick campaigned to make the blueberry the official state fruit since nearby Whitesbog is the home of the commercial blueberry we know today.

But I wanted to make a pie based on a different food that was my awakening to the state of New Jersey. One morning after tying one on, my friend Jill's brother TJ made me my first-ever Taylor ham, egg, and cheese sandwich on a toasted everything bagel with salt, pepper, and ketchup. It was one of the most delicious things I have eaten while sitting with my sins from the night before.

The sandwich also introduced me to a great divide in the Garden State. Is it Taylor ham or pork roll? North of I-78 you will only hear Taylor ham, to the south it's pork roll. Central Jersey is a bit of a toss-up. All is fair in love and breakfast meat.

Taylor ham was developed by John Taylor in Trenton in 1856. This wonderful processed meat is cured with a mix of spices, salt, sugar, and preservatives and smoked before packing. It's perfect for sandwiches and lunches on the go. It was put on the market as Taylor's Prepared Ham but later renamed Original Taylor Pork Roll because the cured meat in its tube casing did not meet the requirements to be considered "ham." It is more of a lunch meat than a traditional ham. The rebranding posed a great headache for John Taylor as his company scrambled to trademark its new name. Alas, the trademark was denied, and other versions popped up—including one from Case Pork Company.

George Washington Case started his own company, selling his own version of minced smoked and cured pork roll from his farm in Somerset County in 1870, a little over a decade after John Taylor started making Taylor ham. Both companies, ironically, are now headquartered in Trenton, which is not only the state's capital but the geographic center point of the pork roll vs. Taylor ham debate.

So New Jersey is a state divided by delicious breakfast meat. But whether it's called Taylor ham or pork roll, it is New Jersey's greatest breakfast offering.

The pie is a Jersey breakfast sandwich pie with a poppy seed crust divided down the middle. On one side, Taylor ham, and on the other, Case's pork roll. Both sides are baked with melty American cheese, topped with fried eggs, and served with SPK: salt, pepper, and ketchup.

JERSEY BREAKFAST SANDWICH PIE

ACTIVE TIME: 30 MINUTES — BAKE TIME: 1 HOUR — TOTAL TIME: 1 HOUR 30 MINUTES — MAKES ONE 10-INCH PIE

CRUST

Poppy Seed All-Butter
Crust (single, page
332), rolled out (see
page 339)

FILLING

4 slices Case pork roll,
⅛ inch thick (or your
desired thickness)

4 slices Taylor ham,
⅛ inch thick (or your
desired thickness)

8 slices American
cheese

6 large eggs

Unsalted butter or olive
oil

Kosher salt and freshly
ground black pepper

Ketchup

PREPARE THE CRUST: Preheat the oven to 375°F. Take a 10-inch pie pan, using foil to build a divider in the center of the pie: Fold a strip of foil until it is 1 inch wide and stand it up vertically, making a barrier to divide the pan in half. (Be sure to make the strip long enough so that you can wrap the ends around the edge of the pie pan so it is secure and won't move.) Grease the pan and the divider. Transfer the rolled out dough to the pan and use your fingers to gently fit the dough into the pan, going up and over the foil divider. Cut away the excess around the edges and crimp, then use a fork to prick all over the bottom and sides of each compartment. Place the crust in the freezer for 15 minutes. Line the crust with foil, fill with pie weights, and place on a baking sheet. Blind bake for 20 to 30 minutes, until golden brown and cooked through. Set aside to cool until ready to fill.

MAKE THE FILLING: Make four small cuts around each slice of Case pork roll and Taylor ham to prevent them from curling. Fry the slices of Case pork roll and Taylor ham in a medium skillet over medium-high heat until crispy and warmed through.

ASSEMBLE AND BAKE THE PIE: Preheat the oven to 400°F. Place the baked crust on a baking sheet. In one compartment, layer on the Taylor ham, then slices of the cheese. Repeat to fill the section. Do the same on the other side with Case pork roll and cheese. Bake until the cheese melts, 10 to 12 minutes.

MAKE THE EGGS AND SERVE THE PIE: While the cheese melts between the ham in the oven, in a medium skillet over medium heat, fry your eggs the way you like them (I like mine sunny-side up) in butter or olive oil. Top the pie with the eggs, along with salt, pepper, and ketchup. Serve and enjoy while listening to the Boss. (May I suggest my personal favorite, "Dancing in the Dark"?)

THE DEDICATION!

The Garden State belongs to my friend of sixteen years, Alex Flannery, whom I affectionally call the Prince of the Tri-State Area.

I met Flannery sophomore year of college in Savannah. He was sitting on the front steps of his house with his then-roommates, Kyle and Marc, smoking cigarettes. I was with my friend Katie, who lived three houses down. As we walked by, Kyle hollered at us and invited us to a party that evening. We said okay and the rest is history.

Flannery and I bonded that evening over our shared love of the Gaslight Anthem, the Lawrence Arms, and smoking cigarettes. From that party on, I would find myself escaping the party to hang out with Flannery on the front porch. We would sit and smoke copious amounts of cigarettes, drink many beers, crank our own tunes, and shoot the shit. I talk to him almost every ding dang day and couldn't imagine my life in America without him.

New Jersey promises liberty and prosperity for all, but what I hope most is that everyone in life gets to have a friend as top-shelf as Alex Flannery.

New Mexico

PIE

31

OF 50

LAND OF ENCHANTMENT

STATE COOKIE: BIZCOCHITO ★ STATE VEGETABLES: CHILE & FRIJOL

THE STATE!

New Mexico is the southeast state of the Four Corners, meeting Colorado, Utah, and Arizona at the Four Corners Monument. The Spanish were in New Mexico long before the Mayflower bumped up against Plymouth Rock, and Native Americans long before them. The Spanish went to New Mexico in 1540 in search of cities made of gold that were rumored to exist in the Americas. They found not treasure but land similar to that in Mexico, so they dubbed the area Nuevo Mexico.

Santa Fe is the oldest European city west of the Mississippi River and the oldest capital city in North America, dating to 1610. And though the state is home to the oldest continuously inhabited towns on the continent, it is one of the youngest states in the nation. New Mexico entered statehood in 1912, making it the forty-seventh state.

New Mexico is known as the Land of Enchantment, with scenery that varies from forests to deserts and everything in between. Even though Denver, Colorado, is the Mile High City, it has nothing on Santa Fe, which sits 7,199 feet above sea level and is the highest capital city in the nation. The Rio Grande runs through the whole state. The state also boasts White Sands National Park, home to the world's largest field of sand dunes—4.1 billion tons of gleaming white gypsum sand.

I visited Santa Fe with my father and sisters two decades ago. I don't remember much about the trip except I was blown away by the sunsets.

THE PIE!

Chiles are to New Mexico what potatoes are to Idaho—and the Hatch chile, also known as the New Mexico chile, is king. The chile became the official New Mexico state vegetable in 1965, along with the frijol, or pinto bean.

The village of Hatch is the Green Chile Capital of the World, but chiles, though synonymous with the Southwest, are not native to the region. Spanish settlers brought the plant to New Mexico from the Valley of Mexico, where the Aztecs had cultivated it for centuries. Although the plants require massive amounts of water, something not readily available in most of New Mexico, the pepper thrived due to its versatility and unique flavor. Pungent chile peppers are harvested in the early fall, toasted, peeled, and served in stews, stuffed with cheese, or made into sauces to top anything your heart desires, such as breakfast burritos.

Green chile stew, traditionally named caldillo, is a thin stew made with a meat base usually consisting of beef, pork, chicken, and/or mutton, along with potatoes and green chiles. The stew dates to the 1600s and is served at all times of the day. It is a perfect complement to eggs, tortillas, and rice.

My New Mexico pie is a beef, pork, and green chile pie with a blue cornmeal crust. A simple-looking pie on the outside with complex, robust flavors inside. The earthiness of the blue cornmeal brings the vibrant colors of Santa Fe sunsets into pie form and cradles the slow cooked green chile stew within. This hearty pie will stick to your bones and keep you warm on a cold desert night.

GREEN CHILE STEW PIE

ACTIVE TIME: 30 MINUTES — BAKE TIME: 1 HOUR — TOTAL TIME: 18 HOURS 30 MINUTES — MAKES ONE 10-INCH PIE

CRUST

Blue Cornmeal Crust (double, page 335), rolled out for top and bottom crusts (see page 339)

Egg wash (see page 346)

FILLING

½ pound beef tenderloin, cubed

½ pound pork loin, cubed

2 tablespoons masa harina

1½ teaspoons extra-virgin olive oil

1 cup low-sodium beef broth

1 cup chopped green chiles

½ medium yellow onion, diced

½ large potato, diced

3 tablespoons diced red pepper

2 cloves garlic, chopped

1½ teaspoons ground cumin

1 teaspoon chopped fresh cilantro

Pinch of cayenne pepper

Kosher salt and freshly ground black pepper to taste

SPECIAL EQUIPMENT

Slow cooker

MAKE THE FILLING: In a large bowl, toss the beef and pork in the masa harina, making sure each piece is coated evenly. In a large pan, heat the olive oil over medium-high heat. Add the meat in batches and brown on all sides, roughly 10 minutes per batch. Transfer the meat to the slow cooker and stir in the broth, chiles, onion, potato, red pepper, garlic, cumin, cilantro, cayenne, and salt and pepper. Cook on low for 8 hours. Let the stew cool, then refrigerate overnight.

ASSEMBLE AND BAKE THE PIE: Preheat the oven to 375°F. Fit the bottom crust into a greased 10-inch pie plate and fill with the stew. Place the top crust on top and roll and crimp to seal (see page 343). Cut a vent in the middle of the top and brush the top with egg wash. Bake on a baking sheet on the center rack for 1 hour, rotating the pie 90 degrees every 15 minutes, until the pie is golden brown and fragrant. Let cool for at least 15 minutes before slicing and serving. Best enjoyed viewing a Santa Fe sunset!

THE DEDICATION!

The pie for this gem of a state is for Viridiana Lieberman. I met Viri almost a decade ago at my friends Haley and Bryce's apartment in Hell's Kitchen while watching *Game of Thrones*. We had elaborate viewing parties where Haley and I would cook from the official cookbook *A Feast of Ice and Fire*, by Chelsea Monroe-Cassel and Sariann Lehrer, timing the dishes to line up with where they were in the episode. Over a meal fit for a Stark, we bonded over our love of pop culture and all things movies.

Viri is from Albuquerque, where her family still lives in the house she grew up in. She is New Mexico proud, waxing poetic constantly about the food, the music scene, and how she would wake up to a sky littered with hot air balloons. Viri has a smile as bright as a thousand flash bulbs going off on a red carpet. She is my Golden Globe of a friend and an Academy Award of a person to have on my team.

New Mexico, crescit eundo: They say it grows as it goes and my love for you grows with every sunrise and sunset.

New York

PIE
32
OF 50

THE EMPIRE STATE

STATE MUFFIN: APPLE MUFFIN ★ STATE FRUIT: APPLE ★ STATE SNACK: YOGURT

THE STATE!

New York is the state I call home! As of this book's publication, I will have lived in the same Brooklyn apartment for thirteen of my fourteen years in New York City. When I see the skyline in movies, when I cross the Manhattan Bridge on the train, and when I wander the streets aimlessly with tunes in my ears, I still can't fully believe that I made it here.

At the tender age of 15, I wrote a letter to myself, setting intentions and manifesting what I wanted to do with my life. I wrote that I would move to New York when I graduated from high school (did not happen), I would go to Parsons School of Design (I got in but went to Savannah instead), and right after college I would buy one of those amazing lofts where the elevator opens right into your apartment. (Because I would have a casual three million bucks to drop on an apartment right out of college. Okay, Stace!)

Life and the real estate market had a very different plan for me, but I wouldn't have it any other way. I eventually made my way to New York after college with my best friend Patrick, barreling through the Lincoln Tunnel in a Penske truck after driving through the night from Georgia.

That first year, Patrick and I shared the tiniest apartment on Manhattan's Upper East Side. Many evenings we spent crying, wondering if we made the right decision, and eating cheese and potatoes because that was all we could afford. When I got my first big-girl fashion job paycheck, I bought an aqua sky Le Creuset Dutch oven that I still use. The struggle of those first years finding our footing made us more thankful for where we find ourselves now. I don't have it fully together, but at least I know where my favorite slice joint is and where I can wet my whistle on the weekend to drown those sorrows a little.

New York entered statehood in 1788, the eleventh state to join the Union. A year later, George Washington was sworn in as the first president of the United States in New York City, then the country's capital. The state got its name from the English Duke of York, and its nickname, the Empire State, because George Washington called it "the seat of the Empire."

New York is so much more than NYC's towering skyscrapers, loud trains, and constant honking of traffic. It is the only state that borders both the Atlantic Ocean and the Great Lakes. The concrete jungle of Manhattan pales in comparison to the mountains, forest, waters, and lakes the state has to offer, from the Adirondacks to the beaches of Long Island. One of my earliest memories of New York is not of the city but of Niagara Falls, bordering New York and Canada: I am 4 years old, wearing Little Mermaid leggings and an Australian sweatshirt, with 75,000 gallons of water per second roaring from the falls behind me.

My dream for myself in the city has evolved since I moved here. Now I want a full brownstone instead of a loft, but one constant is that I can't imagine living anywhere else. New York is my bad boyfriend. Every time I think I'm done with it, it pulls me back in.

THE PIE!

New York is the second largest apple producing state in the nation, producing 25 million bushels of apples annually. Named the state fruit in 1976, apples are grown all over New York with fruit that is sweet, crisp, and tart.

Apples are not a native crop but were introduced by Europeans in the 1500s. For those settlers, dried apples were a staple snack and hard apple cider was a popular drink. Along with the apple itself, the state also adopted the apple muffin as the official muffin in 1987 as a result of student efforts.

I wanted this pie to capture something uniquely New York, like the yellow taxi cab once was. Entenmann's crumb cake gave me the inspiration. What makes the Entenmann's crumb cake "New York style" is that the top of the cake is HEAVY with a cinnamony crunchy buttery topping that sinks into the batter underneath it. Sometimes the cake is almost all crumb.

The Entenmann's crumb cake made its debut in 1898 on Rogers Avenue in Brooklyn, the brain child of William Entenmann, a German immigrant from Stuttgart who learned baking from his father. The bakery grew in popularity because of home delivery along thirty routes that crossed the city. Frank Sinatra was among its weekly customers. The crumb cake became a staple part of the Saturday afternoon grocery list for Sunday breakfasts in homes across the city, a weekend necessity paired best with a hot cup of coffee and the Sunday newspaper.

The pie for the state that is my home and has my heart is an apple pie with a coffee cake crumble on top—piled higher than the Empire State Building and best enjoyed with a strong cup of coffee. I originally made 150 mini pies, and gave them to all my favorite businesses and threw a big party for my friends where we got to feast and trade all our New York horror stories. Don't worry, you don't have to bake 150 mini pies to enjoy this state's pie! A 10-inch big boi version of the recipe is included for your Sunday morning enjoyment.

VERSION 1: APPLE PIE
WITH COFFEE CAKE CRUMBLE

ACTIVE TIME: 30 MINUTES — BAKE TIME: 1 HOUR — TOTAL TIME: 2 HOURS 30 MINUTES — MAKES ONE 10-INCH PIE

CRUST

All-Butter Crust (single, page 332), rolled out, fit into a greased 10-inch pie pan, crimped, and frozen (see page 339)

FILLING

½ cup granulated sugar

½ cup packed light brown sugar

¼ cup all-purpose flour

½ teaspoon ground cinnamon

¼ teaspoon ground ginger

¼ teaspoon ground nutmeg

7 Granny Smith apples (about 1 pound), peeled, cored, and cubed

2 teaspoons lemon juice

CRUMBLE TOPPING

1 cup packed light brown sugar

2 cups all-purpose flour

2 teaspoons ground cinnamon

½ cup (1 stick) unsalted butter, softened

MAKE THE FILLING: Combine the granulated sugar, brown sugar, flour, cinnamon, ginger, and nutmeg in a large bowl. Stir to combine. Toss the cubed apples in the lemon juice and coat with the spice mixture. Set aside.

MAKE THE TOPPING: In a large mixing bowl, stir together the brown sugar, flour, and cinnamon to combine. Add the softened butter and mix until it resembles coarse breadcrumbs.

FILL AND BAKE THE PIE: Preheat the oven to 375°F. Fill the crust with the filling and top with the crumble topping. Bake on a baking sheet on the center rack for 1 hour, rotating the pie 90 degrees every 15 minutes, until golden brown. Allow to cool for at least 1 hour before serving. Enjoy à la mode or with the strongest cup of coffee you've got while "New York, New York" blares loudly!

TOWN HALL
113-123 West 43rd Street
Between Broadway & Sixth Ave.

SEPT.
25
1969

Thurs. 8:30

Admission $3.00

VERSION 2: MINI APPLE PIES
WITH COFFEE CAKE CRUMBLE

ACTIVE TIME: 3 HOURS — BAKE TIME: 6 HOURS — TOTAL TIME: 13 HOURS — MAKES 150 (3-INCH) MINI PIES

CRUST

All-Butter Crust (double, page 332) x 7, rolled out ¼ inch thick and cut into 150 (3-inch) rounds

FILLING

2½ cups granulated sugar

2½ cups packed light brown sugar

1 cup all-purpose flour

5 teaspoons ground cinnamon

1½ teaspoons ground ginger

1½ teaspoons ground nutmeg

35 Granny Smith apples (about 5 pounds), peeled, cored, and diced

5 tablespoons lemon juice

CRUMBLE TOPPING

1½ cups packed light brown sugar

1½ cups all-purpose flour

1½ tablespoons ground cinnamon

¾ cup (1½ sticks) unsalted butter, softened

SPECIAL EQUIPMENT

3-inch cookie cutter with scalloped edge

12-cup muffin tin

MAKE THE FILLING: Combine the granulated sugar, brown sugar, flour, cinnamon, ginger, and nutmeg in a large bowl and stir to combine. Toss the diced apples in the lemon juice and coat with the spice mixture. Set aside.

MAKE THE TOPPING: In a large mixing bowl, stir together the brown sugar, flour, and cinnamon to combine. Add the softened butter and mix until it resembles coarse breadcrumbs.

FILL AND BAKE THE PIES: Preheat the oven to 375°F. Fit each cup of the muffin tin with a dough round. Fill each with about ¼ cup filling and top with about 2 tablespoons crumble topping. Bake for 25 to 30 minutes, until golden brown.

Repeat until all dough, filling, and topping are used. Keep dough rounds in the fridge in between batches to keep them nice, cool, and workable. After baking, allow to cool for at least 1 hour before removing from muffin tin. Enjoy!

THE DEDICATION!

New York's pie can't go to just one person. There are too many people and places that have touched me and made NYC—which can sometimes seem like the busiest but loneliest place—feel like home.

So I dedicate this pie to all my favorite places in the city, including R&D Foods on Vanderbilt Avenue, the Double Windsor in Windsor Terrace, Big Night in Greenpoint, Fishs Eddy off Union Square, and Finback Brewery and Four & Twenty Blackbirds in Gowanus, to name a few. The list could go on for days.

Most of all this pie is dedicated to the people who live in this city with me, my friends who are my family. Thank you for making a hard place to live in very easy to love. I am blessed and thankful for the spontaneous after-work beers, nights tying one on at a show or restaurant, wandering the streets, long drives out to the Rockaways. Every moment here is magic because of you. My work keeps me here, but you give me the perfect reason to stay.

North Carolina

PIE

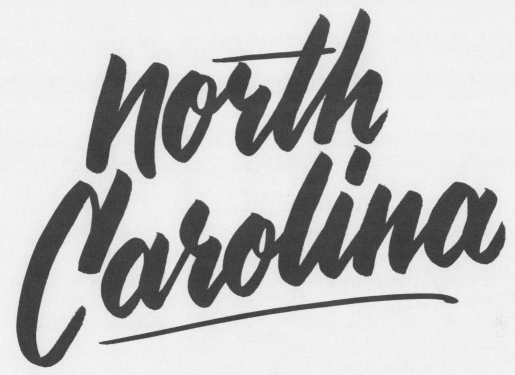

33

OF 50

FIRST IN FLIGHT

STATE BLUE BERRY: BLUEBERRY ★ STATE RED BERRY: STRAWBERRY
STATE FRUIT: SCUPPERNONG GRAPE ★ STATE VEGETABLE: SWEET POTATO

THE STATE!

North Carolina was the twelfth state to enter the Union in 1789, but it is in the top five in my heart. A song by Hurray for the Riff Raff has the lyrics, "My heart is a Blue Ridge Mountain / My head an overflowing fountain," and there's no better way to describe my love for this state.

My first visit to North Carolina was for Christmas with my best friend Patrick's family. His parents live in Hayesville in the west, close to the Georgia border. Whenever we stay there, we wake up to a favorite tradition, making pigs in a blanket for breakfast. We pour ourselves cups of coffee, and I get to rolling the Nathan's cocktail franks in the dough from a freshly popped can of Pillsbury Grands with Patrick's dad, Tony. These pigs in a blanket make me feel the utmost comfort and love.

My second visit was to spend time with a group of friends that call themselves "the Island," because no man is an island. With them, I got to see Asheville for the first time, for an Avett Brothers concert no less! I felt cradled by the mountain and charmed by every sunset, especially the ones viewed from the steps of the Grove Park Inn. On that trip the Blue Ridge Mountains took hold of me. They rise steeply from the Piedmont to peaks that reach up to 6,000 feet. In the far west of the state are the Unaka Mountains, home to the Great Smoky Mountains that twist and turn, rolling you westward.

North Carolina, you're First in Flight and first in my heart.

THE PIE!

The state is home to pimento cheese, thicc big boi biscuits, hoppin' John, and so much craft beer you could kayak down a river of India pale ale. But I knew exactly what I needed to put in this pie: pulled pork, Cheerwine, and hush puppies.

North Carolina is home to various forms of barbecue, but two are the most famous: In the eastern part of the state it's all about "whole hog" barbecue, where a whole pig is smoked and seasoned with a vinegar-based pepper sauce. In Lexington, in the west, it's all about the pork shoulder and a sweet, tomato-based sauce. Since smoking a whole hog was impossible in my apartment, I used my oven to smoke a pork shoulder.

The barbecue sauce is where the Cheerwine comes in. Cheerwine was created in 1917 in Salisbury by L.D. Peeler and was the first bottled cherry soda. Cheerwine contains zero alcohol, but was named for its resemblance to red wine in color; the brand's original slogan was "For health and pleasure." Many North Carolinians hold it up as the best drink to wash down smoky barbecue because of its balance of effervescence and sweetness. It's also hailed as an effective digestive agent and has even become the official soft drink of the NBA, the National Barbecue Association.

Whichever way chosen to smoke and sauce barbecue, the side dishes I have come to love are red slaw and fried hush puppies—so that's what I use to top the pie. Red slaw, or barbecue slaw, is an essential part of Lexington-style barbecue. Unlike traditional coleslaw, red slaw doesn't use mayonnaise and can be stored for longer periods without refrigeration. It consists of green cabbage, vinegar, water, and ketchup for its color.

And hush puppies—those small, salty, savory, deep-fried cornmeal batter bois! The fried morsels of deliciousness got their name from when people on fishing trips would cook their catch of the day and their dogs would howl in anticipation of the meal. While frying the fish, the cook also fried bits of dough and threw them to the pups to "hush" them.

North Carolina, here's a pig pickin' in a pie, with pulled pork with a Cheerwine barbecue sauce in a cornmeal crust, topped with red slaw and hush puppies. Make sure you have a napkin, a cold beer, and a Cheerwine on ice ready for sippin'.

PULLED PORK PIE

WITH CHEERWINE BARBECUE SAUCE, CAROLINA RED SLAW, AND HUSH PUPPIES

ACTIVE TIME: 1 HOUR 30 MINUTES — BAKE TIME: 1 HOUR — TOTAL TIME: 3 HOURS 45 MINUTES — MAKES ONE 10-INCH PIE

CRUST

Cornmeal Crust (single, page 335), fully blind baked (see page 348)

PULLED PORK FILLING

Dry Rub and Pork

2 teaspoons packed light brown sugar

1½ teaspoons hot paprika

1½ teaspoons celery salt

1 teaspoon mild paprika

½ teaspoon garlic salt

½ teaspoon dry mustard powder

½ teaspoon freshly ground black pepper

½ teaspoon onion powder

¼ teaspoon kosher salt

½ pound pork shoulder

Cheerwine Barbecue Sauce

2 tablespoons unsalted butter

½ teaspoon garlic powder

1 cup ketchup

1 cup Cheerwine soda

¼ cup A.1. steak sauce

3 tablespoons Worcestershire sauce

2 tablespoons white vinegar

½ teaspoon dry mustard

½ teaspoon cayenne pepper

½ teaspoon freshly ground black pepper

MAKE THE FILLING: In a large mixing bowl, mix all the ingredients for the dry rub. Take the pork butt, give it a good pat dry, and cover thoroughly with the rub. Let sit in the fridge, uncovered, for 1 hour.

Cover the bottom of a roasting pan with a single layer of cherrywood chips, cover the chips with water, and let them soak for 1 hour. Drain the water, leaving a film of water on the bottom of the pan.

Preheat the oven to 250°F, with one rack in the bottom third of the oven, removing all other racks. Put a metal rack into the roasting pan on top of the wood chips and place the pork on the rack. Make a tent of foil, completely sealing the pan but leaving room on the top for smoke to circulate around the pork. Cook the pork for 1 hour, making sure it reaches the internal temperature of 180°F. Let the meat rest for 15 minutes before shredding with two forks. Set aside in the fridge until ready to assemble pie.

MAKE THE CHEERWINE BARBECUE SAUCE: While the pork is smoking: In a medium saucepan, melt the butter over medium heat. Add the garlic powder and cook for 30 seconds. Whisk in the ketchup, Cheerwine, A.1., Worcestershire, vinegar, mustard, cayenne, and pepper. Bring to a boil then reduce heat to medium-low and simmer until slightly thickened, about 20 minutes. Cool to room temperature. Set aside until ready to assemble pie.

MAKE THE CAROLINA RED SLAW: Combine the green and purple cabbage in a large bowl. In a medium bowl, mix the

Recipe continues ★★★

Carolina Red Slaw

½ cup shredded green cabbage

½ cup shredded purple cabbage

¼ cup ketchup

1 tablespoon apple cider vinegar

2 teaspoons granulated sugar

1 teaspoon kosher salt

1 teaspoon freshly ground black
   pepper

½ teaspoon cayenne pepper

Hush Puppies

1 cup yellow stone-ground cornmeal

¼ cup all-purpose flour

1½ teaspoons baking powder

½ teaspoon kosher salt

1 large egg, beaten

¾ cup whole milk

1 small onion, chopped

Canola or vegetable oil for frying

Flaky salt

SPECIAL EQUIPMENT

Large roasting pan with rack

6 cups cherrywood chips

Meat thermometer

Dutch oven

Deep-fry thermometer

ketchup, cider vinegar, sugar, salt, pepper, and cayenne. Pour over the cabbage and mix well. Allow the slaw to sit in the fridge for at least 1 hour, or until ready to assemble pie.

MAKE THE HUSH PUPPIES: Combine the cornmeal, flour, baking powder, and salt in a medium mixing bowl. Whisk the egg, milk, and onion in a separate large mixing bowl. Stir in the dry ingredients until just combined; do not overmix. Refrigerate the batter for 30 minutes before frying.

Fill a Dutch oven at least halfway with oil and heat to 365°F over medium-high heat. In batches of five or six, drop tablespoon-size dollops of batter into the hot oil and fry for 2 to 2½ minutes, flipping throughout to make sure they cook evenly, until golden brown. Transfer to paper towels to drain and sprinkle with salt.

ASSEMBLE THE PIE: Reheat the pulled pork on the stove or in the microwave until warmed through. Mix the pulled pork with 1 cup of the Cheerwine sauce. Fill the fully baked crust with the pulled pork. Pile the red slaw in the center and surround with freshly fried hush puppies. Serve warm with more Cheerwine barbecue sauce. Enjoy!

THE DEDICATION!

This pie is for my first friend from North Carolina, Susannah McInerney. This fine mountain mama hails from the mountains of Asheville. We met in college but our friendship didn't bloom until New York, where we danced the nights away and got in all sorts of trouble in the East Village. My first Thanksgiving in the city was with Suzy; her mom sent us an Edible Arrangement and I learned about the wonders of broccoli casserole and Cool Whip.

Suzy is one of my greatest and most cherished friends. Thinking of her is like when I hear the first chords of the Fleetwood Mac song "Gold Dust Woman," when the center of my chest starts to swell and my body tingles with joy and happiness.

And a special NC shout-out goes to Katie, Anne, Valerie, Olivia, Gigi, and Katie Peeler. The female friendships and comfort this state has given me know no bounds.

North Carolina, my heart is a blue ridge mountain. See you soon for biscuits, beer, sweet tunes, and lifelong friendships.

North Dakota

PIE

34

OF 50

LEGENDARY!

STATE FRUIT: CHOKECHERRY

THE STATE!

The geographic center of the North American continent is marked with a stone in Rugby, North Dakota. Dakota is a Sioux word that roughly translates as "friend" or "ally," and for years the region was called the Dakota Territory, including what is now both North and South Dakota. It wasn't until 1889, when railroads were built bringing American settlers, that North and South Dakota were each declared their own state.

Theodore Roosevelt arrived in 1883 to hunt bison, but soon fell in love with the land's scenic beauty and wildlife. He was instrumental in the founding of the country's national parks system, and Theodore Roosevelt National Park in western North Dakota is the only national park named after a person. One of the passports I am most proud to have is my National Parks Passport. It makes me so happy to get a new stamp at each park I visit.

The state is also home to the International Peace Garden, at the border between North Dakota and Canada, which represents the 1932 pledge by the United States and Canada to never go to war with one another.

Lake Sakakawea has 1,300 miles of shoreline—more than California's Pacific Coast. The state is filled with more sunflowers than any other state and its state tree is the American elm, which grows to an epic 100-plus feet! It is also home to the elusive rare white buffalo, the Dakota miracle that can be seen at the National Buffalo Museum, and the world's largest (fake) buffalo in Jamestown: Called "Dakota Thunder," the statue stands 26 feet tall.

North Dakota, you are truly Legendary!

THE PIE!

I'm going to skate right past the state fruit, the chokecherry, to celebrate a different food in this pie. The hotdish is a casserole commonly served in North Dakota and throughout the Midwest at family reunions, potlucks, and church gatherings. While every home has its own version, hotdish usually consists of a starch, a meat, and a gravy or cream of mushroom soup. The origins of hotdish are believed to be from Norwegian settlers whose word varmrett translates as "warm dish." These easy-to-make and filling meals came about when farm wives needed an inexpensive way to feed their families or congregations. Tater Tots became the staple topping of the hotdish in 1953 when they were invented and no one has looked back since.

North Dakota, here's your Tater Tot hotdish pie. Filled with ground beef, mixed veggies, the GOAT of all Campbell's soups (cream of mushroom), and topped with Tater Tots.

TATER TOT-HOTDISH PIE

ACTIVE TIME: 30 MINUTES — BAKE TIME: 1 HOUR 15 MINUTES — TOTAL TIME: 2 HOURS — MAKES ONE 10-INCH PIE

CRUST

All-Butter Crust (single, page 332),
rolled out, fit into a greased
10-inch pie pan, crimped, and
frozen (see page 339)

FILLING

1 pound ground beef

½ medium onion, chopped

½ (8-ounce) package frozen mixed
vegetables

1 (10.75-ounce) can cream
of mushroom soup

½ (16-ounce) package frozen
Tater Tots

MAKE THE FILLING: Preheat the oven to 350°F. In a large skillet over medium-high heat, cook the beef and onions until browned, then drain the fat. Transfer the meat and onions to a large bowl and add the frozen vegetables.

ASSEMBLE AND BAKE THE PIE: Fill the frozen pie crust with the filling. Spread the cream of mushroom soup on top of the pie and cover the surface with the frozen Tater Tots. Cover with foil and bake for 1 hour. Uncover and bake for 15 to 20 minutes longer, until the Tater Tots are golden brown. Let rest for 15 minutes before slicing and serving. Enjoy!

THE DEDICATION!

This pie is dedicated to Jane from North Dakota, who I met in a Lyft car share in Los Angeles when I was there for my sister's wedding in 2017. Jane is the only person I have met from North Dakota, and we spent the 45-minute ride from the airport to my sister's apartment chatting about a little bit of everything. Once during her time in 4H, she won a blue ribbon at the North Dakota State Fair for her blueberry muffins. Later, she moved to Louisville, Colorado, where she has run an annual pie contest with up to sixty kinds of pies on display.

My time with Jane, though wonderful, was fast and fleeting and we never exchanged details. But her pie stayed on my mind, and when I baked my own, I shared it with my roommate Steph and her sweet pup Jake.

Until I come to visit, North Dakota, you will be my great white buffalo!

Ohio

PIE

35

OF 50

THE BUCKEYE STATE

STATE FRUIT: TOMATO

THE STATE!

Half of the population of the United States lives within 500 miles of the seventeenth state to enter the Union, Ohio. No one is exactly sure where Ohio got its name but some experts think it originates from the Iroquois word O-Y-O, which roughly translates as "great river." The Ohio River begins in present-day Pennsylvania, where the Iroquois live. The Buckeye State gets its nickname from a common tree whose nuts look like a deer's eyes.

Ohio is home to the world's largest basket, in Dresden. It is also home to the inventors of the first airplane, the Wright Brothers, and to Neil Armstrong, the first man to walk on the moon. The Shakers, a religious community that lived in Ohio for many years, sped up the processing of fruit for pie baking by perfecting the apple peeler and cherry pitter. However I think the most important thing Ohio has given us is the hot dog. It was created by Niles resident Harry M. Stevens in 1900.

The first time I went to Ohio was to visit the town of Bellefontaine, not far from Columbus, accompanying my friend Meredith on a trip home. What I remember most about that trip was getting drunk on Bud Lights with Meredith at Mad River Mountain, where she used to ski growing up. We drank and danced to a live band that played one of my top-ten favorite songs, "Brandy (You're a Fine Girl)" by Looking Glass. Light beer, music, and a great friend...there is a reason this state is called the Heart of It All.

THE PIE!

The buckeye candy is a sweet, fudgy peanut butter ball dipped in chocolate that first made an appearance in the 1960s and is said to be invented by Ohio resident Gail Tabor. She was trying to dip peanut butter balls in chocolate, and noticed that when they were partially dipped they looked just like the buckeye nuts shed by the state tree. Tabor would bring these sweet treats to Ohio State football games for years—to the joy of everyone who got to eat them.

The recipe for buckeyes I use in this pie was given to me by my friend Meredith's grandma, Maggie Patterson. My favorite part of the recipe, which was handwritten in the most beautiful cursive, is that at the bottom it says, "The Best"—underlined.

For Ohio, here's a buckeye-inspired pie with a chocolate graham cracker crust and a creamy peanut butter filling topped with buckeyes and a drizzle of chocolate. Best enjoyed with the roar of an Ohio State game in the background after a large plate of Skyline Chili.

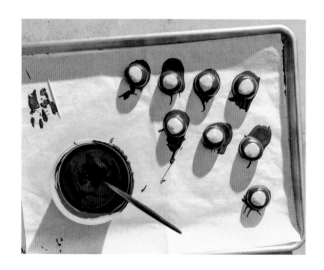

BUCKEYE PIE

ACTIVE TIME: 2 HOURS — CHILL TIME: OVERNIGHT — TOTAL TIME: 10 HOURS — MAKES ONE 10-INCH PIE

CRUST
Chocolate Graham Cracker Crust (page 336), blind baked as directed

TOPPING
½ pound confectioners' sugar (about 3¾ cups)
¼ cup (½ stick) unsalted butter, melted
1¼ cups creamy peanut butter
¾ cup semisweet chocolate chips

BUCKEYE FILLING
1 (8-ounce) package cream cheese, softened
½ cup creamy peanut butter
½ cup confectioners' sugar
1 (16-ounce) tub Cool Whip whipped topping, thawed

SPECIAL EQUIPMENT
Chopsticks or toothpicks
Waxed paper
Stand mixer with paddle attachment or hand mixer

MAKE THE BUCKEYE TOPPING: In a medium bowl, mix the confectioners' sugar, melted butter, and peanut butter together. Form the mixture into about twelve 1-inch balls and place on a baking sheet lined with waxed paper. Chill overnight.

Set up a double boiler: Place a heat-safe mixing bowl on top of a medium saucepan. In the saucepan bring water—just enough so the bottom of the bowl does not touch the water—to a simmer. Put the chocolate chips in the bowl and melt over the simmering water.

Using either chopsticks or a toothpick to help you hold the ball steady, dip each peanut butter ball into the chocolate, leaving a circle or "eye" of peanut butter visible. Place the dipped balls on a baking sheet lined with waxed paper and chill for 15 minutes. Save the remaining melted chocolate.

MAKE THE FILLING AND ASSEMBLE THE PIE: Using a stand mixer with the paddle attachment, mix the cream cheese, peanut butter, and confectioners' sugar until smooth. Fold in the whipped topping until fully incorporated. Spoon the filling into the fully baked graham cracker crust. Chill in fridge for at least 2 hours, or up to overnight.

FINISH THE PIE: Drizzle the remaining melted chocolate on top of the chilled filled pie. Place the buckeyes around the edge of the pie. Slice, serve, and enjoy!

THE DEDICATION!

Ohio is dedicated to not one but two special Ohio women: Meredith Passaro from Bellefontaine and Kristen Kyle Ginn from Troy.

I met Meredith at a garden party through our mutual friend Kate. We got to talking about how much we both loved the outdoors and hiking. The following weekend Kate and Meredith asked me if I wanted to go climb a mountain with them in the Catskills. We now are many miles and peaks into our friendship, countless nights spent sleeping in tents and shooting the shit by the fire. One thing we will always agree on is that at the end of a big hike all we want is a large plate of onion rings and a cold beer.

I met Kristen at the ripe old age of 19 in Savannah. We met in an accessory design class and have been friends ever since. Kristen has been with me through most if not all of the milestones of my adult life and I couldn't be more thankful for all our nights listening to the Lilith Fair playlist and drinking Mike's Harder Lemonade.

Until I look the Buckeye State in the eyes once again!

Oklahoma

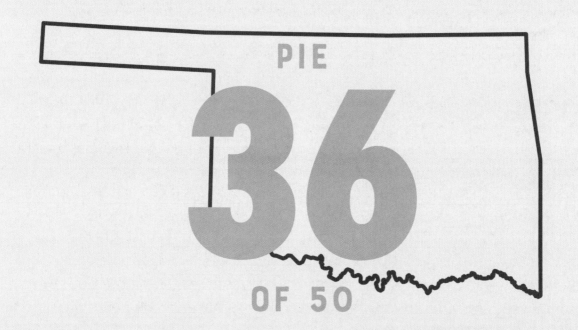

NATIVE AMERICA

STATE BEAN: BLACK-EYED PEAS ★ STATE TREAT: CORNBREAD
STATE DESSERT: PECAN PIE ★ STATE FRUIT: STRAWBERRIES

THE STATE!

Growing up, I watched Rodgers and Hammerstein musicals constantly with my dad, and I first came to know the great state of Oklahoma through the musical by the same name, which celebrates frontier life in 1906.

Oklahoma did not enter the Union until 1907, making it the forty-sixth state. Before that, it was designated "Indian Territory" by the U.S. government. In 1830, President Andrew Jackson signed the Indian Removal Act, which forcibly relocated more than 60,000 Cherokee, Seminole, Muscogee (Creek), Choctaw, and Chickasaw people from their homelands in the Southeast. This terrible journey came to be known as the Trail of Tears.

Oklahoma's name is derived from two words in the Choctaw language: okla, meaning "people," and humma, meaning "red." Together they loosely translate as "land of the red man."

Oklahoma is home to more than fifty languages, over thirty distinct tribes, and a colorful history that includes cowboys, battles, oil, dust storms, settlements, resettlements, and free land.

One favorite piece of history I learned from Derek Waters's show, *Drunk History*: During the Land Rush in 1889, settlers were allowed to race into parts of the state and claim it for themselves to create homesteads. Settlers who crossed the border sooner than they were allowed were called Sooners, which led to the state's nickname, the Sooner State.

THE PIE!

Oklahoma is home to many state foods and many regional favorites including the pecan pie. It even held a record for baking the largest pecan pie: about 40 feet wide and weighing about 16 tons. But Arbuckle Mountain Fried Pies in Davis has stolen my heart. These wonderful fried pockets of goodness started as a simple recipe developed in the quiet town of Springer near the Arbuckle Mountains by Maude Pletcher.

In the 1980s, Maude's son Ace opened a Cattle Company restaurant and started serving his mother's famous fried pies, sharing their family classics with people near and far. Today Ace's brother's son Jerry and his wife Diane Pletcher own the former gas station in Davis where the fried pies are now sold (in addition to other outlets in neighboring states). Through the years the flavors have expanded but the memories of their grandmother's original pies live on.

I love this story of how a family held on to something so special and shared it with as many people as possible. For Oklahoma, I too had to make fried pies: blueberry and strawberry, fried in Crisco and showered with confectioners' sugar. Best eaten piping hot with a large cup of black coffee, on a pit stop on your way to explore Oklahoma's beautiful lands.

STRAWBERRY AND BLUEBERRY
FRIED HAND PIES

ACTIVE TIME: 1 HOUR — FRY TIME: 1 HOUR — TOTAL TIME: 2 HOURS — MAKES 24 (2-INCH) HAND PIES

CRUST

All-Butter Crust (double, page 332)

Egg wash (see page 346)

1 (12-ounce) can blueberry pie
  filling

1 (12-ounce) can strawberry pie
  filling

1 (48-ounce) can Crisco shortening
  for frying

1 cup confectioners' sugar
  for dusting

SPECIAL EQUIPMENT

2x2-inch square scalloped cookie
  cutter, or pizza cutter

Deep-fry thermometer

ROLL OUT THE DOUGH: Roll the dough into sheets that are ⅛ inch thick. Using either the cookie cutter or pizza cutter, cut the dough into 48 (2x2-inch) squares.

ASSEMBLE THE HAND PIES: Place a heaping tablespoon of pie filling into the center of a square of dough. Brush the edges of the dough with egg wash and then place another square of dough on top, pressing the edges to seal the pocket. Place on a baking sheet. Repeat with the remaining dough and fillings to make 24 hand pies. Refrigerate until ready to fry.

FRY THE HAND PIES: In a large heavy-bottom pot over medium-high heat, melt the Crisco and bring up to 350°F. Fry the hand pies in batches of 2 or 3, flipping each over halfway through, until both sides are golden brown, 3 to 4 minutes. Drain on paper towels to soak up excess oil and sprinkle with sifted confectioners' sugar.

Best eaten piping hot while making the good open-mouth steam release face and with a black cup of coffee!

THE DEDICATION!

This pie is dedicated to Bob and Reta Wagner, who hail from Gore, although I met them in Hawai'i in 1995 when I was 7 years old. Uncle Bob worked with my dad as the chief engineer at the former Kahala Hilton on O'ahu.

I am blessed that my dad's job allowed me to have such wonderful relationships with people who have played such a role in making me fall utterly in love with this country. Auntie Reta has since passed, but I think of her fondly and often. They were a lovely addition to my American family and filled my childhood with many happy memories.

Oklahoma, I can't wait to visit you, soon enough!

Oregon

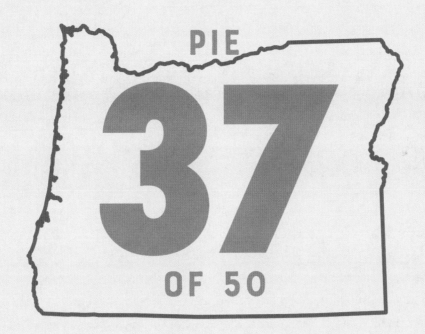

PIE

37

OF 50

PACIFIC WONDERLAND

STATE FRUIT: PEAR ★ STATE MUSHROOM: PACIFIC GOLDEN CHANTERELLE
★ STATE NUT: HAZELNUT ★ STATE PIE: MARIONBERRY PIE

THE STATE!

Before I die, I have to see Oregon's Crater Lake. At 1,943 feet deep, it is the deepest lake in the United States. Its crystal blue waters are some of the cleanest in the continent. Can you imagine just sitting at the edge of it trying to take it all in while drinking a Miller Lite and listening to sweet tunes?

In 1840, American settlers arrived to the area we now know as Oregon by way of the Oregon Trail. In 1859 Oregon became the thirty-third state to join the Union.

Some people think Oregon got its name from the French word ouragan, which means "hurricane," a term that was used by French explorers to describe the windy parts of the state. Others think it could have derived from the Chinook word oolighan, a type of fish eaten by Native Americans in the area. We do know that the state was nicknamed the Beaver State because early settlers trapped the animals, which were abundant, for their fur.

In addition to Crater Lake, Oregon is home to Hells Canyon, the deepest river gorge in North America. Running up and down the state are the Cascade Mountains, which include Mount Hood, a dormant volcano and Oregon's highest point at 11,245 feet. And if you grew up watching *The Goonies*, like I did, note that Cannon Beach's long, sandy shore and Haystack Rock were featured in the last scene of the movie.

This state is a Pacific Wonderland I cannot wait to get lost in!

THE PIE!

The marionberry was developed by the U.S.D.A. breeding program in cooperation with Oregon State University. A cross between Chehalem and Olallie blackberries, a marionberry is medium-sized, conical in shape, and dark purple in color. The flavor is tart, earthy, and sweet—my favorite combo! Marionberries are grown exclusively in the Pacific Northwest, one of the few regions that specialize in the type of harvesting and processing the berry needs. In July of 2017 the marionberry pie was designated the official state pie of Oregon.

Meanwhile, the pear is the state fruit, likely because 84 percent of the United States' pear crop comes from the Pacific Northwest due to the region's unique climate.

Besides marionberry and pear in my pie filling, I wanted a creamy element to elevate what I was offering the state: I found it in Salt & Straw's Arbequina olive oil ice cream. It is incredible; the first time I had it I was blown away by its earthy and rich flavor. Salt & Straw is a Portland-based ice cream company and flavor lab started by cousins Kim and Tyler Malek.

Oregon is the only state in America whose official nut is the hazelnut. Nearly 99 percent of all hazelnuts grown in the United States are grown in the Willamette Valley. So it seems only fitting that a salty hazelnut crumble tops the pie.

The pie for the great state of Oregon is best eaten in the shadow of Mount Hood or with the perfect view of Crater Lake.

PEAR AND MARIONBERRY PIE
WITH OLIVE OIL ICE CREAM AND SALTY HAZELNUT CRUMBLE

ACTIVE TIME: 1 HOUR — BAKE TIME: 1 HOUR — TOTAL TIME: 4 HOURS — MAKES ONE 10-INCH PIE

CRUST

All-Butter Crusts (double, page 332), rolled out, one for bottom crust, one cut into 2-inch-wide lattice strips (see page 344)

1 teaspoon granulated sugar

1 teaspoon all-purpose flour

Egg wash (see page 346)

Finishing sugar (see page 346)

FILLING

5 cups marionberries, fresh or thawed frozen; or use blackberries

1 cup shredded pear

1 cup granulated sugar

¼ cup cornstarch

TOPPING

½ cup (1 stick) unsalted butter, softened

½ cup packed light brown sugar

1 teaspoon kosher salt

¼ cup all-purpose flour

1¼ cups almond flour

½ cup finely chopped hazelnuts

Salt & Straw olive oil ice cream; or vanilla ice cream with a finishing olive oil drizzle

SPECIAL EQUIPMENT

Parchment paper

Stand mixer with paddle attachment

MAKE THE FILLING: In a large bowl, mix all the filling ingredients together; set aside for 30 minutes to macerate.

ASSEMBLE AND BAKE THE PIE: Preheat the oven to 375°F. Fit the bottom crust into a greased 10-inch pie pan. Sprinkle the teaspoons of sugar and flour on the bottom of the pie crust. With a slotted spoon, fill the crust with the filling, leaving the majority of the juices in the bowl.

Arrange the lattice strips on top of the filling in desired pattern; roll and crimp edge (see page 343). Brush with egg wash and sprinkle with finishing sugar. Bake on a baking sheet on the center rack for 1 hour, rotating the pie every 15 minutes, until the filling is bubbly and the crust is golden brown. Set aside to cool for at least 2 hours.

MAKE THE TOPPING: Reduce the oven to 325°F. Line a baking sheet with parchment paper and spray with nonstick spray. In a stand mixer with paddle attachment, cream the butter, brown sugar, and salt. Add the all-purpose flour and almond flour and mix until a soft paste forms. Add the hazelnuts and mix until combined. Crumble the mixture with your hands until the texture of wet sand. Scatter the crumble on the prepared baking sheet and bake for 5 to 7 minutes, stirring once halfway through, until golden brown.

FINISH AND SERVE THE PIE: I recommend serving in shallow bowls. Slice the pie and top each slice with a scoop of ice cream and a drizzle of olive oil. Sprinkle the crumble on top. Best enjoyed while basking in the glory of Crater Lake or admiring a sunset over the Cascade Mountains!

THE DEDICATION!

The pie is dedicated to Joe Lipski and Leah Maghini, who used to call Portland home! I met Joe and Leah in Hartford, Connecticut, at a Fourth of July party at our friends Shanel and Dan's house. We spent the weekend playing beer pong, blasting Bruce Springsteen, shooting fireworks, and partying. We bonded over '90s music and food and, since Leah spent time in China, the nuances of tofu types and our favorite dumplings. Before they made the move to Oregon (they have since moved back) I would take the bus to Hartford for the weekend and we would have nothing but fun in the sun or at Two Roads Brewery knocking back their infamous Two Juicy IPAs.

Oregon, I am told things look different there. You're a wonderland.

Pennsylvania

PIE

38

OF 50

STATE OF INDEPENDENCE

NO STATE FOODS

THE STATE!

When I was college, my friend Vytenis would tell me all about how he and his Lithuanian friends would go to the Poconos every summer. I begged him to take me just once, thinking that it was an island getaway à la "Kokomo" from the Beach Boys. Alas, I came to find out that the Poconos are actually mountains when I finally made the journey myself for a ski trip.

The British colony of Pennsylvania was founded by Englishman William Penn, a Quaker, in 1681. The name means "Penn's woods," in honor of William Penn's father. The colony offered religious freedom, attracting people of various denominations to the state, including German immigrants, Quakers, Mennonites, and Amish people. The settlers developed their own dialect, and descendants of these first settlers are now known as the Pennsylvania Dutch.

Pennsylvania was the second state to enter the Union in 1787, and is home to many of the country's pivotal moments in history. The Declaration of Independence was signed in Philadelphia in 1776, it is home to the Liberty Bell, and it's where Betsy Ross sewed the first American flag.

The state is home to cheesesteaks, water ice (aka Italian ice), soft pretzels originally brought by German settlers, whoopie pies, and Tastykakes. And if you find yourself in Philadelphia, get one of my fave combos at the Sassafras Bar in Olde City: mac and cheese that is topped with pretzel bits and the French Drip Cocktail, an absinthe drip that is bitter and herbaceous. The perfect combo to ease your sorrows and bring you joy in the dark woody bar.

THE PIE!

I took a deep dive into the history books and found only one pie that could represent this state in all its glory: the shoofly pie!

The funny thing is that the shoofly pie didn't start off as a pie, but as a crustless molasses cake known as centennial cake. It was first baked in 1876 to celebrate the 100th anniversary of the Declaration of Independence. The recipe was developed as a play on the treacle tart, a traditional British dessert. Colonial Americans substituted molasses for the treacle and a crust was added to make it easier to enjoy without a plate or a fork.

The pie was traditionally served for breakfast, in the evening with dinner, or as a field snack with a cup of black coffee. The absence of eggs suggests that it was created during the winter months when eggs were scarce and the pantry was more bare.

Some people believe the name comes from when bakers would have to shoo flies away from their pies cooling on the windowsill because it was so thick and sweet. Others think it was named after Shoofly the Boxing Mule, a popular traveling circus animal. Shoofly was so beloved that household products were named in his honor, including a brand of molasses produced in Philadelphia that was used in the pie. Shoofly's name may have originated from a popular song at the time, "Shoo, Fly, Don't Bother Me!"

The pie, the pride of Lancaster Country and the Pennsylvania Dutch, is delicious dunked in a cup of strong black coffee.

SHOOFLY PIE

ACTIVE TIME: 30 MINUTES — BAKE TIME: 45 MINUTES — TOTAL TIME: 3 HOURS 15 MINUTES — MAKES ONE 10-INCH PIE

CRUST

All-Butter Crust (single, page 332), rolled out, fit into a greased 10-inch pie pan, crimped, and frozen (see page 339)

TOPPING

1½ cups all-purpose flour

½ cup packed dark brown sugar

1 teaspoon ground cinnamon

1 teaspoon grated nutmeg

⅛ teaspoon kosher salt

½ cup (1 stick) cold unsalted butter, cubed

FILLING

¾ cup molasses

¾ cup boiling water

½ teaspoon baking soda

SPECIAL EQUIPMENT

Pastry cutter

MAKE THE TOPPING: In a large bowl, mix together the flour, brown sugar, cinnamon, nutmeg, and salt. Using the pastry cutter, cut in the cold butter until the mixture resembles cornmeal. Set aside in fridge while you make the filling.

MAKE THE FILLING: Preheat the oven to 450°F. In a large mixing bowl, combine the molasses, boiling water, and baking soda.

ASSEMBLE AND BAKE THE PIE: Pour the filling into the frozen pie crust and spoon the topping over the filling, making an even layer. Place the pie on a baking sheet and bake on the center rack for 15 minutes. Lower the oven temperature to 350°F and bake for an additional 30 minutes, or until set and firm. Let cool for at least 2 hours before slicing, and serve with a cup of hot black coffee. Enjoy!

THE DEDICATION!

This pie is dedicated to Andy Mangold, who hails from West Chester, Pennsylvania!

I met Andy through Massachusetts pie recipient Matt. We cemented our friendship when both of us were asked to be in Matt's wedding party. We spent a weekend in Upstate New York for Matt's bachelor party, where Andy made the most delicious chicken tacos and chestnut soup I've ever had.

A core memory for me is Andy picking me up at the bus station when I went to deliver this pie to him and us just driving around Baltimore, where he lives, and chatting about nothing in particular and just enjoying each other's company. It's a blessing in life to have people you enjoy so much.

To the State of Independence, thank you for a lifetime of memories and for forever friends.

Rhode Island

PIE
39
OF 50

THE OCEAN STATE

STATE FRUIT: RHODE ISLAND GREENING APPLE ★ STATE DRINK: COFFEE MILK

THE STATE!

The smallest state of all the fifty, a mere 48 miles long and 37 miles wide, this tiny seaside state has taken my whole heart. Rhode Island was lucky number thirteen to enter the Union in 1790, but the first colony to declare independence from Britain.

The most common explanation for its name is that the explorer Giovanni da Verrazzano compared the land to the Greek island of Rhodes, inspiring Roger Williams, the founder of Rhode Island, to name the colony Rhode Island. Another is that Dutch explorer Adriaen Block called the land Roodt Eylandt, or "Red Island," because of the red clay on its shores. Either way, there is nothing better than sitting on a tiny part of the 400 miles of coastline this Ocean State has to offer and drinking a Del's Lemonade at sunset.

Newport is my home away from home in the summer, all thanks to my friend Christine Alber and her family. Newport pastimes include the Cliff Walk trail, touring mansions, eating the best food at restaurants like TSK (Thames Street Kitchen) and Mission (both owned by my friends the Jenkinses and Burnleys), and drinking at the oldest operating tavern in the United States, the White Horse, built in 1673.

I love the Newport Folk Festival at Fort Adams State Park, right on the water. Think about listening to beautiful tunes, sipping on a Narragansett shandy while an ocean breeze kisses your skin: What more could a girl want? I have seen some of my favorite bands on its stage, such as the Avett Brothers, Maggie Rogers, Lucius, Wilco, and more. At the sixtieth festival, a surprise guest walked on stage: the love of my life, DOLLY PARTON! When she started singing, I burst into tears.

Rhode Island may be tiny but the impression it has left on me is everlasting. See you soon for a shandy at sunset.

THE PIE!

Coffee milk is top on the list of uniquely Rhode Island food products. Though the state is home to a shandy made with Del's Lemonade and Narragansett beer, you can drink lemonade and beer anywhere. But if you ask for coffee milk outside of Rhode Island, you'll be met with utter confusion.

In the late 1930s, two companies, Eclipse (in Warwick) and then Autocrat (in Lincoln), began selling bottles of a sugary, mildly caffeinated coffee syrup that was used to make coffee milk, a mixture of the sweet syrup and milk—similar to how you make chocolate milk with chocolate syrup. The syrup wars ended in 1991 when Autocrat purchased their longtime competitor, but instead of shutting down production, they made the classy move to continue producing both brands to keep Rhode Islanders happy. Two years later, in 1993, coffee milk became the official state drink.

For a state I love so dearly, here's an Autocrat coffee milk pie: a chocolate pie crust filled with coffee custard and topped with whipped cream and chocolate shavings. The pie is best enjoyed after a long day at the Newport Folk Festival, softly swaying to all your favorite tunes.

COFFEE MILK PIE

ACTIVE TIME: 30 MINUTES — CHILL TIME: 2 HOURS — TOTAL TIME: 2 TO 4 HOURS AND 30 MINUTES — MAKES ONE 10-INCH PIE

CRUST

Chocolate All-Butter Crust (single, page 333), rolled out, fit into a greased 10-inch pie pan, crimped, and fully blind baked (see page 339)

FILLING

2¼ cups whole milk

4 large egg yolks, beaten

2½ tablespoons Autocrat coffee syrup

1½ teaspoons instant coffee

½ cup cornstarch

¾ cup granulated sugar

¼ teaspoon kosher salt

2 tablespoons unsalted butter, cubed

TOPPING

1 cup heavy whipping cream

2 tablespoons confectioners' sugar

½ teaspoon vanilla extract

¼ cup dark chocolate shavings

SPECIAL EQUIPMENT

Stand mixer with whisk attachment

MAKE THE FILLING: In a medium bowl, whisk the milk, egg yolks, coffee syrup, and instant coffee. In a medium saucepan, combine the cornstarch, sugar, and salt. Whisk in the milk mixture. Whisk over medium heat until the mixture thickens and coats the back of a spoon, 7 to 9 minutes. Remove from the heat and whisk in the cubed butter, a little at a time, until fully incorporated.

ASSEMBLE THE PIE: Pour the filling into the fully baked crust. Cover with plastic wrap, pressing it against the surface of the filling to prevent a skin from forming. Refrigerate the pie for 2 to 4 hours, until it is completely chilled.

MAKE THE TOPPING AND FINISH THE PIE: In the bowl of a stand mixer combine the cream, confectioners' sugar, and vanilla and beat until soft peaks are formed, about 2 minutes.

Top the chilled pie with the whipped cream, using swooshing motions with a spoon or offset spatula to cover the top. Sprinkle the chocolate shavings all over the whipped cream. Slice and serve with a Narragansett–Del's Lemonade shandy on Ocean Drive in Newport, Rhode Island!

THE DEDICATION!

This pie is dedicated to Christine Alber of Portsmouth. Christine and I went to college in Savannah, but didn't meet until we were both on a train to Montauk for New Hampshire pie recipient Kelsie's bachelorette party. We bonded over our love for Tim Riggins, the power of good side-eye, and the joy of a great breakfast sandwich. Soon after, Christine invited me to my first Newport Folk Festival. Six fests and four Thanksgivings later, here we are.

The Ocean State has captured my heart, my mind, my soul, and my tummy! I await the day when I am washed by its ocean breezes once again.

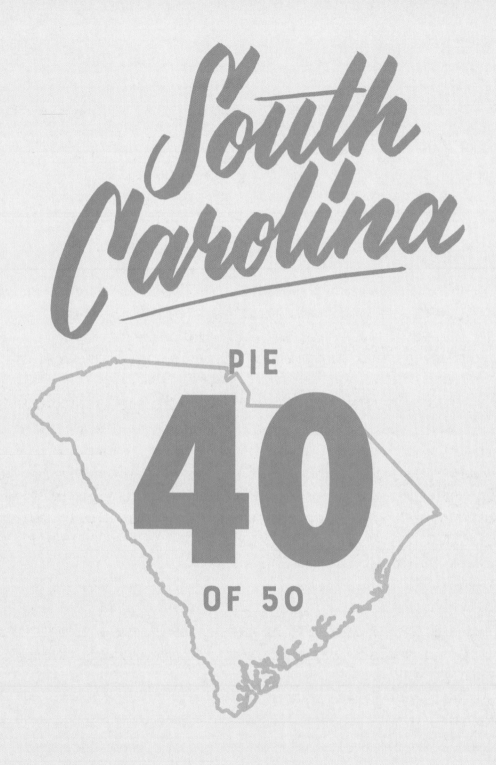

South Carolina

SMILING FACES, BEAUTIFUL PLACES

STATE FRUIT: PEACH ★ STATE VEGETABLE: COLLARD GREENS
STATE SNACK FOOD: BOILED PEANUTS

THE STATE!

This gem of the South became the eighth state to join the Union on May 23, 1788. But then became the first state to *leave* the Union in the lead up to the Civil War, which started in 1861. It rejoined the United States in 1868. The state was named after King Charles I of England and its nickname, the Palmetto State, honors the state's tree, the sabal palmetto.

South Carolina was the leading rice producer in the United States and home to Carolina Gold rice, beloved today by chefs for its flavor and texture. The strain was brought from Madagascar in 1685 by a merchant ship that docked in Charleston. At one point, about 100,000 acres of the rice were planted in the South, becoming an engine of economic growth that was built on slavery. The variety fell out of favor in the 20th century before its current revival.

After one visit, I fell in love with how romantic the city of Charleston is. You are surrounded by buildings that are rich in history, cooled under the shade of large trees with Spanish moss draped all over them, and can enjoy an ocean breeze that cannot be beat. And I have eaten my fill of boiled peanuts from gas stations on the drive from Savannah to Charleston.

I can't wait to smile back at this state's Smiling Faces, sooner rather than later.

THE PIE!

Yes, Georgia is known as the Peach State, but to some, South Carolina is known as the Tastier Peach State. South Carolina has a long heritage of peach production because of its temperate climate, rich soil, and sloping terrain; it boasts 18,000 acres of peaches and ranks second in fresh peach production, behind only California. The state started growing them in the early 1860s and hasn't looked back. With over fifty varieties of peaches grown in the state, it was officially designated the state fruit in 1984.

I wanted to incorporate peanuts into a peach pie, since boiled peanuts are one of my favorite snacks. They were made the official state snack in 2006, but South Carolinians started boiling them way back in the 1800s to make use of surplus peanuts. (Peanuts had been eaten boiled for centuries in Africa, and the practice came to the United States with enslaved plantation workers.) It's now part of modern-day South Carolina's culinary landscape.

So the pie for South Carolina is a peach pie with a crushed peanut crust! It's best enjoyed with a cold glass of white wine while the soft breeze off the Atlantic rolls onto your front porch.

PEACH PIE
WITH CRUSHED PEANUT CRUST

ACTIVE TIME: 30 MINUTES — BAKE TIME: 1 HOUR — TOTAL TIME: 3 HOURS 30 MINUTES — MAKES ONE 10-INCH PIE

CRUST

Crushed Peanut All-Butter Crust
(double, page 333), bottom
crust rolled out, top crust cut into
½-inch-wide lattice strips (see
page 344)
1 teaspoon granulated sugar
1 teaspoon all-purpose flour
Egg wash (see page 346)
Finishing sugar (see page 346)

FILLING

6 cups peeled, pitted, and sliced
peaches (7 or 8 medium
peaches)
¾ cup granulated sugar
¼ cup cornstarch
¼ teaspoon ground cinnamon
½ cup (1 stick) unsalted butter,
cubed

MAKE THE FILLING: In a large bowl, mix the peaches, sugar, cornstarch, and cinnamon together. Set aside until ready to fill pie.

ASSEMBLE AND BAKE THE PIE: Preheat the oven to 375°F. Fit the bottom crust into a greased 10-inch pie pan. Sprinkle the bottom with the teaspoons of sugar and flour. Fill with the filling and sprinkle the cubed butter on top. Top the pie with lattice strips in desired pattern; roll and crimp (see page 343). Brush the pie with the egg wash and sprinkle with the finishing sugar.

Bake the pie on a baking sheet on the center rack for 1 hour, rotating 90 degrees every 15 minutes, until the crust is golden brown and the filling is bubbling. Cool for at least 2 hours before serving alone or à la mode. Enjoy after a Low Country boil with a coastal breeze and a side of boiled peanuts to snack on!

THE DEDICATION!

The pie for South Carolina is dedicated to Kristin Winters of Columbia. I met Kristin in college in Savannah. One of my most vivid memories is us scream-singing at the top of our lungs and dancing the night away in the pit at a Mutemath concert.

In New York after college, we've spent many afternoons wandering around the Metropolitan Museum of Art and many nights on the dance floor, with many delicious meals in between. The most delicious meal we shared together was at Gabrielle Hamilton's restaurant Prune, where we ate a carrot that had been cooked slowly for 48 hours.

To this state's most beautiful Smiling Face, Kristin!

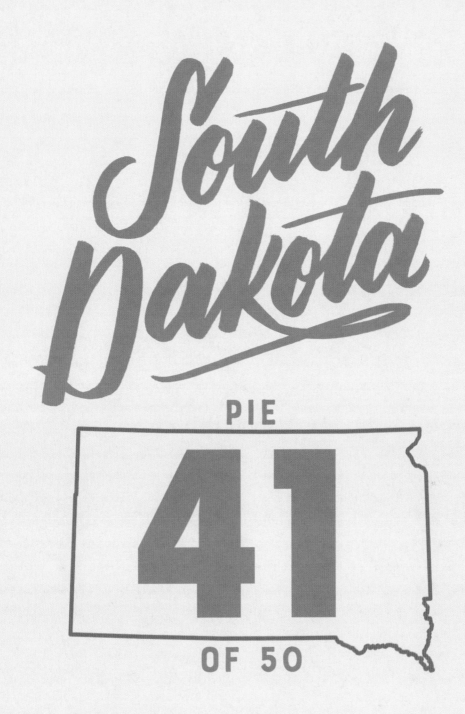

South Dakota

PIE
41
OF 50

GREAT FACES, GREAT PLACES

STATE DESSERT: KUCHEN ★ STATE BREAD: FRY BREAD

THE STATE!

South Dakota changed everything for me. Researching the pie for this state opened me up to what this project could mean, and showed me the vast knowledge and connections I could gain from it. I started with nothing, stumped about what to say about or do for the fortieth state of the Union. But I love a challenge.

I vented my stress to Massachusetts pie recipient Matt, who told me he had just finished a project for a historian in South Dakota! It felt like the universe weirdly gifted this connection to me.

I emailed with the historian, Eric Zimmer, picking his brain on everything South Dakota. He led me to chef Sean Sherman, whose book, *The Sioux Chef's Indigenous Kitchen*, was essential to this pie's creation. Eric even invited me to Rapid City for dinner with his friends and family.

For thousands of years before Europeans set foot on the land, Native American tribes such as the Cheyenne, Arikara, Ponca, Lakota, and Dakota Sioux lived on the land that is now South Dakota. Today, nine Native American tribes still reside there. The state was claimed by the French in 1743 and bought by the United States in 1803 through the Louisiana Purchase. The Dakota Territory, which included what's now North Dakota, was made into two states in 1889.

The state has sprawling prairies, farmlands, glacial lakes, and the Black Hills, which include the state's highest point, Black Elk Peak, at 7,242 feet. South Dakota is also home to the Badlands, a national park that has striking rock formations that rise up from the prairie in all different shades of colors. It's a maze of buttes, canyons, pinnacles, and spires.

While visiting the great state I drove through the Badlands with my friend Lauren while we listened to classic country music and saw the sun slowly set over the sprawling 244,000 acres of the park. While on our mini tour of the state, we also saw the Crazy Horse Memorial and Mount Rushmore, visited the geographical center of the United States in Belle Fourche, and had the free ice water at Wall Drug. Just the two of us, a cooler full of snacks, and the open road! My favorite kind of vacation.

South Dakota is full of Great Faces, Great Places and I cannot wait to roam the lands again.

THE PIE!

I wanted to pay tribute to the Native American tribes whose land forms this state and leaned heavily on Sean Sherman's work as inspiration for the pie.

Sean is Oglala Lakota and was born into the Pine Ridge Reservation in South Dakota. His career focus has been to foster the revitalization and awareness of Indigenous food systems. Mexican, Chinese, and Korean restaurants are becoming more abundant throughout the states, but what is missing is readily accessible Native American cuisine. It is rich and flavorful, full of wonderful textures, flavors, and interesting techniques. Sean and his team at the Sioux Chef, the company he created devoted to Native foods, make Indigenous foods more available to communities, allowing people to learn about Native cuisine.

I was intrigued by the use of nuts and berries for sweeteners in his dessert chapter, and captivated by the idea of bergamot leaves adding a floral quality to sauces.

So here is South Dakota's wild rice pudding pie flavored with homemade sunflower milk and blueberry and strawberry bergamot spoonsweet (which is a bright jammy sauce) and topped with a maple pumpkin and sunflower seed crunch in a blue corn crust. A complex textural dreamscape inspired by a state that I cannot wait to visit again. This pie is best eaten while the sun sets over the Badlands.

WILD RICE PUDDING PIE
WITH BERRY-BERGAMOT SPOONSWEET AND MAPLE SUNFLOWER-PEPITA CRUNCH

ACTIVE TIME: 30 MINUTES — CHILL TIME: 1 HOUR — TOTAL TIME: 9 HOURS 30 MINUTES — MAKES ONE 10-INCH PIE

CRUST
Blue Cornmeal Crust (single, page 335), rolled out, fit into a greased 10-inch pie pan, crimped, and fully blind baked (see page 339)

FILLING
Sunflower Milk
2 cups shelled raw sunflower seeds
2 cups water
¾ cup maple syrup, plus more to taste
Pinch of kosher salt
Wild Rice Pudding
2 cups cooked wild rice
1 cup sunflower milk
Pinch of kosher salt
Maple sugar to taste

TOPPINGS
Spoonsweet
2 cups mixed berries (blueberries, raspberries, blackberries)
1 tablespoon bergamot leaves
2 tablespoons maple sugar
Maple Sunflower-Pepita Crunch
½ cup shelled raw sunflower seeds
½ cup raw pepitas
⅓ cup maple sugar

SPECIAL EQUIPMENT
Blender
Parchment paper

MAKE THE SUNFLOWER MILK: In a large bowl, soak the raw sunflower seeds in the water overnight. Pulse the seeds and their soaking water with the maple syrup in a blender for 3 to 5 minutes, until smooth. Pass the mixture through a sieve and add the salt. Taste and add more maple syrup to sweetness preference. Refrigerate until ready to make the filling, up to 2 days ahead. Makes about 2 cups. Use the remaining sunflower milk as you would regular milk in coffee or smoothies—it's delicious!

MAKE THE SPOONSWEET TOPPING: In a medium saucepan, combine the berries, bergamot, and maple sugar. Cover and bring to a simmer over medium-low heat, pressing the berries to release their juices. Uncover and simmer until the mixture is thick enough to coat the back of a spoon, 3 to 5 minutes. Remove from the heat and cool completely. Blend in the pot with an immersion blend until smooth. Set aside to cool until ready to assemble pie.

MAKE THE MAPLE SUNFLOWER-PEPITA CRUNCH: In a large nonstick skillet, toast the sunflower seeds and pepitas over medium-high heat until the air fills with a nutty fragrance, about 3 minutes. Sprinkle in the maple sugar and stir constantly until the sugar is melted and all the seeds are coated nicely. Transfer the seeds to a baking sheet lined with parchment paper, spreading evenly. Cool completely, then set aside until ready to assemble pie. Try not to snack on them too much.

Recipe continues ★★★

MAKE THE WILD RICE PUDDING: In a large pot, simmer the cooked wild rice in the sunflower milk until the rice is soft and tender, about 15 minutes. Blend 1 cup of the mixture until smooth. Return the pureed mixture to the pot, add the salt, and sweeten with maple sugar to taste. Set aside to cool for at least 15 minutes before filling pie, to give the pudding a chance to set up a little bit.

ASSEMBLE THE PIE: Fill the fully baked crust with the pudding. Using a spoon or offset spatula, make a well in the center of the pudding about ¼ inch deep. Fill the well with the spoonsweet. Around the edge where the pudding and spoonsweet meet, sprinkle some of the sunflower-pepita crunch. Place the pie in fridge for at least 1 hour before slicing and serving with additional maple sunflower-pepita crunch. Enjoy while watching a wonderful sunset over the Badlands!

THE DEDICATION!

This pie is for Eric Zimmer. Eric grew up in the Black Hills of South Dakota and is a historian and author who specializes in Native American history, the history of U.S. social policy, and public and environmental history. Eric invited this pie-bearing stranger into his home and arranged a get-together with his fellow historians, authors, gallery curators, and friends so everyone could taste the pie I made as an ode to the state they call home. Thank you to Eric, Sam, Sam, Lois, Denise, and sweet puppo Nigel for the best conversation, the best meal, and new friends. You never know where pie will take you!

This pie is also dedicated to Emily & Melissa Elsen of Four & Twenty Blackbirds Pie Shop in Brooklyn, who hail from Hecla, South Dakota. Their cookbook ignited my love of pie baking.

South Dakota is truly full of Great Places and Great Faces.

Tennessee

THE STAGE IS SET FOR YOU

STATE FRUIT: TOMATO

THE STATE!

Tennessee, you're the only ten I see! The sixteenth state is thought to have gotten its name from an old Yuchi word tana-see, which means "the meeting place." Which is what it was for me when I first visited the state. For my 30th birthday, my friends Suzy, Katie, Val, and Anne took me to Pigeon Forge to visit Dollywood! We ate foot-long corn dogs, rode a roller coaster that went so fast that I for sure thought the eyelash extensions I got for the trip had blown right off, and toured Dolly Parton's museum and tour bus. We did it *all*. We even stayed at the DreamMore Resort in a family room that had bunk beds and butterfly details everywhere.

In addition to Dollywood, the Great Smoky Mountains, Graceland, and the Grand Ole Opry all call Tennessee home. Great Smoky Mountains National Park is the most visited national park in North America. The Grand Ole Opry started as a country-music radio show in 1925 and today it is the place where legendary musicians take the stage and charm massive crowds with their sweet songs. Tennessee is also home to the "meat and three," hot chicken, red-eye gravy, and one of my favorite things, country ham.

A state that is rich in history, lush in nature, and the birthplace of my favorite person on the planet, the Stage Is Set for You, Tennessee!

THE PIE!

I knew that for this state pie there was no other option than to make an ode to Dolly Parton. I have read that one of Dolly's favorite things to do is to wake up early and start her day in the kitchen with her husband Carl Dean. When Dolly cooks breakfast for Dean, it consists of biscuits, sausage patties, and her signature tried-and-true milk gravy.

The origins of biscuits and gravy date back to the 1700s in Southern Appalachia. It was the ideal cheap, calorie-dense food that sawmill workers, who were lifting heavy logs all day long, needed. In the early days of America, biscuits weren't the flaky fluffy wonderful tender clouds we have come to know today. They were hard, tooth-breaking lumps of flour and water. You needed something rich and creamy to even it out. Enter gravy. Pork was usually the protein of the poor since sausage released so much fat when cooked that the roux for the gravy created a rich and hearty meal that would keep you full all day.

The sausage for this pie is Swaggerty's. The name Swaggerty's in East Tennessee is about as common as McDonald's. It is a family-owned business started in the Great Depression by the family's patriarch, Lonas Swaggerty. Food and money at the time were scarce but from the Swaggerty's farm in Kodak, the family created a delicious and affordable sausage whose name and taste spread through the Great Smoky Mountains.

The pie for Tennessee honors the queen of the world, Dolly Parton. A gravy pie made with Swaggerty's sausage all the way from Tennessee with a portrait of Dolly as a crust topper. Like this hearty pie, my love for her sticks to my bones. This savory dream is best eaten while listening to "Tennessee Mountain Home" while the sun rises over the Great Smoky Mountains.

SWAGGERTY'S SAUSAGE GRAVY PIE
WITH PORTRAIT OF DOLLY PARTON

ACTIVE TIME: 30 MINUTES — BAKE TIME: 1 HOUR 15 MINUTES — TOTAL TIME: 2 HOURS 45 MINUTES — MAKES ONE 10-INCH PIE

CRUST

All-Butter Crust (double, page 332, or triple if you are making portrait of Dolly), rolled out (see page 339)

Egg wash (see page 346)

GRAVY FILLING

1 pound Swaggerty's Farm breakfast sausage patties

¼ cup all-purpose flour

2 cups whole milk

Pinch of cayenne pepper

Kosher salt and freshly ground black pepper to taste

Flaky sea salt for finishing (optional)

SPECIAL EQUIPMENT

Cast-iron skillet

Instant espresso for painting (if making portrait of Dolly)

Paintbrush (optional)

FOR DOLLY PARTON
DESIGN TEMPLATE, SCAN CODE

MAKE THE FILLING: In cast-iron skillet over medium heat, cook the sausage, breaking it up with a wooden spoon, until cooked through, about 10 minutes. Add the flour and cook for 1 minute. Pour in the milk and stir to combine. Add the cayenne and salt and pepper to taste. Bring the mixture to a boil, then reduce the heat to low and simmer on low until thick, about 5 minutes. Let cool for 1 hour.

ASSEMBLE THE PIE: Preheat the oven to 375°F. Fit the bottom crust into a greased 10-inch pie pan and fill with the cooled gravy filling. Cover with the top crust and roll and crimp the edges to seal (see page 343). Brush with egg wash and sprinkle with flaky sea salt and fresh cracked pepper. Cut a vent in the center of the pie to release some steam. Place the pie on a baking sheet and bake on the center rack for 1 hour and 15 minutes, rotating the pie 90 degrees every 15 minutes, until golden brown and fragrant.

If making portrait of Dolly Parton, take the third rolled-out crust and place on a flour-dusted sheet pan. Cut out the shape of Dolly and, using the stencil as your guide, use the remaining crust to create shapes for Dolly's hair. Use a mixture of espresso powder and water to paint the facial details. Freeze for 30 minutes before baking at 375°F for 20 minutes, checking and rotating every 5 minutes. Let cool completely.

Once the whole pie is baked, let it cool for 15 minutes before slicing. Best enjoyed while listening to "Tennessee Mountain Home" by Dolly Parton and gazing over the Great Smoky Mountains!

THE DEDICATION!

The pie is dedicated to my friend Myles Robinette of Knoxville, and the woman who is my North Star, Dolly Parton.

Myles and I both went to SCAD, attended the same parties, and went to the same bars—but we didn't meet until New York. Before he moved to Austin, I would spend almost every Friday with Myles. We would drink whiskey where we could and dance where we shouldn't, and he was always my first pick to do a karaoke duet with. Hanging out with Myles is like a really good hug. You feel it all the way in your soul.

Where do I even begin with Dolly Parton? I discovered her music as a little girl in Hong Kong and was in awe of her musicality, her sass, and the bright light that seemed to shine off her. Her music has helped me understand growth, life, and most of all love. Listening to "Do I Ever Cross Your Mind" while watching the sun rise on my 30th birthday at the Grand Canyon is one of the most special ways I have ever rung in a new year of life. I will always love her.

Thank you, Tennessee, for giving not only a five-star friend but the role model of my whole darn life. At every crossroads in my life, every time I wake up and at the end of each day, I think to myself, "What would Dolly do?"

Texas

PIE

43

OF 50

THE LONE STAR STATE

STATE BREAD: CORNBREAD ★ STATE DISH: CHILI CON CARNE

STATE FRUIT: TEXAS RED GRAPEFRUIT

STATE PEPPER: JALAPEÑO ★ STATE PIE: PECAN PIE

THE STATE!

Everything is truly bigger and, in more than one case, better in the twenty-eighth state.

Texas is unique. It got its nickname, the Lone Star State, because in 1836 it declared itself an independent nation from Mexico and flew its flag with a single star on it, until its annexation by the United States in 1845, when it became the twenty-eighth state. The state is home to the Alamo, dubbed the Cradle of Texas Liberty and the state's most popular historic site.

For half of my career in fashion I worked for Plano-based JCPenney, allowing me to visit the wonderful state and eat buckets of queso so frequently that the top button of my jeans buckled under the tension. I spent my first Thanksgiving ever in McKinney, a suburb of Dallas, with my college friend Karis and her family. They taught me all about all the different foods and most importantly about the long nap you take on the couch while the gentle murmur of a football game plays from the television.

One of my most favorite places in America is the Circle Star Ranch in Wolfe City. This ranch belongs to the Phillips family and is one of the most special places I have ever visited. I have so many good memories there, drinking beers around a bonfire, eating some of the best barbecue these lips have ever tasted, and taking naps on one of the plethora of leather couches that grace the home.

Until the next time I am in the Long Star State with a ranch water in hand marveling at the open skies...Tim Riggins said it: "Texas Forever."

THE PIE!

The Lone Star State does have a state pie, but my pie just could not be pecan, no matter how delicious. I wanted a pie to capture all the drunken nights and the spicy mornings I've had in Texas. This is where the state fruit and the state pepper come in.

The Ruby Red grapefruit was designated the official fruit of Texas in 1993. Texans have grown grapefruit in the Rio Grande Valley since the 1700s, but it wasn't until 1929 that a mutation on a single tree created the sweet Texas Ruby Red. This grapefruit has been carefully nurtured and perfected over time to be the sweetest grapefruit to touch your lips, with a perfect jewel-toned interior. The grapefruit now flavors things like Deep Eddy vodka based in Austin and the seasonal Ruby Redbird brewed in Shiner.

The jalapeño became the state's pepper on May 10, 1995. Texas leads the nation in jalapeño consumption. It is an essential ingredient in Texas chili, salads, and queso and is added to everyday dishes for a little extra spice.

For Texas: a red grapefruit custard pie topped with candied jalapeños. A pie packed with big flavor, booze, and spice for a state with the prettiest open skies. Texas Forever!

RUBY RED GRAPEFRUIT PIE
WITH CANDIED JALAPEÑOS

ACTIVE TIME: 30 MINUTES — BAKE TIME: 50 MINUTES — TOTAL TIME: 3 HOURS 20 MINUTES — MAKES ONE 10-INCH PIE

CRUST

All-Butter Crust (single, page 332), rolled out, fit into a greased 10-inch pie pan, crimped, and partially blind baked (see page 339)

FILLING

1½ cups granulated sugar

2 tablespoons all-purpose flour

½ teaspoon kosher salt

2 tablespoons unsalted butter, melted

3 large eggs plus 1 large egg yolk

1 cup heavy cream

Dash of orange bitters

1 cup fresh grapefruit juice

3 tablespoons Deep Eddy Ruby Red vodka

CANDIED JALAPEÑO TOPPING

1 cup water

1 cup granulated sugar, plus more for sprinkling

½ pound jalapeños, sliced and seeded

MAKE THE FILLING: Preheat the oven to 325°F. In a large bowl, whisk the sugar, flour, salt, and melted butter together. Whisk in the eggs and yolk one at a time, making sure each is fully incorporated before adding the next. Whisk in the cream and bitters. Whisk in the grapefruit juice and vodka last to make sure the filling doesn't curdle. Strain the filling through a sieve into another bowl.

ASSEMBLE AND BAKE THE PIE: Place the partially baked crust on a baking sheet and fill with the filling. Bake on the center rack for 50 to 55 minutes, rotating 90 degrees after 30 minutes, until the edges are set but the center jiggles like a soft thigh. Let the pie cool for at least 2 hours.

MAKE THE CANDIED JALAPEÑOS AND FINISH THE PIE: Bring the sugar and water to a boil in a large saucepan. Reduce the heat and simmer for 5 minutes. Add the jalapeños and simmer for 4 minutes. Transfer the jalapeños to a cooling rack placed on a baking sheet. Sprinkle with additional sugar and toss the jalapeños so they are evenly coated in the sugar. Let dry for at least 1 hour.

Arrange the candied jalapeños around the edge of the pie. Slice, serve, and enjoy under the Texas sun, y'all!

THE DEDICATION!

This pie is for one of my most cherished friends, Bryce Tilman Phillips. Many years have passed since we first met, with dozens of tequila and whiskey shots taken and countless memories made.

Bryce grew up in Arlington, Texas, in one of the most loving households I have come to know. His family is truly the best. Bryce's family's ranch in Wolfe City is one of my most favorite places in the world. His mom, Patty, taught me all about eating black-eyed peas on New Year's and handed me my first bowl of them ever. The year after that was one of my best yet.

Bryce is responsible for taking me on my first-ever long-haul backpacking trip. It was a real "go big or go home" moment; we hiked 50 miles of the Appalachian Trail. After many days on the trail, most of which were wet and rainy, we were forever bonded by the miles, trail names, and blisters on our feet.

It's good in life to have people you trust and love so whole heartedly and unconditionally the way I do with my buddy Bryce. I messed with Texas and I turned around and fell in love.

Utah

PIE

44

OF 50

LIFE ELEVATED

STATE FRUIT: CHERRY ★ **STATE HISTORIC VEGETABLE: SUGAR BEET**
STATE SNACK FOOD: JELL-O ★ **STATE VEGETABLE: SPANISH SWEET ONION**

THE STATE!

Utah, the only "U" state in the fifty. The forty-fifth state got its nickname, the Beehive State, from the Mormons who came to Utah in 1847: The early pioneers considered themselves as hardworking as bees.

Driving through southern Utah feels like driving on Mars with its red rocks and swooping rock arches. The state is bordered by Idaho and Wyoming to the north, Colorado to the east, Arizona to the south, and Nevada to the west. At its southeastern corner, Utah is part of the Four Corners, the only place in the country where four states come together. Utah has five national parks: Arches, Canyonlands, Zion, Bryce Canyon, and Capitol Reef.

On my way to the North Rim of the Grand Canyon for my solo 30th birthday sojourn, I got the chance to spend a night in Kanab. I wiggled my toes in the Coral Pink Sand Dunes and laid my head that evening in a lovely hotel called Canyons Lodge. Kanab was the perfect place to stop on the way to the Grand Canyon. It got its nickname, Park Central, because it is located minutes away from three national parks, three national monuments, one national recreation area, and two state parks. The center of it all.

Utah, Life truly Elevated!

THE PIE!

Funeral potatoes got their unique name from being a crowd-pleasing casserole often served as a side dish at funeral luncheons. There is nothing more comforting and delicious than warm cheesy potatoes with a crispy, buttery cornflake topping. The dish became particularly popular along the Mormon Corridor of Utah, western Wyoming, eastern Idaho, and Southern California. No one is sure where funeral potatoes originated, but most sources attribute their spread to the Relief Society, a women's organization within the Church of Jesus Christ of Latter-day Saints. One responsibility of society members was attending to the needs of the bereaved, including meals. Making funeral potatoes became a way to show support and sympathy for a grieving family. The long-lasting ingredients of funeral potatoes are almost always in a Mormon's pantry, a result of the church's practice of maintaining a three-month food supply at all times, so the dish is able to be cooked at a moment's notice.

It is now also served at church potlucks and alongside ham for Christmas and Easter. It was even featured as a motif on a commemorative pin at the 2002 Winter Olympics that Salt Lake City hosted.

This pie is best eaten at any dang time of day. It is a warm hug for your tummy and your soul and will most definitely soothe any sadness away. Here's to putting funeral potatoes at the forefront of more meals, dinners, and potlucks in the future.

FUNERAL POTATO PIE

ACTIVE TIME: 15 MINUTES — BAKE TIME: 50 MINUTES — TOTAL TIME: 1 HOUR 20 MINUTES — MAKES ONE 10-INCH PIE

CRUST

All-Butter Crust (single, page 332), rolled out, fit into a greased 10-inch pie pan, crimped, and frozen (see page 339)

FILLING

1 cup sour cream

1 (10.5-ounce) can cream of chicken soup

3 tablespoons unsalted butter, melted

½ teaspoon dried minced onion

½ teaspoon kosher salt

¼ teaspoon freshly ground black pepper

1 (20-ounce) package frozen hash browns, thawed in fridge overnight

1 cup shredded cheddar cheese

CORNFLAKE TOPPING

1 cup cornflake cereal

2 tablespoons unsalted butter, melted

MAKE THE FILLING AND TOPPING: In a large bowl, combine the sour cream, soup, melted butter, dried onion, salt, and pepper. Add the potatoes and cheese and stir to combine. Set aside until ready to assemble pie.

Crush the cornflakes and mix in the melted butter, stirring to combine well.

ASSEMBLE AND BAKE THE PIE: Preheat the oven to 375°F. Fill the frozen crust with the filling and sprinkle on the cornflake topping. Place the pie on a baking sheet and bake on the center rack for 40 to 50 minutes, until golden brown and the cornflakes are crispy. Let cool for at least 15 minutes before slicing and serving. Best enjoyed warm with someone you love!

THE DEDICATION!

This pie is dedicated to the lovely people I met who run the Canyons Lodge in Kanab. When I made my reservation to stay there I had no idea what it would be like. I had such a lovely evening with them chatting about the area, getting great tips on where to stop on my road trip, what sights to see. You never know who you are going to meet on your journey.

When I first made it, the pie was consumed by my lovely friends Alex Collins (DC pie recipient), Lauren Rinaldi (Connecticut pie recipient), and Bryan Moreno (Nebraska pie recipient), all of whom have been to Utah like myself. We spent the evening drinking tequila, eating the pie, and enjoying each other's company like we always do.

This pie is a representation of stepping out of your comfort zone and exploring something no matter how foreign it is to you. I cannot wait to return and explore the state more, meet more people, and eat more funeral potatoes!

Utah! Life Elevated!

Vermont

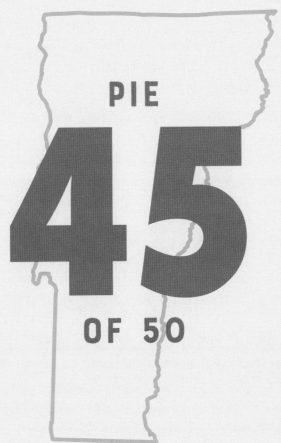

PIE

45

OF 50

VERMONT NATURALLY

STATE FRUIT: APPLE ★ STATE PIE: APPLE PIE
STATE VEGETABLE: GILFEATHER TURNIP

THE STATE!

In 1764, King George III folded the area we know as Vermont into New York. A mere year after the Declaration of Independence was signed, Vermont declared its own independence. The Green Mountain State would remain separate from the United States for fourteen years. Vermont had its own currency, postal service, constitution, and president until it became the fourteenth state in 1791.

Vermont gets its name from two French words, vert ("green") and mont ("mountain"), since much of the state is covered in mountains and forests and is home to the most famous Green Mountains. They were formed over 400 million years ago and the rocks are thought to be some of the oldest in the world. About 78 percent of the land in Vermont is forests, which are home to the state's liquid gold, maple syrup. As the largest producer of maple syrup in the United States, Vermont churns out almost two million gallons a year.

My first time in Vermont was to visit Chittenden in 2012 for a wedding. As always, my friends and I really tied one on. The morning after, sitting with our sin from the night before, we drove to the Maple Sugar & Vermont Spice diner and ate stacks on stacks of pancakes. That was the first time I tasted real maple syrup. I left with a half-gallon and have been hooked ever since.

One of my favorite bacons comes from Singleton's General Store in Proctorsville. It is smoky as heck but so delicious, it's unreal. My buddy Pete's family has a place at the Okemo Mountain Resort in Ludlow that we have had the honor of visiting and we never forget to stop at Singleton's on the way home to stock up.

I can't wait until I am back in Vermont. I hope to drive up slowly from New York, enjoy the fresh air, mountain breezes, and finally get to visit the King Arthur Baking Company campus in Norwich.

THE PIE!

My buddy Pete's pop used to always say, "An apple pie without the cheese is like a kiss without the squeeze." Apple pie became the state pie on May 10, 1999, and Vermont even has a 1999 law on the books requiring that proprietors of apple pie make a "good faith effort" to serve it with ice cream, cold milk, or "a slice of cheddar cheese weighing a minimum of ½ ounce."

The idea of adding cheese to pie originated in England in the 17th century. In Yorkshire, apple pie was served with Wensleydale, which *may* be where Pete's pop's phrase originally came from. Whether the phrase originated in America or England is a hot debate, so let's just chalk it up to cultural collaboration. What we know for sure is that people were so passionate about apple pie and cheese that poetry was written about it. Eugene Field wrote, "But I, when I undress me / Each night, upon my knees / Will ask the Lord to bless me / With apple pie and cheese."

This is an apple pie with a Cabot cheddar cheese crust, served with extra cheese on the side for a state that deserves nothing less.

APPLE PIE

WITH CABOT CHEDDAR CHEESE CRUST

ACTIVE TIME: 30 MINUTES — BAKE TIME: 1 HOUR — TOTAL TIME: 3 HOURS 30 MINUTES — MAKES ONE 10-INCH PIE

CRUST

Cheesy All-Butter Crust (double, page 333), rolled out, one for bottom crust, one cut into 1-inch-wide lattice strips (see page 344)

1 teaspoon all-purpose flour

1 teaspoon granulated sugar

Egg wash (see page 346)

Finishing sugar (see page 346)

FILLING

6 medium Granny Smith apples, peeled, cored, and thinly sliced

2 tablespoons lemon juice

¾ cup plus 2 tablespoons granulated sugar

¾ cup packed light brown sugar

¼ cup all-purpose flour

1 teaspoon ground cinnamon

1 teaspoon ground nutmeg

¼ teaspoon kosher salt

FOR SERVING

Sliced extra-sharp Cabot cheddar cheese

MAKE THE FILLING: In a large mixing bowl, toss the apples with the lemon juice and the 2 tablespoons granulated sugar. Set aside for 30 minutes.

In a medium mixing bowl, mix the ¾ cup granulated sugar, the brown sugar, flour, cinnamon, nutmeg, and salt. Drain the apples and add to the sugar mixture. Mix together until well incorporated and all the apple slices are coated.

ASSEMBLE THE PIE: Preheat the oven to 375°F. Fit the bottom crust in a greased 10-inch pie pan. Sprinkle the teaspoons of flour and sugar on the base of the pie. Fill with the filling.

Weave the lattice strips in a simple basket weave pattern (see page 345) on the top. Trim any excess crust along the edge leaving enough to roll and crimp to seal (see page 343). Brush the crust with egg wash, sprinkle with finishing sugar, and place on a baking sheet.

BAKE THE PIE: Bake the pie on the center rack for 1 hour, rotating every 15 minutes, until golden brown and the filling is bubbling. Bake an additional 5 to 10 minutes if the lattice needs additional browning. Let cool for at least 2 hours before serving with slices of cheddar cheese. Best enjoyed after a little kiss on the cheek too!

THE DEDICATION!

The pie is for my fine friend Annie Gormley Kraus. Annie is from Chittenden, near Killington. I met her in 2013 at a scavenger hunt my friends from SCAD and I played every year in the city. We instantly hit it off. Annie recently shared with me that pie was something her mom always made for their family, friends, and anyone that would come round their house, even when Annie insisted she not bother. For her mom, cooking for people was her way of saying, "Welcome to our home." Her mother and I have that in common. All Annie's recollections of pie are centered around special days, her mom, and family and friends being together. Pie is home.

Vermont, Naturally: Like the fall leaves, I have fallen for you.

PIE

46

OF 50

VIRGINIA IS FOR LOVERS

NO STATE FOODS

THE STATE!

Virginia is home to Jamestown, which in 1607 was the first permanent English settlement in what would become the United States. In 1788, after the Revolutionary War, Virginia became the tenth state. It was named after Queen Elizabeth I, who was called the Virgin Queen.

I have vague memories of stopping by Virginia's Colonial Williamsburg, where actors recreate what life was like in the 18th century, with my family when I was very little. My dad had taken my sisters and me on a long road trip from New York to Disney World in Orlando. There were blacksmiths at work, colonial meals, and many of the buildings in the village are originals from the 1700s.

Many foods that are seen as traditionally American, like cured ham, collard greens, fried oysters, and black-eyed peas, have a connection to Virginia. In Colonial Virginia, country ham was cured with so much salt that it could go unrefrigerated. At her Mount Vernon home, Martha Washington cured 400 hams a year.

One of my favorite Thanksgivings was with my friend Paul's family in Hopewell. I got to spend time in Paul's childhood bedroom, which was heavily decorated with horse themed items—down to the light switch covers. I got to meet his horse Lucky, drink my first Cheerwine, and eat all the casserole my heart desired. We spent the evening in stitches laughing and chatting around the kitchen table with his mom, Melanie.

To me, Virginia is not just for lovers, it's about family.

THE PIE!

Virginia is known as the birthplace of a nation. It is also said to be the birthplace of the chess pie, so I made one for Virginia with candied peanuts on top. The earliest known recipe appeared in the cookbook *The Virginia Housewife* by Mary Randolph in 1824. The recipe was titled Transparent Pudding and variations have appeared in New England and Southern cookbooks since then. There are many stories about the origin of the name. Some claim chestnut flour was used in the pie, others claim that "chess" is the interpretation of a Southern accent saying "just pie." Chess pie is the base recipe for many of the pies we enjoy today, including derby and pecan pies.

Virginia is also responsible for the largest of the four peanut types grown in the United States. By 1902 Virginia had become the largest peanut producer in the country. Candied peanuts add a little texture to the chess pie, right on top.

CHESS PIE
WITH CANDIED PEANUTS

ACTIVE TIME: 1 HOUR — BAKE TIME: 50 MINUTES — TOTAL TIME: 3 HOURS 50 MINUTES — MAKES ONE 10-INCH PIE

CRUST

All-Butter Crust (single, page 332), rolled out, fit into a greased 10-inch pie pan, crimped, and fully blind baked (see page 348)

FILLING

2 cups granulated sugar

2 tablespoons cornmeal

1 tablespoon all-purpose flour

¼ teaspoon kosher salt

½ cup (1 stick) unsalted butter, melted

¼ cup whole milk

1 tablespoon white vinegar

½ teaspoon vanilla extract

4 large eggs, beaten

TOPPINGS

Candied Peanuts

½ cup granulated sugar

¼ cup water

1 cup salted peanuts

Whipped Cream

1 cup heavy whipping cream

¼ teaspoon vanilla extract

SPECIAL EQUIPMENT

Stand mixer with whisk attachment or hand mixer

PRO TIP: *Make the filling the night before so it has time to thicken in the fridge. Whisk before filling the pie and baking. You'll know the filling is set when it jiggles like a soft thigh.*

MAKE THE FILLING: In a large mixing bowl, stir together the sugar, cornmeal, flour, and salt. Add the melted butter and mix well. Add the milk, vinegar, and vanilla. Add the eggs and stir well.

ASSEMBLE AND BAKE THE PIE: Preheat the oven to 350°F. Pass the filling through a fine-mesh sieve. Fill the fully baked crust with the filling and place on a baking sheet. Bake on the center rack for 50 to 55 minutes, until the filling is slightly jiggly. Check 30 minutes in, and use foil to shield the edges if they are getting too brown. Let cool for at least 2 hours.

MAKE THE CANDIED PEANUTS: Preheat the oven to 300°F. In a medium saucepan over medium heat, combine the sugar and water and stir until the sugar dissolves. Add the peanuts and cook over medium heat, stirring constantly, until the peanuts are completely coated and no sugar syrup remains, 10 to 12 minutes. Pour the peanuts onto a baking sheet and spread out in an even layer. Bake for 30 minutes, stirring every 10 minutes, until the peanuts are fragrant. Allow to cool completely before crushing into smaller pieces. The candied peanuts can be made ahead and stored for up to 3 months in an airtight container.

Recipe continues ★★★

WHIP THE CREAM: While the peanuts are cooling, in a stand mixer with a whisk attachment or using a hand mixer, whip the cream and vanilla to stiff peaks. Cover and refrigerate until ready to finish pie.

FINISH AND SERVE THE PIE: Top the completely cooled pie with the whipped cream. Sprinkle the crushed candied peanuts on top. Slice and serve! Best enjoyed on the front porch while dusk rolls in on a summer's eve!

THE DEDICATION!

The pie is dedicated to my friend of fourteen years, Paul Frederick, who hails from Hopewell. I first met Paul in his apartment in Savannah when I came over to see his roommate Dave. I will never forget the image of Paul in a beautiful seersucker shirt, white jeans, and loafers cooking chicken teriyaki on a George Foreman grill at 11 p.m. We weathered Hurricane Irene together in my Brooklyn apartment, surviving on his mom's pasta salad and frozen Reese's Cups and watching a three-DVD set of terribly wonderful rom-coms we got at Target. Paul and his partner Will took me on my first sail around the Hudson, where we drank Heady Toppers and watched the sun set. So many wonderful memories of my time in America include Paul.

Virginia, you birthed a nation for lovers.

Washington

PIE

47

OF 50

THE EVERGREEN STATE

STATE FRUIT: APPLE ★ STATE VEGETABLE: WALLA WALLA SWEET ONION

THE STATE!

Washington was once owned by both the British and the United States. In 1846, the two nations signed a treaty dividing the land, which included the U.S. portion of the Oregon Territory. Some of this land became the state of Washington we know today, while the British took control of the land to the north, now Canada. In 1889 Washington became the forty-second state to join the Union, and the only state to be named after a president.

Washington's nickname, the Evergreen State, is fitting for a state half covered with lush and dense rainforests and filled to the brim with beautiful plants and so much wildlife. It is home to Mount Rainier, standing tall in the horizon at 14,410 feet, and Mount St. Helens, whose volcanic eruption in 1980 was the largest the Lower 48 had seen since 1917.

What captivates me most about this state is its lush bounty of produce, from wild mushrooms to berries, and all the seafood in its rivers and ocean. The Evergreen State, I cannot wait to get lost in you with a coffee in hand, en route to slurp on briny raw oysters while smelling that lush, humid air.

THE PIE!

To capture Washington in all its glory, the pie had to include Rainier cherries and apples. But I had to take it up a notch with a potato chip crumble on top, with crispy crooks and craggles as rocky as the Cascade Mountains.

The state grows more sweet cherries than any other region in the nation. Named after the state's famous volcano peak, the Rainier cherry was developed at Washington State University in Prosser by cross-breeding the Bing and Van varieties. The Rainier cherry's skin is thin and sensitive; they bruise easily and their season of June to August is more fleeting than summer itself. They are so special because of their short harvest time and because conditions have to be just exactly right for them to flourish, making them the jewels of summer.

Washington is also a top apple-producing state, responsible for 50 percent of the nation's apples, from Red Delicious to my personal favorite baking apple, the Granny Smith.

The potato chips I use for the topping are, of course, from Washington: Tim's Cascade Style chips from Auburn. In 1988, Tim's was named the best potato chip in Seattle. As a diehard Cape Cod chip fan, I must admit that Tim's are delicious: salty and so crisp, truly a perfect sandwich chip. If you can get your hands on the iconic red and white striped bag with the blue Cascade Mountains on them, consider yourself a real lucky bud.

I hope this pie captures the flavor of a state filled with such lush bounty.

RAINIER CHERRY AND APPLE PIE
WITH POTATO CHIP CRUMBLE

ACTIVE TIME: 30 MINUTES — BAKE TIME: 1 HOUR — TOTAL TIME: 5 HOURS 30 MINUTES — MAKES ONE 10-INCH PIE

CRUST

All-Butter Crust (single, page 332),
    rolled out, fit into a greased
    10-inch pie pan, crimped, and
    frozen (see page 339)
1 teaspoon all-purpose flour
1 teaspoon granulated sugar

CRUMBLE TOPPING

⅓ cup crushed Tim's Cascade Style
    lightly salted potato chips
⅓ cup all-purpose flour
⅓ cup rolled oats
¼ cup packed light brown sugar
⅛ teaspoon baking soda
Pinch of ground cinnamon
Pinch of kosher salt
6 tablespoons (¾ stick) unsalted
    butter, softened
Flaky sea salt

FILLING

3 cups pitted and halved Rainier
    cherries
2 cups shredded peeled Granny
    Smith apples (2 or 3 medium
    apples)
½ cup granulated sugar
¼ cup cornstarch
Pinch of kosher salt

MAKE THE CRUMBLE TOPPING: Preheat the oven to 325°F. In a medium bowl, combine the potato chips, flour, oats, brown sugar, baking soda, cinnamon, and salt. Incorporate the softened butter into the dry mixture until it resembles a coarse sand or granola. Spread the mixture on a parchment-lined baking sheet and bake for 10 to 15 minutes, until dry and golden. Set aside until ready to bake the pie.

MAKE THE FILLING AND ASSEMBLE THE PIE: Preheat the oven to 375°F. In a large bowl, mix all the filling ingredients together until fully incorporated. Sprinkle the teaspoons of flour and sugar onto the base of the frozen crust. (This will ensure there is no soggy bottom.) Fill the crust with the filling.

BAKE THE PIE: Place the pie on a baking sheet and bake on the center rack for 50 minutes, rotating the pie pan clockwise every 15 minutes. Sprinkle the crumble topping onto the pie and bake for 10 minutes longer, until the crumble is golden brown and crispy.

Let the pie cool for at least 4 hours. Sprinkle with flaky sea salt before serving. Enjoy with a hot cup of coffee while watching the rain fall through the trees from the comfort of a kitchen table window in Seattle!

THE DEDICATION!

This pie is dedicated to my friend Dave Stine. Dave is originally from New Jersey but has called the great state of Washington home for the past decade. He lives there with his lovely wife, Amy. All of us went to SCAD together. One of my favorite memories is dancing the night away at our friend's wedding in Vermont. No shoes and a lot of arm and finger gesturing as the stars lit up the sky above us.

I couldn't survive the turmoil of life as an Asian American in this country without Dave. He is my constant support and the person I go to when everything gets too overwhelming. We talk it out, we relate it to an episode of *Love Island*, we process, and we move through it as gracefully as we can.

This is a top-shelf pie for a top-shelf friend. The Evergreen State, I long to visit you. I am constantly green with envy.

West Virginia

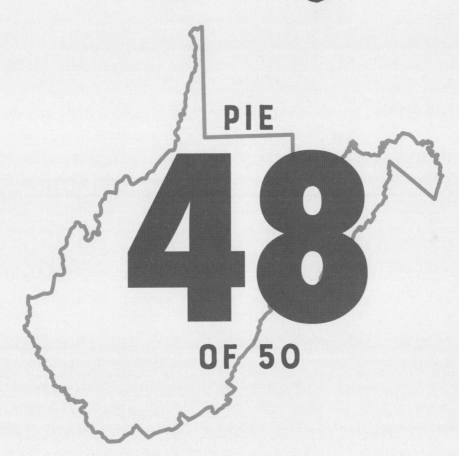

PIE

48

OF 50

ALMOST HEAVEN

STATE FRUIT: GOLDEN DELICIOUS APPLE

THE STATE!

West Virginia is considered the southernmost Northern state and the northernmost Southern state. Colorado may be known for its towering peaks out West, but West Virginia is the only state completely within the Appalachian Mountain region; its elevation is higher than any other state east of the Mississippi. I guess that's why John Denver said it's Almost Heaven—'cause you *can* just about touch the clouds.

West Virginia had an arduous road to statehood. In the 1600s, after the British arrived, the region encompassing West Virginia, Virginia, Kentucky, parts of North Carolina, Delaware, Pennsylvania, and New York was all called Virginia. In 1730, a thousand acres of land were offered by the British to each European family willing to move to the area that would eventually become West Virginia. The land was offered without the consent of the Native Americans whose homelands were taken. The Native tribes began supporting the French in a land war against the British from 1756 to 1763, which the British won. West Virginia remained part of Virginia during the Revolutionary War. In the Civil War, part of the state refused to secede from the Union along with the rest of the state, and rumblings of it becoming its own state started. It continued to be part of Virginia in 1861, but two years after that, it became the thirty-fifth state.

West Virginia, you're Almost Heaven, and I can't wait for your country roads to take me home.

THE PIE!

The pepperoni roll is a West Virginia staple that is often referred to as the unofficial state food—and might be named an official state food soon! A resolution to do that was introduced in March of 2019 and passed in the State House. It is now up to the State Senate rules committee for further discussion...and we all know how long bureaucracy can take in America! This state emblem has a younger history than biscuits and gravy, but it's no less of a West Virginia staple.

The first known pepperoni roll was sold by Giuseppe Argiro at the Country Club Bakery in Fairmont in 1927. A historical marker sits outside the bakery, commemorating the origin of the "West Virginia delicacy created by Italian families in Fairmont to feed local coal miners. Variants now popular statewide." The pepperoni roll, nearly ubiquitous throughout West Virginia, particularly in convenience stores and gas stations, is an Italian American stuffed bread roll: a soft white yeasted bread roll with pepperoni baked in the middle. During baking, the fats of the pepperoni melt, infusing the bread with spicy oil.

The pie for this state is a cheesy pepperoni pie with a marinara swirl and pepperoni-stuffed crust. I had a picture in my head of a pie with pepperoni in the crimps and I just *had* to make it happen! It's cheesy, salty, and satisfying—best enjoyed hot, in the parking lot of a gas station.

PEPPERONI-ROLL DIP PIE
WITH PEPPERONI-ROLL STUFFED CRUST

ACTIVE TIME: 1 HOUR 30 MINUTES — BAKE TIME: 55 MINUTES — TOTAL TIME: 2 HOURS 55 MINUTES — MAKES ONE 10-INCH PIE

CRUST

All-Butter Crust (single, page 332)

About 6.5 ounces pepperoni (about half a log), cut lengthwise into quarters and then into twelve 1-inch-long pieces

FILLING

1 (8-ounce) package cream cheese, softened

1 cup shredded low-moisture mozzarella

½ cup chopped pepperoni

½ cup whole milk

¼ cup mayonnaise

1 (2.64-ounce) packet McCormick original country gravy mix

1 cup marinara sauce (store-bought is fine)

¼ cup sliced pepperoni

Chopped fresh parsley for serving (optional)

Red pepper flakes for serving (optional)

STUFF AND BAKE THE CRUST: Roll out the crust to a 13-inch round. Fit the dough into a greased 10-inch pan so there is at least 2 inches hanging off the edge. Make about 24 cuts all around the overhang, about 1 inch apart. Roll one 1-inch piece of pepperoni up in one of the crust sections, like a pig in a blanket, until you get to the edge of the pie pan. Press down to secure. Work your way around the pie, rolling up a piece of pepperoni in every other crust section. For the overhanging dough in between, roll each section up onto itself and crimp down. Repeat until your crust is stuffed and crimped all the way around. Place in the freezer and freeze until solid, about 30 minutes.

Partially blind bake the crust (see page 347): Line the dough with foil and fill with pie weights. Bake on the center rack of a 375°F oven for 30 minutes. Let cool before removing pie weights and filling the crust.

MAKE THE FILLING: In a large bowl, mix the cream cheese, ½ cup of the mozzarella, the chopped pepperoni, milk, mayonnaise, and gravy mix until well blended. Put in the fridge until ready to assemble pie.

ASSEMBLE THE PIE: Preheat the oven to 350°F. Fill the partially baked stuffed crust with the filling. Dot marinara sauce onto the top of the filling, then swirl it into filling with a spoon or table knife. Sprinkle the remaining ½ cup mozzarella on top and place the sliced pepperoni around the edge of the pie, inserting half of the slice into the filling and leaving half to peek out the top.

BAKE THE PIE: Place the pie on a baking sheet and bake on the center rack for 25 minutes, or until the filling is heated through and the cheese is bubbly and melty. Let cool for at least 1 hour. Sprinkle on parsley and red pepper flakes before slicing and serving. Enjoy while blasting John Denver with some of your finest friends on your way home!

THE DEDICATION!

This pie is dedicated to my friend of sixteen years, Jeffrey Caldwell Hart. I met Jeffrey sophomore year of college; he picked me to be his friend. We were both in the same Survey of Western Art class. I had a class right before, so I would come bounding into art history with an arm full of shoe lasts and leather poking out of my tote and throw my body into the last seat just as class was about to start. During a smoke break the second day of class Jeffrey joined me. He told me that next class, his friend Taylor and he would save a seat for me. We have been friends ever since.

Jeffrey was born in Charleston and introduced me to pepperoni rolls. Both of us moved to New York right after college. During the first few tumultuous years in the city, whenever I was anxious, I would go sleep over at Jeffrey's. We would lie in his bed, listen to Fleetwood Mac, and enjoy the soft light pouring through his Williamsburg apartment's curtains. I felt so safe being in his bedroom lying next to him.

West Virginia, you are Almost Heaven. Whenever I'm with Jeffrey I am home, and all my memories gather 'round him.

Wisconsin

PIE

49

OF 50

AMERICA'S DAIRYLAND

STATE FRUIT: CRANBERRY ★ STATE GRAIN: CORN ★ STATE PASTY: KRINGLE

THE STATE!

America's Dairyland was first called the Wisconsin Territory in 1836, but didn't become the thirtieth state until 1848. The state's name is said to have come from the Miami word meskonsing, which roughly translates as "it lies red" or "this stream meanders through something red," referring to the state's reddish sandstone. The state got its nickname of the Badger State not because of the badgers that live throughout the state, but because the 19th-century miners who cut into the Wisconsin hills to find lead were called badgers: They would sleep in the caves they dug, just like badgers burrow to create dens.

Before moving to the States, if you asked me about Wisconsin, I could name two things: cheese and the Green Bay Packers. Cheesemaking was brought to Wisconsin by Swiss immigrants in the 1800s. Today, the state produces an average of 2.6 billion pounds of milk per month (as someone who is lactose untalented, that would bring me to my knees!), and more than 3 billion pounds of cheese each year.

Around 2019, I was recruited for a job at Lands' End in Dodgeville, and thought I ought to explore the possibility of shaking up my life again. They flew me out for the interview and I spent the weekend exploring Madison. I looked at apartments, went on a long hike at Devil's Lake, got delicious food from the Willy Street Co-op and a mini cheese plate from Fromagination, and had one of the best ham and cheese croissants ever at Batch Bakehouse. What I loved most was the Saturday I spent walking around the Dane County Farmers' Market. I bought an ear of corn and ate it raw on a park bench while admiring the city of Madison and listening to some choice tunes. Although I got the job offer in Madison, I turned it down to stay in New York. I wasn't fully done with the city yet—but that doesn't mean Madison won't be a part of my future.

Wisconsin, America's Dairyland, I fall in love with you with every squeak of a cheese curd on my teeth. A toast to you with a Miller High Life in a glass bottle.

THE PIE!

The pie for this state is a cranberry pie with a cornmeal crust and Bucky Badger fried cheese curds on top!

The cranberry was designated the state fruit in 2003 as the result of a class project by fifth-grade students from Trevor Grade School in Kenosha County. They decided that the cranberry, rather than the cherry, was the best candidate for Wisconsin's state fruit. Wisconsin leads the nation in cranberry production, accounting for over half of the nation's output.

Corn was designated the state grain in 1989. This came about during a legislative debate. Sponsors claimed designating corn as the state grain would draw attention to its importance as a cash crop. This in turn would make people more aware of corn's many uses.

In 2017, fourth-graders at Mineral Point Elementary School in Mineral Point proposed a bill to make cheese the official dairy product. About 90 percent of the milk produced in the state goes on to become about 3 billion pounds of cheese. That's a lot of curds and whey!

I wanted to combine all these elements for a true ode to this wonderful state. What better way to consume a cheese curd than fried? And with the tartness of cranberries to cut the richness?

This pie is best eaten while having a grand old time drinking Milwaukee's Champagne of Beers or a Mountain Dew and whiskey, and shooting the shit while football plays faintly in the background.

CRANBERRY PIE
WITH FRIED CHEESE CURD TOPPING

ACTIVE TIME: 1 HOUR 30 MINUTES — BAKE TIME: 1 HOUR — TOTAL TIME: 6 HOURS 30 MINUTES — MAKES ONE 10-INCH PIE

CRUST

Cornmeal Crust (single, page 335), rolled out, fit into a greased 10-inch pie pan, crimped, and frozen (see page 339)

CRANBERRY FILLING

2 cups fresh cranberries

½ cup granulated sugar

1 medium apple, cored, peeled, and shredded

⅓ cup orange juice

¼ cup cornstarch

3 tablespoons all-purpose flour

1 tablespoon grated orange zest

½ teaspoon ground ginger

¼ teaspoon kosher salt

1 tablespoon vanilla extract

FRIED CHEESE CURD TOPPING

8 cups corn oil for frying

¾ cup beer (preferably Miller High Life)

¼ cup milk

2 large eggs, beaten

1 cup all-purpose flour

½ teaspoon kosher salt

1 (12-ounce) package cheese curds (preferably Bucky Badger brand)

SPECIAL EQUIPMENT

Heavy-bottomed pan for deep frying
Deep-fry thermometer

MAKE THE FILLING: In a large mixing bowl, combine the cranberries and sugar and let it sit for 1 hour to macerate. Drain the cranberries and stir in the apple, orange juice, cornstarch, flour, zest, ginger, salt, and vanilla. Transfer to a medium saucepan and cook over medium heat, stirring constantly, for 3 minutes, until thickened. Set aside to cool for 15 minutes before filling the crust.

ASSEMBLE AND BAKE THE PIE: Preheat the oven to 375°F. Sprinkle a teaspoon each of flour and sugar on the bottom of the frozen crust and fill with the cranberry filling. Place the pie on a baking sheet and bake on the center rack for 1 hour, rotating 90 degrees every 15 minutes, until the filling is bubbly and the crust is golden brown. Cool for at least 4 hours.

FRY THE CHEESE CURDS: Heat the corn oil in a heavy-bottomed pan until it reaches 375°F. While the oil heats up, in a large mixing bowl, whisk together the beer, milk, eggs, flour, and salt to form a thin smooth batter. Add the cheese curds and turn to coat, then remove them from the batter with a strainer or slotted spoon. When the oil is at the correct temperature, fry the curds in batches of five to ten, until golden brown, 1 to 2 minutes each batch. Drain excess oil on paper towels.

FINISH AND SERVE THE PIE: Arrange the freshly fried cheese curds around the edge of the cooled pie. Slice, serve, and enjoy while watching the Packers with a cold Miller High Life in a glass bottle!

THE DEDICATION!

This pie is dedicated to Brian Kaspr of Milwaukee. I met Brian through Kickstarter in 2015. I backed his demolition derby campaign to send a 1986 Caprice that he painted "Cry Cry Cry" on to the automobile afterlife and then again in person at a Baggu event.

Brian was one of the first people to know about my pie project. After I wrote out the general plan for the project and made a mood board for what I wanted the general aesthetic to be, I reached out to him to ask if he would be interested in doing the branding and state titles, and if he thought it was even a good idea in the first place. After a few emails back and forth, we were like LFG!!!! He's been on this journey with me since day one.

Brian is an incredible friend, cheerleader, and support system. I couldn't imagine living, laughing, and loving through this project or life without him.

Wisconsin, you are America's Dairyland. Your people and your heart are always whole, never 2 percent.

Wyoming

PIE

50

OF 50

LIKE NO PLACE ON EARTH

NO STATE FOODS

THE STATE!

Wyoming is truly Like No Place on Earth. It started off as a U.S. territory in 1868, while the U.S. cavalry and Native Americans battled for control of the land. In 1890, Wyoming became the forty-fourth state.

There are many theories on how Wyoming's name originated. It might come from the Lenape word meaning "mountains and valleys alternating" or "large plains." Others believe it could have come from a Munsee language word meaning "at a big river flat," or an Algonquin word meaning "a large prairie place."

I have been to Jackson Hole, driven through the Teton Pass, and stood at the foot of Devils Tower. Jackson Hole is an absolute dream. A town full of ski resorts, dude ranches, and wildlife safaris, it is home to the Million Dollar Cowboy Bar, a landmark watering hole in the heart of town. It was established in 1937 and the walls have seen performances of the likes of legends like Waylon Jennings, Glen Campbell, and Hank Williams.

The first time I visited the state, I drove there from South Dakota with my friend Lauren to see the Devils Tower National Monument, a massive flat-topped hill with steep sides. I had seen pictures of it, but standing in its shadow was something else.

Wyoming is the last state on my pie trip, but home to many of the country's firsts. Besides being the first state to grant women the right to vote, it is home to the first national monument (Devils Tower), the first national park (Yellowstone), the first national forest (Shoshone), and JCPenney.

From the descent in the plane to the drive through Teton Pass, there isn't one moment where the views aren't postcard perfect. Wyoming may be the least populated state in the Union, but it is filled to the brim with magic in its nature and heart in its people.

THE PIE!

Wyoming is known as the Cowboy State and has acres and acres of land for riding horses and raising cattle. Vast ranches are scattered all over Wyoming, and rodeo is the official state sport. Cowboys and cowgirls work up an appetite at cattle ranches and dude ranches all day, often sitting down for a dinner full of meat. Game is widely hunted here and elk meat is commonly found on the table in the form of burgers, chili, steaks, and stew.

I captured the adventure and spice that fills this state with an elk chili pie with a Teton-inspired lattice on top, served with a huckleberry sauce.

Elk range from mountainous wilderness areas to lowland deserts and plains and are plentiful on both public and private lands. They are abundant, delicious, and lean.

The huckleberry is often confused with the blueberry. Although they are very similar in taste, the big differences are the seeds within the huckleberry that give it a crunchy texture when fresh, and its thicker skin. The flavor is like an intense blueberry, but more tart.

Enjoy a slice of this pie by the fire under the blanket of stars, looking at the Teton Mountains in the distance. Wyoming, truly Like No Place on Earth.

ELK CHILI PIE
WITH HUCKLEBERRY SAUCE

ACTIVE TIME: 1 HOUR — BAKE TIME: 1 HOUR — TOTAL TIME: 2 HOURS 45 MINUTES — MAKES ONE 10-INCH PIE

CRUST

All-Butter Crust (double, page 332), rolled out (see page 339), one for the bottom crust, one cut into lattice strips (see page 344) or in the shape of the Teton Mountains

Egg wash (see page 346)

ELK FILLING

1 tablespoon olive oil

1 medium yellow onion, diced

2 tablespoons bourbon

1 pound ground elk

2 tablespoons tomato paste

2 tablespoons granulated sugar

1½ tablespoons chili powder

1 tablespoon garlic powder

1 tablespoon cumin seed

1 teaspoon cayenne pepper

1½ teaspoons kosher salt, plus more to taste

1 cup beef stock

1 cup black coffee

1 cup tomato sauce

2 tablespoons maple syrup

¼ cup tahini

1 teaspoon instant coffee

MAKE THE FILLING: In a large Dutch oven or saucepan, heat the olive oil over medium heat. Add the onion and sweat for 5 to 6 minutes, cooking gently. Deglaze the pan with the bourbon and let the alcohol cook off for 2 minutes. Add the elk and cook for 6 to 7 minutes, breaking up the meat. Stir in the tomato paste, sugar, chili powder, garlic powder, cumin, cayenne, and salt. Add the beef stock, coffee, and tomato sauce. Stir and bring to a boil, then add the maple syrup, tahini, and instant coffee. Reduce the heat and simmer for 20 to 25 minutes, until thick and fragrant. Remove from the heat and allow to cool completely.

MAKE THE DEMI-GLACE: Simmer the broth and butter in a medium saucepan over medium-low heat until reduced by half. Slowly add the cornstarch mixture, whisking to combine. Simmer until smooth and rich. Set aside until ready to make huckleberry sauce.

MAKE THE HUCKLEBERRY SAUCE: In a heavy-bottomed saucepan, heat the olive oil over medium heat. Add the mirepoix and sauté for 8 minutes, until softened. Add the demi-glace, port, and 1 cup of the huckleberries. Simmer to reduce the mixture by a third, about 20 minutes. Strain through a sieve and return to the clean saucepan. Just before serving, bring the sauce to a simmer and add the remaining 1 cup huckleberries, the butter, and chocolate. Stir until the chocolate has melted.

Demi-Glace

2 cups beef broth

1 tablespoon unsalted butter

1 teaspoon cornstarch dissolved
   in 3 tablespoons water

Huckleberry Sauce

1 tablespoon olive oil

2 cups mirepoix (equal parts chopped
   onion, carrot, and celery)

4 cups port wine

2 cups huckleberries, fresh or frozen,
   or blueberries if unavailable

1 tablespoon unsalted butter

2 teaspoons dark chocolate chips

SPECIAL EQUIPMENT

Paintbrush (if painting Teton mountains)

Instant espresso (if painting Teton mountains)

FOR TETON MOUNTAIN
DESIGN TEMPLATE, SCAN CODE

ASSEMBLE AND BAKE THE PIE: Preheat the oven to 375°F. Fit the bottom crust into a 10-inch pie pan. Fill with the prepared filling. Arrange the lattice strips horizontally on top of the filling in desired pattern (see page 345) or in the shape of the Teton Mountains, painting the mountains with the dissolved espresso. Crimp the edge and brush with egg wash. Place the pie on a baking sheet and bake for 1 hour on the center rack, rotating 90 degrees every 15 minutes, until golden brown. Allow to cool for at least 15 minutes. Slice, serve, and spoon the warm huckleberry sauce on top. Best enjoyed around a fire with friends with a view of the Tetons!

THE DEDICATION!

This pie is dedicated to my friend of sixteen years, Maia Oustinoff Albers. I first met Maia at a house party in Savannah and we became instant friends. I remember driving around Savannah in her VW Golf blasting Shiny Toy Guns and spending hours buying vintage clothes at Civvies. When we moved to New York, we continued to hang out at shows at Music Hall of Williamsburg, drinking many Tecates at the Levee and getting into all sorts of sweet trouble.

Maia made the move to Jackson Hole almost a decade ago. At the time I was so sad, yet so excited to have another place to visit and to see what the next chapter of her adventure would look like.

It's rare in life you find people who sing the same tune as you. Like Wyoming, there is no place on earth like our friendship.

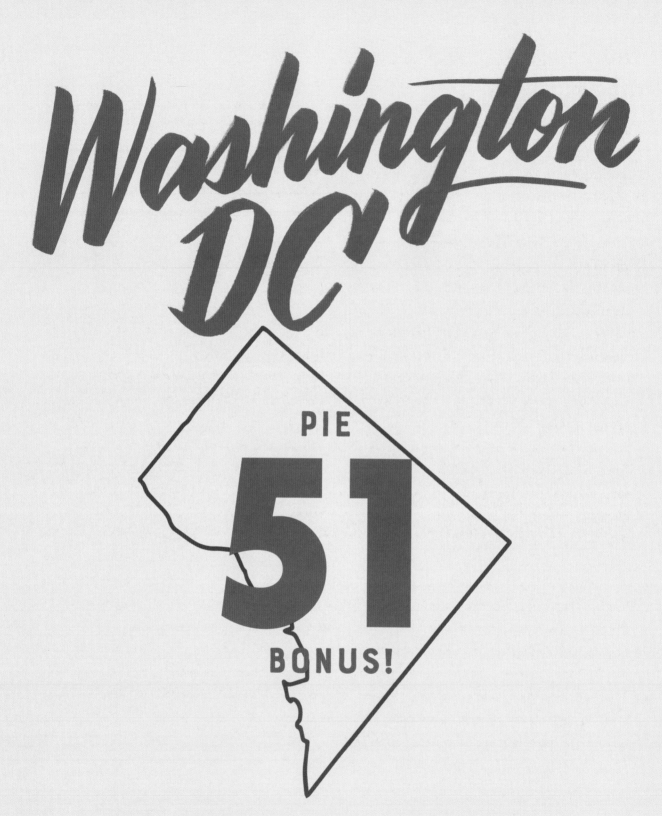

The District of Columbia may not yet be a state, and is formally known as Washington the Federal District of Columbia. With an official name like that, it's worthy of its own pie!

When I last visited our nation's capital, sandwiched between Maryland and Virginia, I hit up all the classic sites, from the White House to the Lincoln Memorial. But what touched me most was Julia Child's kitchen in the Smithsonian Institution. Seeing her pegboard system and raised countertops in person (though behind glass) took my breath away. It was a romantic pilgrimage for me. Growing up in Hong Kong I constantly thumbed through my father's copy of *Mastering the Art of French Cooking*. I dreamed of hosting large dinner parties for all my friends and planned fake menus filled with her recipes, and when I went out to dinner with my dad to a French restaurant, I ordered coq au vin or quiche Lorraine. For dessert, I always hoped the restaurant served crêpes Suzette. I knew when I grew up I would have a pegboard wall in my kitchen just like Julia's. And guess what, I do!

My favorite fun fact about DC is that it is home to the largest library in the world. The Library of Congress holds more than 160 million objects in its collection, including 6,000 books that were originally owned by Thomas Jefferson. The history those walls hold is endless and constantly being added to. Maybe one day this book will join the millions of items in the famous stacks!

THE PIE!

For DC: a cherry pie with a crust portrait of George Washington, the first president of the United States! Like so many others, I learned the time-honored story of George Washington and the cherry tree, only to find out that it is actually a myth. As the tale goes, when Washington was 6 years old, he received a hatchet as a gift and damaged his father's cherry tree. When he was confronted by his father, he uttered the words "I cannot tell a lie...I did cut it with my hatchet." His father then told him his honesty was worth more than a thousand trees.

How ironic that a fable highlighting the value of honesty actually turned out to be a fabrication! The story was invented by one of Washington's first biographers, Mason Locke Weems, published for the first time in the fifth edition of *The Life of Washington*. Weems wrote the story because he knew that it would sell books, but at the end of the day his intentions were good: He wanted to present Washington as the perfect role model, especially for young Americans, and emphasize that his public greatness was a reflection of his private virtues.

The cherry tree myth has been retold for more than 200 years. A sweet story that has now taken the form of a thick and jammy cherry pie.

CHERRY PIE
WITH GEORGE WASHINGTON PORTRAIT AND CHERRY BORDER

ACTIVE TIME: 1 HOUR — BAKE TIME: 1 HOUR — TOTAL TIME: 4 HOURS 30 MINUTES — MAKES ONE 10-INCH PIE

CRUST

All-Butter Pie Crust (double, page 332), rolled out, one for the bottom, and one for the portrait and cherry border

Egg wash (see page 346)

½ teaspoon all-purpose flour

½ teaspoon granulated sugar

Finishing sugar (see page 346)

FILLING

5 cups pitted and halved Bing cherries (fresh or frozen)

½ cup granulated sugar

¼ cup cornstarch

Big pinch of kosher salt

SPECIAL EQUIPMENT

2-inch cherry shaped cookie cutter

X-Acto knife, to cut out the portrait of George Washington

Instant espresso (optional)

Paintbrush (optional)

FOR GEORGE WASHINGTON DESIGN TEMPLATE, SCAN CODE

PRO TIP: *Make this pie between the months of April and August when cherries are at their peak! If you're not making the portrait, use the second crust as the top layer of pie.*

MAKE THE CRUST: Fit the bottom crust in a greased 10-inch pie pan and trim the edges so they are flush to the pie pan.

Cut out a portrait of George Washington from the second crust. Use the scraps to create his hair and features, giving the portrait dimension. Place George on a parchment-lined baking sheet. Using espresso, paint George's features, if you like.

Use remaining scraps to cut out cherries for the border. Using a little egg wash, attach the cherries to the border of the bottom crust. Freeze the crust and portrait on parchment-lined baking sheets for 30 minutes before baking.

Preheat the oven to 425°F. Remove only the portrait from the freezer. Brush the portrait with egg wash and sprinkle with finishing sugar. Bake on the parchment-lined baking sheet for 20 to 30 minutes, until golden brown. Set aside to cool completely.

MAKE THE FILLING: In a large mixing bowl, mix the cherries, sugar, cornstarch, and salt. Set aside for 30 minutes to macerate.

Recipe continues ★★★

ASSEMBLE AND BAKE THE PIE: Preheat the oven to 375°F. Sprinkle the ½ teaspoons of flour and sugar on the bottom crust. Fill the crust with the cherry filling using a slotted spoon, leaving juices behind.

Brush the crust with egg wash and sprinkle with finishing sugar. Place the pie on a baking sheet and bake on the center rack for 1 hour, rotating the pie 90 degrees every 15 minutes, until the crust is golden brown and the filling is bubbling. Let the pie cool for at least 2 hours before placing the baked portrait of George Washington on top. Then slice up the pie like young mythical George did to that cherry tree! Serve à la mode and enjoy!

THE DEDICATION!

This pie is for Alexander Collins. I met him when I was at the pit of one of the worst hangovers in my life. Picture this: It is 2014, we are sitting next to each other at the Brazilian restaurant Miss Favela in Williamsburg, Brooklyn, celebrating our girl Lauren's birthday. There is a live band blasting right behind our table. I was in a deep pit of sadness, sitting with all my sins from the night before. But from sadness comes beautiful friendships, built over pão de queijo. Since then, AC and I have been on many trips, have danced at weddings, and have spent countless hours talking about everything and nothing in particular.

DC's pie is also dedicated to my favorite first dog, Bo Obama (sorry Sunny), to Amy Hedgepeth, and to my friend and one-time college roommate who taught me to never trust a big butt with a smile, David "Dr. Dave" Moscati.

DC, thank you for uplifting and embodying the American experience. Unlike the story of the cherry tree, my love for you is no myth.

MAKING CRUST

Every good pie starts with a good crust. But please keep in mind that making your own pie dough is lovely, but it is not essential—so if you are in a bind or making your first pies, know that store-bought dough is totally fine. (I recommend Pillsbury's refrigerated pie crust.) Don't stress: Making pie should be fun.

As for me, I love making crust and find it one of the most therapeutic parts of baking. I blast the tunes and get down in it. I made so many terrible crusts at first, but then I got my technique and the ratio of everything just right after Four & Twenty Blackbirds put me through crust boot camp. If your crusts don't immediately turn out, just keep at it, and once you get the technique down, you'll be set for life—just like riding a bike. Pie dough can also always be made ahead of time and stored, tightly wrapped in plastic, in the fridge for up to 3 days or in the freezer for up to 3 months.

In this section you have everything you need to make every crust featured in this book, with some pro tips weaved in.

The main things to remember are that 1) you should have all your ingredients ready at the start; 2) your butter and liquids must be cold; and 3) your fridge and freezer are your best friends! For more info on tools and ingredients, see the sections that follow.

Let's get to makin' crust!

NOTE: *Please see page 340 for rolling and crimping instructions, page 346 for blind-baking instructions, and each individual pie for final baking instructions.*

TOOLS

As a self-taught baker, I am always on the hunt for tools that make my baking experience more seamless. That said, I hate single-function items because every inch is valuable in my tiny apartment kitchen. A tool I love might not be your favorite, but it's a good place to start. Just remember you don't need to spend a ton of money. Some of my favorite tools have been inherited from friends' grandmothers. Your tools will help you bake better pies and will become an extension of yourself. I also hope they might hold little memories for you. My bench scraper and I go *wayyyy* back; it's been with me for almost every single crust I've ever made!

ROLLING PIN!

There are many kinds of pins; choose what you feel most comfortable using. I am a classic handled rolling pin kinda lady. French rolling pins, which are tapered and don't have handles, just aren't for me. The advantage of a straight rolling pin is that you can apply very even pressure when rolling out your dough, and handles give you an easy grip. Find what works best for you!

PASTRY BLENDER/CUTTER!

I like to make my dough by hand. Using a food processor is an option, but I love the feeling of cutting in the butter and getting a little arm workout in before massive amounts of pie consumption. For cutting in the butter, you'll need a pastry blender. Get a metal one and it will be indestructible. I have used the same one for almost a decade. I got it from Webstaurant.com for $2.99 and it made every crust in this book. Plus it's great for crumbles and biscuits too!

MEASURING CUPS/SPOONS!

You need liquid measuring cups *and* dry ingredient measuring cups/spoons. For dry ingredient measuring cups and spoons, I love metal ones; they are easy to clean and don't hold the scents of your ingredients like plastic cups do. For liquids, I recommend a 4-cup glass Pyrex.

BENCH SCRAPER!

The bench scraper is arguably my favorite kitchen tool. You can use it for so many things: cutting butter, portioning dough, and best of all, cleaning up surfaces at the end of a rolling session. Mine is metal with a wooden handle, from Ateco. I often oil the wooden handle to add to its longevity. It's been with me since the beginning and I want to keep it around for all the pies to come.

PASTRY BRUSH!

You'll need one of these bad bois to egg wash all your pies! You can use whatever you like, from paint brushes from Michael's craft store to silicone ones. I use both, depending on how detailed I need to get.

PIE WEIGHTS!

I have a huge tub of ceramic pie weights (aka baking beads) that I use for blind baking crusts (that is, baking the crust without any filling in it; the weights keep the bottom from puffing up and the sides from slumping down). I have acquired these through the years by buying them in small amounts to fill a 4-quart container. You do not have to buy ceramic pie weights specifically—you can use dried beans, raw rice, sugar, steel beads, or even marbles instead.

PIZZA OR PASTRY CUTTER!

A pizza cutter is not only for when you opt for DiGiorno instead of delivery. It is perfect for cutting lattice strips for your pies. My favorite is from Sur La Table. They make a pastry-specific cutter that is double-headed; one side lets you cut straight and the other fluted.

TIMERS AND THERMOMETERS!

The two T's are your best friends when baking. If you've lived in a rental apartment you know how untrustworthy your oven can be: You turn it to a temp but it isn't accurate, or you aren't sure how long it takes to preheat. The solution is an oven thermometer. I have two in my oven, in the front and back, so I know the exact temperature and where the hot spots are.

Timers! You can use the one on your phone, but I like to set two: one for the full bake time and the second for when I need to rotate the pie. It's just a little insurance.

CONTAINERS! QUARTS! CAMBROS!

Storing all your ingredients is a major part of baking. You want to be organized and keep everything fresh. I love plastic take-out quart and pint containers as much as the next lady, but a specific brand of stackable plastic containers called Cambro has my heart! They are perfect for storing dry goods like flour and sugar. Get some off Webstaurant.com!

PIE PANS!

Every pie pan has a purpose! But in the world of ceramic, metal, and glass, my pick is usually metal. My favorite pie pan to bake in is a 10-inch diameter disposable aluminum pan. Metal pie pans are usually thinner than the other options, so the crust always bakes evenly and you are almost guaranteed no soggy bottom! I get myself a 100

pack from the Dollar General. They're great for easy baking and easy gifting.

I do love a glass pie plate for graham cracker and cold set pies, and ceramic for double-crust stew-filled meaty bad bois. But truly you can bake in whatever you like. That's the beauty of pie: It's a choose your own adventure!

OFFSET SPATULA!

If you want to swoosh-swoosh your meringue and whipped cream, an offset spatula is the weapon of choice. They come in many sizes, but a small 4-inch one from Ateco does the trick.

BAKING SHEETS!

Essential! That is, if you don't want your pies to drip all over your oven and leave you with a smoky, sticky mess. They are also great for prep and laying out your lattice. If you have a couple half sheets (13x18 inches) and a couple quarter sheets (9x13 inches), you can do just about anything.

MIXING BOWLS!

Seems obvious, but having a few sizes is great for dough and filling making. For dough I recommend a wider mouth bowl with a flat bottom and walls that aren't too high so you can really get your hands into the dough and go to town!

LUXURY ITEMS! LOVELY BUT NOT ESSENTIAL!

Like Cher said, "A man is a luxury. Like dessert, yeah. A man is absolutely not a necessity." I may disagree with her about dessert, but while these items are nice they are in no way essential.

FOOD PROCESSOR!
You can use this to make your dough making and vegetable chopping go much much faster!

KITCHEN AID—MY EMMY LOU BLUE!
I love my Kitchen Aid mixer so much that I named her my sweet Emmy Lou Blue. I pined after an aqua sky Kitchen Aid mixer for years until my best friend, Patrick, surprised me with one as a birthday gift. I use her for whipping cream, kneading bread dough, and there is even an apple peeling attachment. You can whip cream by hand or with a hand mixer, and you can knead dough by hand and work on your arm muscles. But if you have one, use her every chance you get!

INGREDIENTS

This is what you need to start your pie baking road trip! I list all my go-to brands so you know exactly what to get in the grocery store.

FLOUR!

All-purpose, unbleached flour is king for pie crust. My favorite brand is King Arthur. I often treat myself to several 5-pound bags and call it "buying myself flours" à la the movie *Stranger Than Fiction*. Good flour = good pie crust.

BUTTER!

In the world of pie crust, butter is the reason you keep coming back for bite after bite. But not all butter is created equal. If you can throw some dough (ha) at one thing in your pie making journey, throw it at the butter. Unsalted butter with a high fat content is your BFF, it is your sunshine after the rain, it is the mix tape your first boyfriend made you—always a good listen.

Try to find butter that is at least 82 percent fat, marked "European-style." The brands I love are Vital Farms and Cabot, but if you cannot get your hands on European-style butter, don't fret! Whatever butter you find will work; just make sure it is unsalted and cold.

GRANULATED WHITE SUGAR!

Domino white sugar: You will use it in your crusts, to sweeten just about every fruit and custard, and even to balance out flavors in savory fillings. This is your kitchen workhorse sugar—especially for that afternoon cup of coffee on a long baking day!

DEMERARA SUGAR!

There is little better than biting into a pie crust with crispy, crunchy, sugary bits on top thanks to the extra-big crystals and flavor that demerara sugar provides. For double-crust pies and on the crimps of single-crust pies, I love to brush on an egg wash and douse the crust in demerara. It makes the crust sparkle!

APPLE CIDER VINEGAR!

The key to a tender crust with a little bite and a lot of personality is adding apple cider vinegar to your liquid while making the dough. This keeps the temperature of the water colder and, when baking, it will burn off first, guaranteeing you a flaky crust. An alternative is vodka; just make sure it's unflavored.

FLAKY FINISHING SALT!

This is utter luxury. For savory pies and some sweet pies, it's so nice to have a little crunch of salt on top to enhance the flavors within. Maldon makes the GOAT of all finishing salts. Nothing compares.

KOSHER SALT

My preferred brand of everyday salt is Diamond Crystal kosher salt. All the recipes in the book were developed with it. Keep that in mind if you are using a different salt, such as Morton's kosher coarse salt or fine-grained table salt, you will need to use less to avoid oversalting. For example, 1 teaspoon of Diamond Crystal equals ⅝ teaspoon (½ plus ⅛ teaspoon) of Morton's kosher coarse salt.

Now it's pie time!

CRUST RECIPES
ALL-BUTTER CRUSTS

ALL-BUTTER CRUST—SINGLE

1¼ cups unbleached all-purpose flour

½ teaspoon kosher salt

1½ teaspoons granulated sugar

½ cup (1 stick) cold unsalted butter, cut into ½-inch pieces

½ cup cold water

2 tablespoons cider vinegar

½ cup ice

ALL-BUTTER CRUST—DOUBLE

2½ cups unbleached all-purpose flour

1 teaspoon kosher salt

1 tablespoon granulated sugar

1 cup (2 sticks) cold unsalted butter, cut into ½-inch pieces

1 cup cold water

¼ cup cider vinegar

½ cup ice

PRO TIP: Use the ingredient amounts for the *single* crust when your pie only has a crust on the bottom. Use the *double* crust when you need to put a crust or lattice on top. Some pies even call for a *triple* crust (like the Tennessee pie, page 270), in which case, make a single recipe *plus* a double recipe.

Crust is the foundation of all your pies. Bakers have their preferences of which fat to use, but I'm all about the butter, baby. Fat is flavor and using a butter with a high fat percentage when making your dough means a pie crust that you're gonna wanna eat crimp first!

The All-Butter Crust recipe is the one I riff on for all the others. So start here. The crust's the limit!

Stir the flour, salt, and sugar together in a large bowl with a flat bottom. Add the butter pieces on top of the dry ingredients. Using your fingers, toss the butter in the dry mixture so each cube is coated. Use a pastry blender or your fingers to cut or rub the butter into the mixture until it is in pieces a bit larger than peas (a few larger pieces are okay; be careful not to over-blend). You want to be able to have big butter chunks in your crust: It helps create a flaky effect, as well as adding delicious buttery hits of flavor!

In a separate large measuring cup or small bowl, combine the water, cider vinegar, and ice. Sprinkle 2 tablespoons of the ice water mixture over the flour mixture; do not add the ice, which is just there to keep your water cold. Using your hands in a circular motion, bring the mixture together until all the liquid is incorporated. Continue adding the ice water mixture, 1 to 2 tablespoons at a time. Carefully mix until the dough comes together in a ball, with some dry bits remaining. Turn the dough out onto a lightly floured surface and knead gently until it comes into one mass; you don't want to overwork it.

Shape the dough into a flat disc (if making double recipe, first separate the dough into two equal portions), wrap in plastic, and refrigerate for at least 1 hour, preferably overnight before using.

Wrapped tightly, the dough can be refrigerated for 3 days or frozen for up to 3 months. Thaw frozen dough overnight in the fridge.

FLAVORED ALL-BUTTER CRUSTS

These fun recipes add a little special something to the all-butter crust. Preparation is the same as for the All-Butter Crust (page 332); add the flavor component when mixing the dry ingredients for the dough. Pie's the limit! Crust flavoring knows no bounds.

These recipes are all for single crusts. Go ahead and double them for your flavored double crust needs.

CHOCOLATE ALL-BUTTER CRUST—SINGLE: Follow the recipe for All-Butter Crust—Single (page 332), but use just 1 cup unbleached all-purpose flour and add ¼ cup unsweetened cocoa powder to the dry ingredients.

POPPY SEED ALL-BUTTER CRUST—SINGLE: Follow the recipe for All-Butter Crust—Single (page 332), but add 1 tablespoon poppy seeds to the dry ingredients.

HERBED ALL-BUTTER CRUST—SINGLE: Follow the recipe for All-Butter Crust—Single (page 332), but add 1 tablespoon chopped fresh rosemary, 1 tablespoon chopped fresh sage, and 1 tablespoon chopped fresh thyme to the dry ingredients.

CHEESY ALL-BUTTER CRUST—SINGLE: Follow the recipe for All Butter Crust—Single (page 332), but add ½ cup shredded sharp yellow cheddar cheese (preferably Cabot cheddar) to the dry ingredients.

EVERYTHING-BAGEL ALL-BUTTER CRUST—SINGLE: Follow the recipe for All-Butter Crust—Single (page 332), but add 3 tablespoons everything bagel seasoning to the dry ingredients.

CRUSHED PEANUT ALL-BUTTER CRUST—SINGLE: Follow the recipe for All-Butter Crust—Single (page 332), but add ½ cup crushed salted peanuts to the dry ingredients.

HOT-OLD-BAY ALL-BUTTER CRUST—SINGLE: Follow the recipe for All-Butter Crust—Single (page 332), but add 3 tablespoons Old Bay hot seasoning to the dry ingredients.

WHOLE WHEAT ALL-BUTTER CRUST—SINGLE

1¼ cups white whole wheat flour

1 tablespoon granulated sugar

1 teaspoon kosher salt

½ cup (1 stick) cold unsalted
   butter, cut into ½-inch pieces

½ cup cold water

2 tablespoons cider vinegar

½ cup ice

Stir the flour, salt, and sugar together in a large bowl with a flat bottom. Add the butter pieces on top of the dry ingredients. Using your fingers, toss the butter in the dries so each cube is coated. Use a pastry blender or your fingers to cut or rub the butter into the mixture until it is in pieces a bit larger than peas (a few larger pieces are okay; be careful not to over-blend). You want to be able to have big butter chunks in your crust to help with flake, plus be extra delish!

In a separate large measuring cup or small bowl, combine the water, cider vinegar, and ice. Sprinkle 2 tablespoons of the ice water mixture over the flour mixture; do not add the ice, which is just there to keep your water cold. Using your hands in a circular motion, bring the mixture together until all the liquid is incorporated. Continue to add the ice water mixture, 1 to 2 tablespoons at a time, until no water (only ice) remains. Carefully mix until the dough comes together in a ball, with some dry bits remaining. Turn the dough out onto a lightly floured surface and knead gently until it comes into one mass; you don't want to overwork it.

Shape the dough into a flat disc, wrap in plastic, and refrigerate for at least 1 hour, or preferably overnight before using.

Wrapped tightly, the dough can be refrigerated for 3 days or frozen for 1 month. Thaw frozen dough overnight in the fridge.

CORNMEAL CRUSTS

CORNMEAL OR BLUE CORNMEAL CRUST— SINGLE

1 cup unbleached all-purpose flour

¼ cup stone-ground white or blue cornmeal

½ teaspoon kosher salt

1½ teaspoons granulated sugar

½ cup (1 stick) cold unsalted butter, cut into ½-inch pieces

½ cup cold water

2 tablespoons cider vinegar

½ cup ice

CORNMEAL OR BLUE CORNMEAL CRUST— DOUBLE

2 cups unbleached all-purpose flour

½ cup stone-ground white or blue cornmeal

1 teaspoon kosher salt

1 tablespoon granulated sugar

1 cup (2 sticks) cold unsalted butter, cut into ½-inch pieces

1 cup cold water

¼ cup cider vinegar

½ cup ice

PRO TIP: Use blue or white cornmeal depending on the recipe or your preference.

Cornmeal adds a hearty element to an all-butter pie crust. It takes the flavor in a nutty, savory direction with delicate toothsome mouthfeel. This is the perfect crust for both savory and sweet applications.

Stir the flour, cornmeal, salt, and sugar together in a large bowl with a flat bottom. Add the butter pieces on top of the dry ingredients. Using your fingers, toss the butter in the dry ingredients so each cube is coated. Use a pastry blender or your fingers to cut or rub the butter into the mixture until it is in pieces a bit larger than peas (a few larger pieces are okay; be careful not to over-blend). You want to be able to have big butter chunks in your crust, it will help create a flake, as well as add delicious buttery hits of flavor!

In a separate large measuring cup or small bowl, combine the water, cider vinegar, and ice. Sprinkle 2 tablespoons of the ice water mixture over the flour mixture; do not add the ice, which is just there to keep your water cold. Using your hands in a circular motion, bring the mixture together until all the liquid is incorporated. Continue to add the ice water mixture, 1 to 2 tablespoons at a time, until no water (only ice) remains. Carefully mix until the dough comes together in a ball, with some dry bits remaining. Turn the dough out onto a lightly floured surface and knead gently until it comes into one mass; you don't want to overwork it.

Shape the dough into a flat disc (if making a double recipe, first separate the dough into two equal portions), wrap in plastic, and refrigerate for at least 1 hour, or preferably overnight before using.

Wrapped tightly, the dough can be refrigerated for 3 days or frozen for up to 1 month. Thaw frozen dough overnight in the fridge.

CRUSHED CRUMB CRUSTS

A crumb crust is an easy way to make a pie quickly with ingredients you might already have in your pantry! It comes together wicked fast and is so delicious! Choose cookies, crackers, graham crackers, or cereal, then pulverize, add butter, and a crust is on your horizon!

These recipes are all for single crusts. I only recommend using a crumb crust for the base of your pie; use a crumble and streusel for topping.

GRAHAM CRACKER OR CHOCOLATE GRAHAM CRACKER CRUST

5 ounces (140 grams) graham crackers or chocolate graham crackers (about one sleeve of 9 crackers), pulsed into fine crumbs in a food processor (about 1 cup)

3 tablespoons granulated sugar

½ teaspoon kosher salt

¼ cup (½ stick) unsalted butter, melted

In a medium bowl, combine the crumbed crackers, sugar, and salt. Stir in the melted butter until the mixture looks like wet sand. Turn the mixture out into a 10-inch pie plate and press it onto the bottom and up the sides, using either a ¼-cup measuring cup or your hands to press the dough down. Take your time, making sure that the crust walls are secure and the base is even. Freeze for at least 15 minutes before filling or blind baking.

If the recipe requires a blind baked crust, bake for 6 to 9 minutes at 375°F. Let cool completely before filling.

CEREAL CRUST

7 ounces (200 grams) cereal of choice (such as Kellogg's Corn Flakes for the Michigan pie, page 155)

3 tablespoons granulated sugar

½ teaspoon kosher salt

¼ cup (½ stick) unsalted butter, melted

Preheat the oven to 350°F. Using a food processor, crush the cereal finely until it resembles coarse sand; stop before it turns to dust. In a large mixing bowl, combine the crushed crackers, sugar, and salt and mix well. Stir in the melted butter until the mixture looks like wet sand and holds together like dough. Press the cereal mixture onto the bottom and up the sides of a 10-inch pie pan. Take your time with this step, using a ¼-cup measure to help pack the sides and bottom evenly if needed. Freeze the crust for 15 minutes. Bake for 12 to 15 minutes, until the crust gets a little toasty.

CREAM CRACKER OR SALTINE CRUST

7 ounces (200 grams) cream
    crackers (preferably Khong
    Guan brand) or saltines,
    crushed

3 tablespoons granulated sugar

½ cup (1 stick) unsalted butter,
    melted

Preheat the oven to 350°F. Using a food processor, crush the crackers finely until they resemble coarse sand; stop before they turn to dust. In a large mixing bowl, combine the crushed crackers and sugar and mix well. Stir in the melted butter until the mixture looks like wet sand and holds together like dough. Press the cracker mixture onto the bottom and up the sides of a 10-inch pie pan. Take your time with this step, using a ¼-cup measure to help pack the sides and bottom evenly if needed. Freeze the crust for 15 minutes. Bake for 12 to 15 minutes, until the crust gets a little toasty.

HASH BROWN CRUST

We all love pie crust, but how about a pie crust made with pretty much everyone's favorite vegetable and breakfast side, *the potato!?*

4 medium russet potatoes,
  peeled and grated
1 teaspoon kosher salt
½ teaspoon freshly ground black
  pepper
2 tablespoons vegetable oil
2 tablespoons unsalted butter

Preheat the oven to 350°F. Toss the grated potato and salt and pepper in a large bowl. Transfer to paper towels or a tea towel and wring out excess water.

Heat the oil and butter in a large skillet over medium-high heat. Add the potatoes and sauté for 10 to 15 minutes, until all the moisture has evaporated. Press the mixture onto the bottom and up the sides of a 9-inch pie pan. Take your time with this step, using a ¼-cup measure to help pack the sides and bottom evenly if needed.

Bake for 15 to 30 minutes, until golden brown. Let cool completely before filling.

TECHNIQUES

This section gives you the basic rundown of the techniques it takes to become a good pie baker. I am a home baker who has learned through a ton of trial and error, and I hope my candid and casual approach to it all gives you the confidence to try it yourself.

Not every crust will come out perfectly, not every crimp will hold its shape, and not every pie will bake evenly. But you know what? You'll still have a delicious creation that you made with your own two hands, and that's pretty darn special. If all else fails, cover it in whipped cream, pour yourself a shot of tequila, and brush it off. Pie is great, but it is still just pie!

ROLLIN'

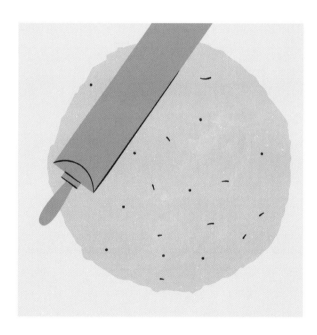

Before you roll out your dough, take it out of the fridge and let it to come to room temperature for about 5 minutes. This is working smarter, not harder, because your dough won't develop cracks while you're rolling it out. If your dough does develop cracks, just break a little off the edge and patch it. Do not fret!

Make sure your surface and your dough are both well floured. When starting to roll (see page 327 for information on rolling pins), start just below the center of the disc and in one swift motion push away from you, applying even pressure across the dough. Pick up the dough and rotate it a quarter turn clockwise and repeat the roll. Continue rolling until the dough is 2 inches wider than the pan you are using. Feel free to grab the pan you are using to eyeball it.

Sprinkle more flour under and on top of the dough as you work, making sure the dough doesn't stick to either the surface or the pin. But use a light hand; too much flour will dry out the dough.

You can roll out the dough ahead of time the day you are baking your pie. The roll-outs will stack in your fridge or freezer with wax or parchment paper in between each piece. Take the rolled-out dough out of the fridge at least 5 to 10 minutes before using so it is at a workable temperature. If it's from the freezer, first thaw it overnight in the fridge.

FITTIN'

Now that your dough is rolled out, you've got to get it into your pie pan. There are many ways you can go about this, but this way works for me:

Start by making sure your pie pan is greased with either butter or cooking spray (Pam works great, or any other vegetable oil spray) for an easy release after baking.

Fold your dough round in half (gently, don't press on the crease), position the fold in the center of the pie pan, then unfold the disc and gently slide the dough into the pan. Go around the edges and gently press the dough into the pan, making sure that the dough is flush against the base. Gently press around the base so there are no gaps between the dough and the pan.

Once your dough has found a snug place in the pan, trim the excess dough around the edges, making sure to leave a 1½-inch allowance. If you did not roll it out enough for there to be this extra bit for crimping, DO NOT FRET! While you crimp you can pull from areas that have more and patch.

Your dough is now snug as a bug in a rug, so let's crimp, cut, and weave!

CRIMPIN'

Crimping is my favorite part of baking pie—besides eating it, of course. I love the action of it; I almost go into a little trance when I do it. When I was at Four & Twenty Blackbirds, I would crimp full stacks of rolled out dough (forty roll-outs! forty crimps!) and have a grand old time listening to tunes and making sure I had a high CPI (crimps per inch)—a metric I brought to the bakery from my days as a handbag designer talking about SPI (stitches per inch). I wanted to try and fit as many crimps as I could onto a pie, within reason of course, for that perfect scalloped edge.

Crimping a pie can be intimidating, but how you crimp your pie is a matter of personal style and it's always a fun journey to discover your signature. For an easier alternative, you can use a fork to press the dough around the edges in fanciful waves. Whichever route you choose, there will be pie!

CRIMPIN' SINGLE CRUST PIES

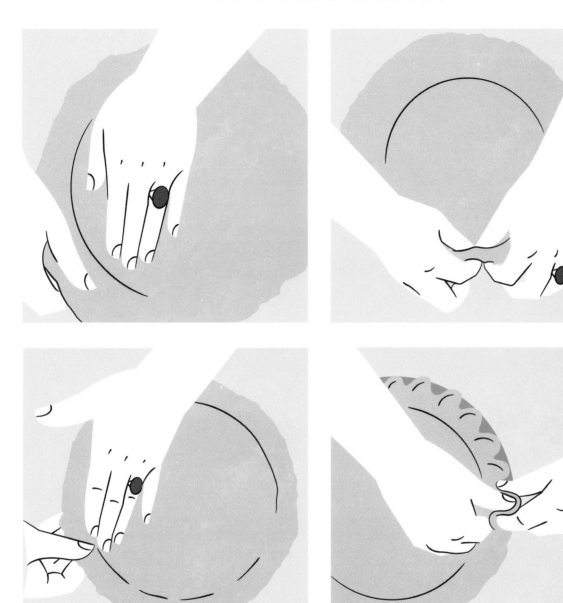

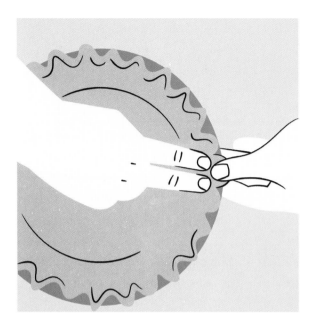

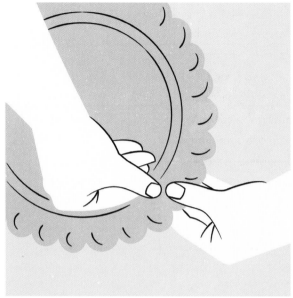

The single crust crimp is used for pies that only have one crust (like Alabama, page 40, or Washington, page 296). The best way to start your crimp for a single crust pie is by rolling the excess dough outward, towards the edge of the pie pan when you are prepping your crimps. This is so there isn't a seam running around the inside of your pie, just seamless crust glory.

To get going, you are going to take your single crust of dough that is snug as a bug in your pie pan and roll the excess dough edge tightly under itself, making a rope that sits directly on top of the pan's rim. You want to make this rope tight so that it doesn't unravel while baking. After you've made the rope, go back around the circumference of the pan and push the rope down with your thumb. This give you a nice circle of dough that can be shaped and pushed into your crimps.

Now take your index finger and your thumb on one hand (I am right-handed so it is my left hand for this) and make a "C" shape. Hold the "C" shape on the outside of your pie pan pushing inward while pushing your opposite thumb into the center of the "C" from inside the pie pan. This is your mold to crimp the edges of the pie all the way around. Once I have gone all the way around making my crimps, I like to use my thumb and index finger on the other hand and push my crimps down to get a flat scallop effect all the way around the pie. Make sure that your crimps sit directly on top of the pan's rim.

YAY! You've crimped your pie! Keep practicing and make up a signature crimp of your own so when you take your pies to a barbecue, they know exactly who brought the beaut!

CRIMPIN' DOUBLE CRUST PIES

The main difference between crimping for a double crust and a single crust pie is that you have a little more dough to work with. With the crust edge you will be rolling the combination of the top and bottom crust towards the center of the pie along the edge. What you aim to do at the end is to make sure there is a tight seal around the edge. Double crusts are usually for juicy fruit pies or saucy stew pies and you want to make sure all the goodness stays nice and tight inside.

To prepare your crust for crimping, take your pie crust that is filled and topped with either lattice or another full crust and trim the edges around so there is only a 1½-inch overhang. Start by rolling any excess dough inward and under itself so it makes a thick rope around the edge, making sure that it is tight all the way around. Once the rope is made, push it down with your thumb. Now you are ready to crimp the same way as you did for the single crust, using your thumb and index finger of one hand as a "C" and your thumb on the opposite hand. Make your crimps all the way around and push them down afterwards to make sure everything is secure.

If it is a full double crust, cut some vents on the top to allow steam to escape while baking

CUTTIN' & WEAVIN' (LATTICE CRUSTS)

To bring your pie together, in some cases you'll want to top it with some sort of lattice (strips of dough that are woven together in a decorative pattern to create a top crust), and then join the top lattice to the bottom through crimping. Once you have the basics covered, the rest is up to you.

This is where you can let your creativity shine: The size of your lattice and how you weave it are entirely personal, and can change from pie to pie. Throughout the book you'll see different examples of lattice width and weaving techniques.

For example, for Wyoming (page 312) I made the lattice in the shape of the Teton Mountains.

Here is what you need to remember when cuttin' and weavin' lattice for your pies: First, roll out your dough as you would do for the base or top of a pie, and chill it in the fridge before you start cutting. Chilled dough is much easier to work with and you'll get much cleaner lines when cutting it.

CUTTIN'

The tools you will need to cut lattice are a floured surface, a pizza cutter, and a clear ruler, which allows you to see what you're doing and create a straight edge, The ruler is optional, but the Virgo deep inside of me craves a little bit of order in the chaos.

Place the rolled-out dough on your floured surface, and, using a pizza cutter, trim one side of the round of dough slightly, so that you have a straight edge to measure from. Using the clear ruler, mark out 1-inch-wide lattice strips. This is the standard size I use in this book, but you can go thinner or thicker depending on your preference.

Once you have the whole thing marked out, cut along each marked line in one swift motion using the pizza cutter and the ruler as your guide. Once your lattices are cut, place them on a floured baking sheet or a baking sheet lined with parchment paper. Chill for at least 30 to 60 minutes before using for the crispest lattice.

WEAVIN'

The easiest lattice weave is a simple basket weave, where the lattice goes over and under itself. You can of course look up fun weaving patterns online and get as fancy as you want! Lauren Ko of @lokokitchen on Instagram is the GOAT of fanciful lattices.

Here, I'll take you through the basics of an over-under weave, which is the one I use most of the time.

To start, take your filled pie base, lay four to seven (depending on how thick your lattice is) parallel strips of your prepared lattice horizontally across the top of the filling, making sure to space the strips evenly, until the pie is covered. Leave about a ¼ inch between each strip of lattice. Fold back every other strip to the point where it connects with the base of the pie. Place one long strip of lattice vertically to the parallel strips at one edge of the pie, then unfold the folded strips back into place. Every other horizontal lattice strip should now be covering the vertical strip. Now take the parallel strips that are underneath the vertical strips and fold them back over the vertical strip. Lay down a second piece of lattice next to the first strip, leaving the same amount of space you did when you laid the horizontal lattice down. Unfold the parallel strips over the second strip. Continue this until the weave is completely covering the top of the pie. Trim the edges of the lattice so that they are flush with the bottom crust. Gently push the lattice onto the bottom crust. You are now ready to crimp the edges of your pie (see page 343)!

BAKIN'

It's time! You're done rollin', fittin', cuttin', and weavin'! Let's pop that baby in the oven! What you need to remember for this step is to preheat your oven! You need to make sure your oven is warm and toasty and ready to receive your pie baby.

PRO TIP: Get an oven thermometer to make sure your oven is at the right temperature.

You're one step closer to servin' and eatin'!

EGG WASH

Dough crusts always require an egg wash to make sure the pie comes out golden brown and that whatever finishing sugar, salt, or spices you add to the top will stick.

For an egg wash, I combine 1 whole large egg, 1 large yolk, and 2 tablespoons milk or water (whichever you have on hand) in a quart container and blend with an immersion blender or whisk until smooth. This has been the recipe that has given me the best golden brown on my bakes.

FINISHING SUGAR

I always have a quart container of finishing sugar mixed and ready to go. It is equal parts granulated white sugar and demerara sugar—the perfect mix to top your double crust fruit pies or the crimps of your sweet crumble pies. The demerara sugar gives you that sugary crunch and the white sugar gives you that golden, caramel-colored finished. Plus, demerara sugar is expensive, so the white sugar helps it go a little further. 'Cause you know we are all people who have champagne taste but a beer budget.

BLIND BAKING

Blind baking is when you pre-bake the crust before filling the pie. You usually blind bake for pies whose fillings don't need as long of a time in the oven to cook through as the crust. By blind baking, you are giving the crust a head start.

You can fully blind bake the crust for a pie that isn't going to go back in the oven, or partially blind bake for a pie that's headed back in for a shorter bake when it's filled. There are a few exceptions to this in the book: recipes that have a filled, fully blind baked crusts that are then baked again, but only oh so briefly!

For blind baking crumb/cookie crusts, see the instructions at the crust recipes. And keep in mind that freezing is the key step! Make sure you freeze your crumb/cookie crust for at least 15 minutes before baking to make sure the crust stays intact and the walls don't slump down.

Blind baking is your friend on the road to no soggy bottoms!

PARTIALLY BLIND BAKED CRUST

The crust is partially blind baked for most custard or cream fillings because custard fillings need less time to bake than the crust, so we want to give the crust a head start. This technique is mostly used for single crust pies. Prebaking or blind baking the crust ensures that you won't have a soggy bottom, the crust will be fully cooked through, and flaky butter goodness will cradle your soft silky custard or cream filling. It is insurance for happy bakes.

Roll out your single crust, fit into the pan, and crimp. Place the prepped crust in the freezer for 10 minutes or until it is frozen solid. Take the dough out of the freezer and use a fork to prick all over the bottom and sides of the crust. This is called docking, which helps eliminate the air bubbles that can form when the dough is exposed to heat and prevents the crust from shrinking. Store in the freezer until ready to use.

Position an oven rack in the center position, place a rimmed baking sheet on the lowest rack, and preheat the oven to 425°F.

Take the crust from the freezer and line it tightly with a piece or two of aluminum foil, making sure the crimped edges are completely covered and there are no gaps between the foil and the crust. Pour pie weights or whatever alternative (beans, rice, sugar, marbles, etc.) you are using into the crust, filling it to the top. Place the pan on the preheated baking sheet and bake for 20 minutes, until the crimped edges are set but not browned.

EGG WHITE GLAZE
   1 large egg white
   1 teaspoon water
   Egg wash (see page 346)

Mix the egg white with the water. This glaze acts as a seal between the crust and the liquid filling and moisture-proofs the crust that is exposed to the filling, preventing soggy bottom.

NOTE: This mixture is not used on graham cracker/crumb crusts.

Remove the pan and the baking sheet from the oven, lift out the foil and pie weights, and let the crust cool for a minute. Use a pastry brush to coat the entire crust with a thin layer of the egg white glaze to moisture-proof the crust. Using a pastry brush, brush just the crimps with the regular egg wash to give the crimps a golden brown. Return the crust to the oven and bake for an additional 5 minutes. Cool completely before filling.

TIPS AND TRICKS FOR BAKING!

★ This is a great tip I learned while working at Four & Twenty Blackbirds. Before filling your fruit pie, sprinkle a little flour and sugar on the crust bottom, ½ teaspoon or 1 teaspoon of each. This protects against soggy bottoms and will lead to a guaranteed Paul Hollywood handshake–worthy bake.

★ For all the pies in this book, bake the pie on a baking sheet: This will save you from unfortunate oven smoke situations and make cleanup faster.

★ If the crust around the edge of your pie is getting too brown but the center isn't quite done, make a crust shield! I learned the best way to do this from my food stylist, Cate. Take a piece of foil about 2 inches larger than the pie and fold it in half. Put it over your pie and mark where you're going to cut the foil by making two incisions at the top and bottom of the inside circle of your pie. Fold the foil once more and cut a circle out of the center. Unfold and lay the foil shield over the pie, covering the outer edge but leaving the center exposed. This is kind of like in *Mean Girls*, when someone cuts the boobs out of Regina George's shirt. You are doing the same with the foil to protect your crimps!

★ How do you know a pie is done?

   For a fruit pie, look for the juices bubbling up throughout. You can also use a wooden skewer to check the doneness of the fruit inside the fruit; it should be feel soft and be easily pierced by the skewer.

   A custard pie is done when the outer edges of the pie are set but the center has a soft jiggle. The jiggle was best described to me by Kathryn (Indiana pie recipient) as to resemble the soft jiggle of a women's upper thigh. The accuracy of this is uncanny. The filling is jiggly but it will continue to set as it cools.

FULLY BLIND BAKED CRUST

The crust is fully blind baked for pies that will not be returning to the oven, such as ice cream pies or cold-set pies, since the fillings do not need to bake. In the book there are some exceptions with pies that go back in the oven with a fully blind-baked crust, until they get extra toasty and golden.

The principles are the same as for partially blind baking (above); you just need to bake it a little longer after the removing the pie weights and brushing with the egg white and egg wash, 10 minutes (instead of 5). When the crust comes out of the oven it should be golden brown in color.

SERVIN'

I cannot stress this enough: *let your pie cool!*

The general rule is that a minimum of 1 hour of cooling time is needed for *all* pies, whether fruit, stew, or custard. Fruit pies and stew pies take longer to cool, but trust me—it will be worth the wait. You can serve some stew pies in the book a little sooner because you want to eat it warm and steamy!

Cooling allows your filling to fully set and come together so it doesn't just all run out into a puddle. Plus it will save you from a lot of roof-of-the-mouth burnage.

For slicing, I recommend a good paring knife that is sharp. Make sure to cut through the crust completely when you slice. The size of the slices is completely up to the server and how much they are trying to butter up the recipient. The first slice will never be the prettiest: Like Cat Stevens and my girl Sheryl Crowe said, "The first cut is the deepest." But cover that bad boy in whipped cream, ice cream, gravy, or sauce, and you'll be grand.

HAPPY PIE EATIN'!

ACKNOWLEDGMENTS

First and foremost I would like to thank my Father, Stephen KK Fong, for giving me every opportunity I have had in life. My father never gave me rules, he always wanted me to make decisions for myself and weigh all my options out to see if the juice would be worth the squeeze. He gave me boundless freedom to express myself, find myself, and become the woman I am today. Daddy, you have supported me through all my life adventures with no questions asked. Thanks for your unconditional love, for letting me believe that no dream was ever too big, and that anything I could want or need was within my reach. And especially for not getting mad at me for charging my first tattoo on a credit card that was for emergencies and lying that it was for art supplies. I love you, Papa Fong!

To my sisters, Stasia and Seraphina: Thank you for always having my back and for always being excited to see what pie I have baked next. All our childhood adventures and turmoil have fueled the fire and passion I have today. Fong sisters forever and ever, amen.

To all my friends I have made in the seventeen years I have lived in America so far: This project is my love letter to the country I have chosen to call home, but most of all it is my love letter to you. To all of you who have taken me into your homes during the holidays and who have supported me here in countless ways. Thank you for all the hugs, the kisses, the handholds, the meals, the phone calls, the texts, and everything in between. You are not only my chosen family, you are my family.

To my wonderful literary agent at the book's conception, Christopher Hermelin. Thank you for letting me vent, stress, and bounce ideas and word vomit on you constantly during the making of this book. Thank you for helping me organize my thoughts when they are racing through my mind and believing in me constantly. Also thank you for coming over whenever I had a surplus of pie and not complaining about how thirsty I am for 6-foot, 5-inch actor Lee Pace. Thanks, too, to Ryan Harbage, for getting me over the finish line.

To my Voracious fam! Thank you for helping me bring my love letter to America to life in a medium I could only dream of. I couldn't have found a better team for this road trip. Like hanging out with the best of the best, in a cabin by the lake where the fire is roaring and the whiskey is bountiful. Thank you a thousand times, thank you. Michael Szczerban, my editor and my friend, thank you for giving me the space, trusting my vision always, and never doubting me in my quest to make this the book that I wanted it to be, no matter how harebrained some of my ideas might have been. When you first reached out to ask if I wanted to make a book, I couldn't believe it. Now that it's real I still can't believe that I was lucky enough to make it with you. Thea Diklich-Newell, thank you for the constant support and for being my twin flame in music taste! The next time I'm in Austin, duh, we are going to a show together and drinking a gazillion ranch waters.

Now I must wax poetic about my C-OVEN!

To my wonderful photographer, Alanna Hale: Thank you for capturing everything so beautifully and being a beacon of light through the whole shoot. I can't think of anyone who could bring my vision to life but you. But what I didn't realize was that I would end the shoot with a friend I'll have for the rest of my life. I hope we are sitting together on a beach soon, sand in our toes, drinkin' and watching the sunset. I am in awe of your grace, your ease, and your talent. This is your book as much as it is mine.

To my food stylist, Caitlin Haught Brown: I am so glad that the universe brought you into my life. No other person can talk me off a ledge like you or give me a sense of calm that can only be felt after breaking open a perfect biscuit (made by you). Thank you for making everything look so gosh darn beautiful. You are the human version of Vicodin. Thank you for the lists, the binders, the Joyce Chens. I am forever indebted to you and the Bed Bath & Beyond return policy. Maybe one day Wegman's will sponsor us so we can eat fancy pecans forever and ever.

To my prop stylist, Maeve Sheridan: Your constant support and enthusiasm could brighten the darkest of nights and light up any room. You are a miracle worker who brought all the pies to life with subtle nods to each state in tiny objects from your treasure trove. Thank you for loving me so well.

To the backbone of the c-oven, Namrata Hegdge, aka Nami Baby! I am so happy that this experience brought you into my life. No one can crush a prep list like you! You are a crimp queen and I cannot wait to see where your career takes you: This is your book after all!

To my hand twin, Kathryn Irizarry: Who knew a global pandemic would bring us together in friendship and in our careers. Thank you for all the dirty chais, late night chats, and your help on prep days and in Rhinebeck. Our hands are small we know, they are not mine, but they could be yours though.

A shout-out to the C-ovens, Zachrifice, Zach! Thank you for putting up with the absolute bombardment of female energy. I owe you a drink and a hug at the Double Windsor.

To my lovely illustrator, Shelby Warwood: From the moment I saw your work I knew you were the one. Thank you for bringing all my wonderful friends and everything in between to life. Your talent and eye of color knows no bounds. Until we get to share a Lone Star and a shot of tequila in person in Austin.

To my lovely designer, Tree Abraham: Thank you for bringing the calm to the chaos and for making my book the most beautiful it can be.

To the king of swoops and loops, Brian Kaspr: Thank you for starting this journey and lending your talents on the long journey we have been together. You are the best bud! I love that we live, we laugh, and we love.

A thousand thank-yous and more to Ben Allen, Pat Jalbert-Levine, Deri Reed, Sarah Clark, Suzanne Fass, and Jeffrey Gantz. It truly takes a village to manage production, copyediting, proofreading, and fact-checking, and y'all took this slice of pie and served it up à la mode. This book wouldn't be where it is without all of your hard work, countless hours spent, and attention to detail.

Never ending thanks to Lauren Rinaldi, Adam Porter, Patrick Racheff, Steph Stilwell, Katie LiButti, Alex Miller, The Love Train, and The Island for believing in me constantly, especially when you knew I didn't have the will or energy to believe in myself. Thank you for pulling me out of all my bouts of sadness and reminding me at the end of the day it is just pie. I am forever indebted to y'all. I love you.

To fellow author Kerri Sullivan: Thank you for being my sherpa through this perilous journey. From helping me get my book proposal together to being a sounding board along the way, I couldn't have ridden the roller coast of a debut book without you.

To Beth Anne and Will: Thank you for opening up your lovely home to me. I will cherish our pre-shoot record listening, whiskey drinkin' time in my heart forever. Also thank you to Will for pulling us out of a literal ditch when the truck got stuck. I love y'all.

To Xenia and Matt: Thank you for lending me your abode Upstate to get the first twenty-five chapters down! Your home is full of magic and good vibes that I was absorbing and channeling throughout my writing.

To the Four & Twenty Blackbirds fam, Rica, Melissa, Emily and the whole team: Thank you for taking a chance on me. Thank you for putting me through pie boot camp, for inspiring me to bake pie in the first place. Your cookbook and shop are the reason I fell in love with making pie. A special shout-out to Rica Borich for mentoring me through my time there and for making me the best baker I could be. Tough Cru Forever!

To my Big Night Fam, Katherine and Alex! Thank you so much for the constant support, snacks, laughs, cheese, and bread. A Big Night snack plate was the perfect fuel for the long writing days. Thank you for loving me so well.

To Nora, the sweet pup I adopted when I had four chapters left to go: Thank you for your calming nature, and for making me feel the most safe I've felt in a long while. To all the future books I'll write with you sitting at my feet.

To the United States of America: You have always been the country I wanted to make my home. It's the movies and the music and the food, but most of all, it's the people. Thank you for welcoming me with open arms. Though at moments my love has been tested, it is undying and unwavering the end of the day because of the people here. The sprawling lands, sunrises, sunsets, and open skies don't hurt either. From sea to shining sea, I love you.

Lastly, to Dolly Parton: You are a constant inspiration in my life. If I could grow up to be half the woman you are, I will die happy. Thank you for always helping me see the light of every clear blue morning.

Your next slice is on me.

Xoxo Stacey

INDEX

Note: Page references in *italics* indicate photographs.

ABOUT THE AUTHOR

STACEY MEI YAN FONG is a home baker living in Brooklyn, New York. She was born in Singapore, lived in Indonesia, grew up in Hong Kong, and moved to the States to pursue a degree from the Savannah College of Art and Design. She spent a decade designing in the fashion industry, and during that time she launched her 50 Pies 50 States project, which led to her slinging pies at Four & Twenty Blackbirds Pie Shop. Now, her pies have been featured by *CBS Sunday Morning*, NPR, Eater, and beyond.

@50pies50states
50pies50states.com